Relevant Ramble

Musings of a Methodist Preacher in Recovery

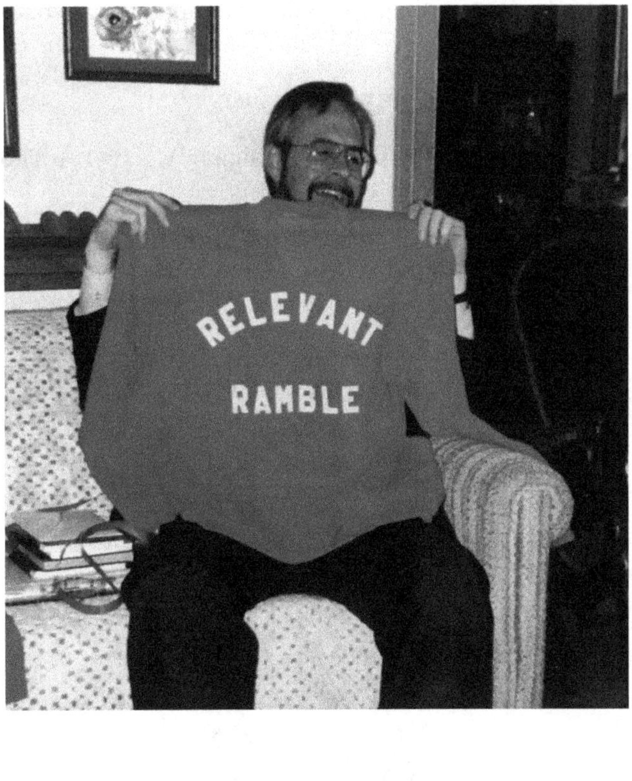

Foreword by Becky Moon

Compiled by Becky Moon and Alex Eash

Relevant Ramble - Musings of a Methodist Preacher in Recovery

First published by Powerful Potential & Purpose Publishing 2020

First printing, January 2021

Cover design, graphics and book design by Candy Lyn Thomen

Front and Back Cover Photo and interior photos
© 2021 Becky Moon - Art From A Moon
Bottom two photos on page 246 © 2020 Harley Sousa Goodman

ISBN: 978-1-7349655-6-8 (BW)
ISBN: 978-1-7361839-1-5 (Color)

Published in USA

Powerful
Potential and Purpose
PUBLISHING

www.PPP-Publishing.com

Hickory, NC - USA

DEDICATION

When Chuck and Alex began working together, he handed over his first handwritten journal. As he was busily crossing out passages of his daily life, Alex was uncovering the essays you will read today. You could say she actually "got" him. She found Chuck's masterpiece in his writing. This book is dedicated to Alex Eash, the brilliant mind who brought to life the thoughts of Chuck Moon. Without her, this book would still be a pile of handwritten journals sitting on a shelf in his office.
Thank you, Alex. You are loved.

And to you, Brian ("my son with whom I am well pleased")
and our grandson Will ~ his love for you spans into eternity.

Contents

JOURNALS VOLUME THREE

A Word from the Editor and Publisher

What is contained in the following pages is the daily written work of an amazing man, Rev. Charles F. Moon. Please keep in mind as you read through this collection of his writings, it is exactly that: a collection of his thoughts and writing from his personal journals. Sometimes jumbled, sometimes out of what we might think of as "sequence" it is, nonetheless, as close as we can come to what he wrote and what he intended with his writing; his last, wonderful gift to a world that may, or may not, deserve it. (As Chuck would say.)

The layout of this book is designed to give you, the reader, room to jot down your own notes and thoughts, just as Chuck did through his years of study and writing. Fill the margins and the lines between the lines with your own words, wisdom and ah-ha moments. Let this be the beginning, or the continuation, of your own sweet journey into the depths of your spirituality, beliefs, heart and soul.

Introduction

To whomever may, or may not, give a shit.

I wrote regularly throughout my life, and devotedly in retirement, filling dozens of journals, bound volumes, and notebooks. My papers include my thoughts, reflections, analysis, and of course sermons from fifty years of life as a preacher, theologian, recovering alcoholic, musician, father, and husband. What's it all about? I would have answered that question differently in different decades. I was called. I sometimes lost my way. At one time, I thought of myself primarily as a musician. I had vowed to quit if I ever couldn't perform at the level I once attained, and to some extent I walked away from music, but never from my love of it. I've always been comfortable as a preacher, because I've always loved God, words, and putting them together in the pulpit. I would rather craft a sermon than do most of the things associated with leading a church. While I was always a minister, I grew into the role of service more once I stopped drinking and realized I could help others do the same. So, here is a meandering memoir, a minister's memories, a drunk's drivel. It contains wisdom and nonsense, truth and profanity, and some of the best of my stories and thoughts.

Foreword

On the day Chuck retired, my mother gave him a $100 bill and said, "This is your first royalty check — now go and write that book you've been talking about." Chuck, however, didn't start writing. He just sat in his chair for the next six months staring at the television or going to AA meetings. He seemed like a lost soul to me and to his friends. We grew more anxious, but I came downstairs one morning and found him in his study. He continued to write day after day with an admirable discipline. My reaction, "Thanks be to God!" Now that he was ready, supplies were needed for a project of this magnitude. Off we went to the bookstore to find just the right journal for his writings. His handwriting was small, precise, and he hand wrote everything–never using a typewriter or a computer for his sermons, essays, or the study materials he wrote. Once he had exactly the right type of journal, which suited his needs, he began to write. Every day he sat at his desk for two to six hours, studying and writing. He documented everything he studied, including all his thoughts and philosophical musings... filling up one black bound journal after another. Today, there's still a stack of them in his office.

Chuck was tall, handsome, and brilliant with a unique way of seeing, thinking, and expressing himself. At his towering 6'6", it was easy for me to find him over the top of a crowd. As his health began to fail, I'd always find him off to the side somewhere, in his wheelchair, surrounded by people. My somewhat shy "Little Gus", as I affectionately called him, always had a following. He was kind and compassionate, and children and animals loved his gentle, kind, and loving nature. He could be wildly sarcastic, quirky, and profane because "we should use *all* the words". As you can imagine, life with Chuck was never dull. We loved to travel, and I dragged this poor fellow all over for 31 years, so the world could see his beauty. He was, however, only totally comfortable in the pulpit, despite my yearning to share this wonderful man with the world.

Chuck graduated from Mississippi Southern with an undergraduate degree in music and from the Candler School of Theology at Emory University. He sang with Robert Shaw and was a choral conductor for 13 years, leaving that behind to go into the pulpit. He served the United Methodist Church from seminary (1965) until his death March 1, 2020.

All the words I've written don't adequately describe my husband, Chuck. He would most want people to remember he loved Jesus, trusted God, that he faithfully served his churches and was a devoted friend of Bill W. and the fellowship of Alcoholics Anonymous. His son Brian and grandson Will were his pride. And he loved me.

I'll end with his favorite expression,
"Everything's gonna be all right."

Becky Moon

August 2020

Art From A Moon

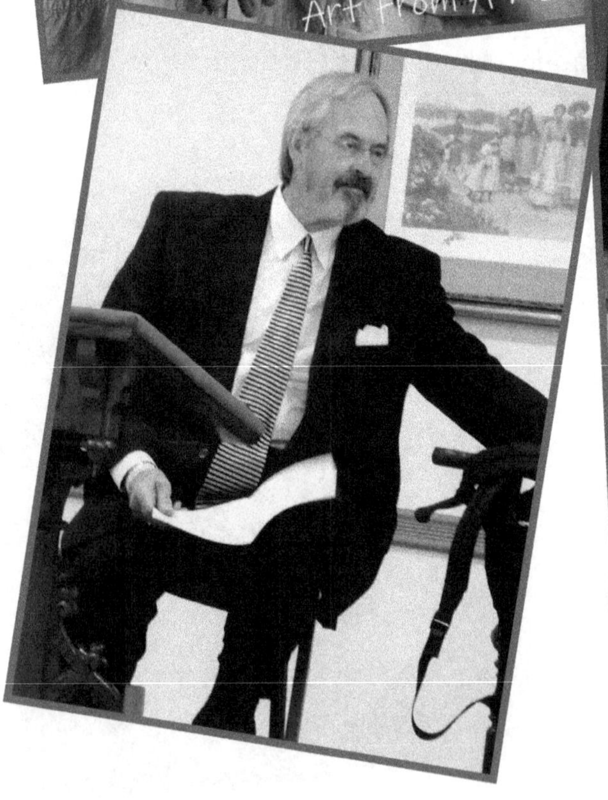

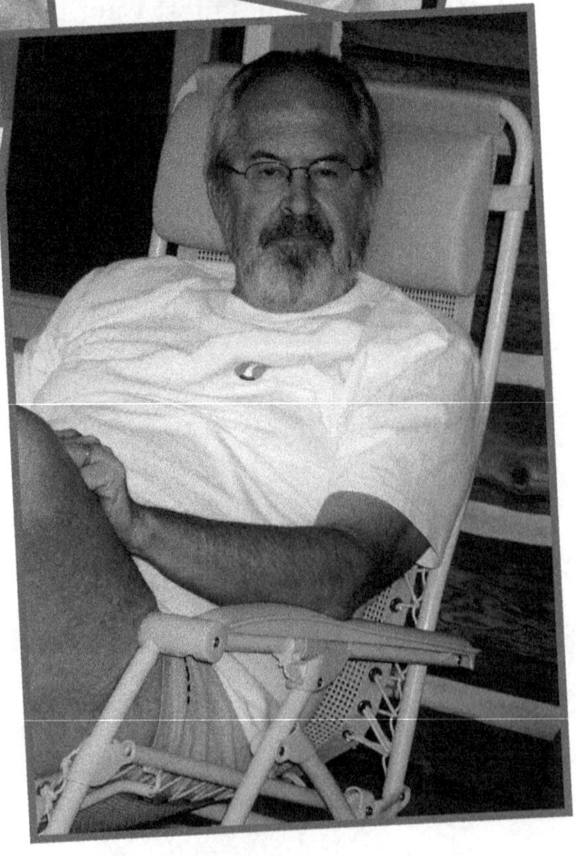

Journals Volume One

In the Beginning

There are currently 7.5 billion of us here on this planet. In our known universe, there are maybe nine galaxies for each of us on planet Earth (80+ billion). Each galaxy contains at least 100 billion suns.

Our little galaxy is called the Milky Way. Here in our local galaxy, there are 400 billion suns, or 69 suns for each person alive.

What does this mean?

Or: what is a quark?

The problem is this: we cannot hold two theories together in a dialectical relationship[1].

The first theory—general relativity—holds what Einstein said is true. This view looks at things on a large scale (really large).

The second theory—quantum mechanics—looks at things on a small scale (really small).

How do these two things work together? Hold one in one hand and the other in your other hand. How do they teach each other?

We don't know.

Since we don't know, it's hard to discern things in a Genesis sense. When God started things, the universe was about the size of an atom. So:

In the beginning...

"In the beginning, God..." (Genesis 1:1)

(In the beginning, God started to create.)

For the person of faith, God didn't finish in the beginning. God still creates.

1 No unified theory has been found.

A quote from Annie Dillard:

> *Only some deeply grounded and fully paradoxical view of God can make sense of the notion that God loves and knows each of the 7.5 billion of us*[2].

How do I know this is true? Well, it has to move from a notion to a "deeply grounded and fully paradoxical" experience in my daily life. How then do I know this is true? "Jesus loves me, this I know, for the Bible tells me so." If that was good enough for Karl Barth, it's good also for me.

Thank you, ancient and present logos, for words.
Let me wallow in them forever.

I like words with power. Here are some from Wendell Berry's "Poem":

Willing to die,
you give up
your will, keep still
until, moved by what
moves all else,
you move.[3]

God is bringing me newness (2 Cor. 5:17); yet there is no newness without a death of the old! When I begin, I start all over. My story is really all I have at this point. So, how do I tell it? I spent years telling stories. Now to tell the tale of myself in a liberating way...

In the beginning, God. It was only 13.7 billion years ago when God said, "let there be light." Things began to happen.[4]

When I came along, I had the sense that something was wrong. There was a discomfort. It was deep and fundamental, and this dis-ease needed treatment. After a short time, I found a solution. I found alcohol, and it

2 Dillard, A. (2000). *For the Time Being*. Alfred A. Knopf. 132.

3 Copyright © 1971, 1972, 1973 by Wendell Berry, from *The Country of Marriage*. Reprinted by permission of Counterpoint Press.

4 13.7 billion is a relatively small number in cosmological terms.

changed things. It really did. When I drank it in, I was born anew. There was a new freedom and a new happiness. It was a lie, of course, but it felt good. I like feel-good. This led to easier and softer solutions to things which required many folks to actually grow up. This led to arrested development. This continued for many years. This was my reality.

Now, I believed all along. I really did! God was real. The stuff I had been taught was true, but alcoholic behavior led me away from the things God had for me, and I got the disease. I acquired the *ism* as they say.

Now, this particular sickness has an easy enough cure: one has only to quit drinking. I saw my son do this in college. He put it away and has not touched it since. How did he do that? Well, I guess that is for him to say. I only know that once I got started, I could not quit. For years and years I could not quit. I tried, of course, because I got in trouble over and over. I told others who loved me I would quit. But I could not.

What I lacked was *power*. I was operating on my own power, and it was not enough. I knew there was a problem, but I could not get a firm grasp on a solution, so I went on for many years without what I have now. The power I needed was a power that could only come to me from outside myself. I was a creature, a created being, and for me, I needed a creator to agree to do for me what I could not do for myself. For years I was functioning, but I was powerless.

What a sad and stupid state that was. I knew there was a problem. I didn't want anyone to find out I was not really who I pretended to be. This led to lying and hiding. That led to being further removed from reality. If one creates their own reality, one will experience inevitable difficulty. I was in trouble. If I was not crazy, I did crazy. Alcoholism is a mental, physical, and spiritual disease.

Sobriety date: St. Patrick's Day, 1990

God, who is infinite, cannot become present because He can never be absent. We do not so much invoke God's presence as we acknowledge it and accept it.

What Is the Truth, and How Can One Know the Truth?

For me, the truth is revealed as I need it in my personal relationship to Jesus. I came to this gradually. In fact, it was after I retired that the best of this relationship developed. So, did I spend a 45-year career not having a fundamentally deep relationship with Jesus Christ? The "truth" was a thing in my head, and I was able to serve it broadly, but it would be interesting to do the whole thing over from my current perspective. (First, no one has ever been able to do such a thing. Second, what God had for me was lived out the first time around, or so it seems, so there could be *now.*)

In order to observe the sunrise, you have to get up early. When one does this, a new day is dawning. That new day is the only one I will ever have. *This* is the day that the Lord has made.

I live out the end of my life now in two communities: *Church,* and *AA.* What a blessing! Church has been enhanced by AA. I am still alive because of AA. When I was still at work in church, I had to give myself, in large part, to the job itself. It then has been a great blessing to sit with Becky and to worship.

The only truth that matters has to be lived out before it can be pondered over. We come to right thinking by right living. If I start with a purely abstract thought, what have I? That would be the world of theory. If I were a theoretical physicist, I could embrace the theories of the very large (relativity and its cousins) or the very small (quantum mechanics), but I would still lack a unified theory. If I could be the first to come up with a unified theory (Einstein failed), then I would still lack the truth that is given daily in my walk with Jesus. There is not enough within me to be self-sufficient. In fact, the Bible says throughout that the person who relies only on their own strength is in for a rough ride (the Qur'an agrees). Now, I like nothing better than to mess with an atheist or a science-only type. I take them on with my head because I am prone to living in my head, but if I really want to relate to them, it must be through the heart. Thus, I can only show them in sharing my daily walk with Jesus. If I'm not walking, I've got nothing to share, anyway. So, truth must be *revealed* truth! Is my daily walk only a theory? No, it can be and *is being* proved. The truth must truth itself, in revelation.

The true meaning of "let there be light" is to be found in the explosion of our universe into being some 13.7 billion years ago[5]. Here is an interesting thing: The Big Bang is not a thing which came out of nothing. How could that be? Current scientific theories can't penetrate to time Zero and describe what was going on before that. Now, science can speak about what was going on one second *after* the Big Bang. (At that point, the universe was already 1,000 times the size of our solar system.) What about before the first second? What was going on at that point? We don't know. If the whole universe was once the size of an atom, the best place to begin is where it says: *In the beginning, when God began to create...*

God has laughed at least twice, at creation and at Easter.

Does anyone really believe the galaxies exist to add splendor to the night sky over Bethlehem?

Does prayer hold things together?
Does God do anything apart from prayer?
Prayer and meditation. Speaking and listening.
Making conscious contact.

When bad things happen to good people, where is God? God seems to hide. I like the concept of the Trinity. They came up with this doctrine (theory) early on to better explain things.

---

5 If it only happened once. Or: is this the only universe or a parallel, one of many?

God, the big starter. (We don't know what went on before the big bang.) After the first second, stuff started moving at a pretty good clip. They figure just before that first second of the universe there must have been a big explosion. Some have pondered silly things like wouldn't it be neat if a camera positioned somewhere could have caught the image of the bang, but God could have begun creation with a mere flick of God's finger if God wanted to. We are creatures. We respond to the creator and the creation, but we just don't know so many things.

Modern medicine is a young science. I'm glad to be one who practices a very old discipline. They (the doctors) tell me to take a pill. I say, "What is a pill?" They say, "You are!" Becky makes an appointment. I go to yet another doctor because some body part seems to be acting up; another pill is called for.

I think back over 45 years of going to various hospitals. I prayed for healing and sometimes healing happened. The doctors would seem surprised. Surprised by joy. The God of my understanding would give that ancient grin.

I take one pill that's made of horse piss. I like to think of how they would get a horse to piss where they could gather it up.

I just read a novel about a nun in a convent who strove for many years for the assurance of God's presence. She lived faithfully and well for many years, and finally the vision was granted. She wrote poems about the process, and the poetry book was published... success. But she had migraines. It became bad enough that a physician was sought... tests... and sure enough, a part of her brain was affected. Epilepsy (the source, the light, the vision?). Surgery and the visions ceased. Does this mean the visions and the gifts of a poet and the sense of the *presence* was a lie?

No, it was all a part of a larger gift (as was finally understood). God is good, no matter what. It's not always about me, is it? It's all to the glory of God. Now, is that good news on every level? Yes! "Yes" is the only really essential word.

Genesis says that all came into being through a word. God spoke the world into existence. Once, there was *nada*, nothing, 'no thing.' Then there was something. All things then are infused, somehow, with the glory of God. How is this true? I don't know. It is not known. It is known in the chores of existence. It is true finally because it *has* to be true. It is truth that truths itself.

Then, after certain trials and errors (the Old Testament is a funny book), the people God appointed were a sorry lot. They were termed stiff-necked. They wandered for a long time in desert places, their eyes straight ahead, looking for deliverance. If only they had a way to get to their purpose. They were in the wastelands. If they had, for instance, a camel, that would be good. Then they could ride into a land of promise. It turns out they were, in fact, seated on a camel while they were wishing for one: a weird bunch, just like my bunch. God just laughed and planned and created.

Many experiments, there were: towers of babbling, floods, earthquakes, manna, conquests, silly little kingdoms and warfare, prophets who wandered around naked and nervous. Really funny stuff like Jonah, who made a whale sick, and David with his smooth, shiny river rock. Then finally God said another fine thing.

What was it? Well, in a way it was the same word that was originally spoken, but this time it came in human form.

Now, humans, it seems, were the strangest of all created things. (Dolphins and wolves are the noblest.) Humans, however, could be counted on to do the opposite of what was in the beginning good. But this new human was different. His name, of course, was Jesus, and even today he is the most highly regarded and most ignored of all the stuff God has done thus far. It is the most amazing story ever told.

Today, of the 7.5 billion of us who live on this tiny blue planet, 100 million of us are children who live on the street and eat garbage when they can get it.

That is why I think we don't really get the point of the story. You can drive down highway A1A in Florida at night and see high-rise after high-rise of beach condos and very few have their lights on. The owners live elsewhere, the homeless live everywhere. I say, move them into the empty high rises and vacation homes. You say to me, "Are you out of your mind? I worked hard to get my beach house, not to mention my 'cabin' in the mountains!" I say, no, you didn't. You didn't *work* for it. You just fell into it. Your hardest decisions were, *what college shall I attend?* You wouldn't last a day on the streets of Calcutta. Oh well.

That's why I say we don't believe a word of the sacred story. But who am I? What have I done? Well, very little. I've got pictures of a few African children on my refrigerator who we sponsor. What an ironic thing that is. Whatever I want to eat and drink is ready and waiting. I have enough money to last me and mine if we are careful and lucky.

If I were God, I would speak a third word. If creation and Jesus didn't do the trick, I think I would put my energy into another planet. There just has to be more than this lovely little thing.

Somewhere, righteousness and truth are kissing each other (Ps. 85:10).

I just looked through the book of Proverbs. It's all there! The reward for seeking wisdom is wisdom itself.

The Universe

Here's a thought: our sun has existed for 5 billion years; it will last another 5 billion years or so before it burns itself out. When it goes, it will take our earth with it.

What does this mean in terms of the end to be expected from God? Not only our universe but also the individual lives we lead are doomed; they will not go on forever and ever. They will burn out. I will die (and not very long from now). Our particular sun will continue to spit out some solar flares which mess with our power grids and such, but I will be gone. "Thou art dust and to dust thou shall return." That is the message that begins lent. The answer is found in Easter, of course, but in the meantime (is time really mean?), I'm stuck wondering and wandering with ashes on my forehead.

Henry David Thoreau said, "The universe is wider than our views of it."[6]

If flesh and blood will not inherit the kingdom of God, how can there be a resurrection of the body?

There is a new creation, a new heaven and a new earth. Easter holds bold promise. I do not despair but have hope and joy despite physical death and the threat which is posed by a finite world and a universe that seems to be wearing itself out.

The problem of coming up with a unified theory is avoiding reductionistic ideas but holding fast to the truth of "on the one hand," but also "on the other hand," and both are true! Science and Theology. A

---

6 Thoreau, H.D. (2017). *Walden*. Enhanced Media. (Originally published in 1854). 173.

dialectical relationship which informs and teaches on a deeper level than is usually the case (a unified theory in practice, if not in truth).

I want to understand the deepest truths of science. I want to know deeply that general relativity and quantum mechanics work together for good, for God's sake. I want to know that the very large and the very small are both a part of a pleasing reality wherein the morning stars sing together, the oceans clap their hands, the honey flows from the rock, righteousness and peace are still kissing each other, and *"the meadows clothe themselves with flocks, the valleys deck themselves with grain, [and] they shout and sing together for joy" (Ps. 65).*[7]

In the Psalms, death comes together with its abode *sheol*. When you die, there you are in the pit. *Abaddon*. You descend. Once there, you are almost never visited by the God of your understanding. But here come the Greeks.

In the Jewish and Christian texts of the Hellenistic period, one need not spend eternity down under, but rising to a new occasion becomes possible. It was probably a welcome notion. In our Bibles the first time the idea of limited individual resurrection is mentioned is in an apocalyptic passage within the book of Daniel: *"Many of those who sleep in the dust of the earth shall awake, some to everlasting life, and some to shame and everlasting contempt."*[8]

Paul could not think of the resurrection without a body (1 Cor. 15). What will the spiritual body be like? I'm just curious, that's all. One thing is clear, no one view captures the universe.

Walter Brueggemann wrote this wonderful thing: "Autonomy and self-sufficiency are finally postures of hopelessness in which free gifts are excluded."[9] Wow. To gain, one must give up. I'm powerless over alcohol and my life was unmanageable. I can live my life now, but I am never the director. It's not that God wants us messed up when we finally get there. We did quite well when we were in charge and large. It's old-fashioned

---

7 See also Ps. 96: 11-13
8 Dan. 12:2
9 Brueggemann, W. (1984). *Message of the Psalms*. Fortress Press. 49.

sin, I guess. If I put something in first place other than God, then I'll lose whatever that is. How many thousands of times must I say something before I accept it?

A few more, at least.

Someone said, "It is always man who is absent, not grace."

The universe itself will eventually evanesce or possibly collapse in a fiery final conflagration (the big crunch). Or, they say, the universe could expand forever, and eventually run down and disperse to the point nothing will remain. This will take trillions of years. Either way, we have a scriptural assurance of forever and ever!

So: death-dealing, or life-generating? I am pro-life here.

Pope Benedict XVI said of Teilhard de Chardin, "It's the great vision that [he] also had: At the end we will have a true cosmic liturgy, where the cosmos becomes a living host." and "Let's pray to the Lord that He help us be priests in this sense... to help in the transformation of the world in adoration of God, beginning with ourselves."[10]

(The Church had oppressed Teilhard in most every way until Vatican II.)

Current cosmologists are much more cynical as to any hope for anything other than eventual futility as regards the end of all things. We make bold to testify to the sciences since all things are in the hands of God, in the end *all will be well.* It's not even that God will erase the board and start over again. God pronounced creation good (Genesis). New creation will consist of the redemption of the *current creation.* If I am cremated, God will sort through the ashes to make a new body out of the old. This will happen because our Lord's risen body bore the scars of the crucifixion but was somehow glorified into the resurrected body. We can hardly prove this to a science type; yet we believe.

---

10 Allen, J.L. (2009, July 29). *Pope cites Teilhardian vision of the cosmos as a 'living host'.* National Catholic Reporter. https://www.ncronline.org/news/pope-cites-teilhardian-vision-cosmos-living-host

Stanley Hauerwas has written "that the first task of the church is to make the world the world."[11] He goes on to say:

> The world simply cannot be narrated—the world cannot have a story—unless a people exist who make the world the world. That is an eschatological claim that presupposes we know there was a beginning only because we have seen the end... Creation names God's continuing action, God's unrelenting desire for us to want to be loved by that love manifest in Christ's life, death, and resurrection.[12]

Well, the cards did their thing, and we have a new Pope. He's a first. He's from America. South America. He calls himself Francis (not his baptized name). He cares for the poor and seems humble. The news people say his emphasis on the poor will lead to controversy with the conservatives. WHAT? Have they (the conservatives) read the scripture? One out of sixteen verses speak of the poor (always favorably). Do we care at all about what Jesus (the reason for the season) has to say? I think not! We don't care enough to get involved. I once thought retirement would be great... I could sit on the boards of some non-profits and thus do a lot of good. Bullshit. First, it's hard to do good. Really hard. Second, I'm too worn out to do much good now. I can't even drive. Becky sold my Jeep! I lost my Jeep, my right leg, and my old dog Alice, all in the same week. That would make a good country song.

John Yoder wrote that the eternal is not atemporal. The eternal "is not less like time, but more like time. It is like time to a higher degree. The Kingdom is not immaterial but is more like reality than reality is."[13] Yes, God is eternal, but the God of the Bible has redeemed time. By the invasion of the Logos (John I), God has made time a sort of hyperreality.

---

11 Hauerwas, S. (2010). *Hannah's Child: A Theologian's Memoir*. Eerdmans. 158.
12 Ibid.
13 Ibid.

The cross and the resurrection have happened (in our little world). It's all about Jesus, and it's all good! Since Jesus was in the beginning *with* God and *was* God, then what God had for us in creation has been fulfilled and is being fulfilled. God is more real than we are. God is all in all, and it is all good because God said it was. I am a child of God. What a concept!

Death is the necessary cost of life. *Christ died*, and all things *became new*. The new possibilities are realized at the edge of chaos. There is then a balance between order and disorder, between continuity and discontinuity. God does not, at this point, start over. After each day of Creation, God pronounced the created order "good." If God cared enough to become invested in the Incarnation, then the body of Christ was not to be discarded and taken out with the cosmic garbage. His crucified body was changed. It was glorified. In Christ there is thus a hope for all matter. We matter! Our bodies are to be raised up at the last day.

To be sure, the dynamic character of life brings change. This change comes from the creator as a characteristic of the cosmos. On the largest of scales as well as the smallest, reality is unpredictable and, well, strange, unexpected. The incredible amount of relatedness on the subatomic level is an indication of the faithfulness of the created order. I believe there is a link between the one who dies in this world to the one who lives re-embodied in the world to come. In fact, we believe that this is the "stuff" of the Church, the body of Christ. We are already part of Christ's body; we shall be a part of Christ's body in the life of the world to come.

The best of science today holds that space, time, and matter all hold together in a package of general relativity theory. If this is true of the world in its scientific reality, then is it not also true of the created order in its spiritual reality?

The body of Christ in the sacrament is more than a mere token! Christ is then really real in the gathered community. Communion is a particular time of covenant in which Christ is actually present, perceived. The new creation will be wholly sacramental (1 Cor. 15:28).

If God is "all in all" now, then surely God will never be absent in the world to come. There will be no need to "go" to church. We will already be in the eternal presence of God.

Karl Barth wrote, just before his death:

> How do I know whether I shall die early or with difficulty? I only know that my dying, too, is part of my life... And then—this is the destination, the limit and the goal for all of us—I shall no longer "be", but I shall be made manifest before the judgment seat of Christ, in and with my whole "being", with all the real good and the real evil that I have thought, said and done, with all the bitterness that I have suffered and all the beauty that I have enjoyed. There I shall only be able to stand as the failure that I doubtless was in all things, but... by virtue of his promise, as a peccator justus. And as that I shall be able to stand. Then... in the light of grace, all that is now dark will become very clear.[14]

That says it all, and I have never read or heard or thought of better words to describe my own end. In my writings, I am not trying to be dark (although I can do dark). I am writing end stuff because that is where I am. That is what I have been musing about. My dear Becky thinks I am too much inclined in this direction, and she is right, because she usually is right. But is it true we are just where God wants us to be? That is a good question, and I am fond of good questions.

We long to live in the moment. We reach out to grasp it, and it is gone. In the twinkling of an eye, every present passes, and what is past never returns. The lived moment passes, and we ourselves pass away.

14 Busch, E. (1976). *Karl Barth: His Life from Letters and Autobiographical Texts.* Fortress Press.

We have expectations. They become experiences which turn into memories and, in the end, the great forgetting.

Then the life after death. That is the life made possible through Christ. It comes to us as a promise in this life. In the present moment of belief, we are grasped by the reality of the resurrection. The covenant which was once broken is reestablished. The Bible says death came through sin. God keeps promises. Life lives on. It is the risen Christ who gives us hope. It is a hope that comes to life and stays alive within the presence of Christ.

T. S. Eliot says in his Four Quartets, "in my beginning is my end—and in my end is my beginning." "Or say that the end precedes the beginning / And the end and the beginning were always there / Before the beginning and after the end."[15]

I Peter 3:15 says

God plants hope within us, and we should not suppress it.

There is, as Martin Luther wrote, a hope that leads across "into the unknown, the hidden, and the dark shadows, so that he does not even know what he hopes for, and yet he knows what he does not hope for."[16] That hope within is God's presence in Jesus Christ. This is what is meant by "hope against hope, it is a gift."

I have to die, but life goes on. This is why we must have church. Science cannot justify hope. It is an act of faith which evokes a living presence that comes to us to sustain us. Therefore, we need not fear the future. We need not fear death.

Ted Peters has written:

> If the law of entropy has the last laugh and the cosmos drifts into a state of irrecoverable equilibrium... then we would have proof that our faith has been in vain... In faith we allied with our

---

15 Sauter, G. (2000).Our reasons for hope. In Polkinghorne, J.C (Ed.), *The End of the World and the Ends of God*. Trinity Press International. 213.

16 Ibid. 215.

> hope, and our hope is based upon the promise... that a new creation is coming by the grace and power of God... The upshot of this is that at the present time we will have to base our eschatological hope on specifically theological resources, not scientific ones.[17]

It reminds me of the person who considered the statement of the scientist who had exhausted all the known disciplines and had climbed the very highest peak of rational inquiry and had finally reached the top of this mountain only to encounter a tribe of theologians who had been sitting there for centuries.

If the Bible is correct when it reports death came through sin, then a good case can be made that God did not intend death in the first place.

The church functions as an interim institution. We are between the Incarnation, the coming of Christ, and the eschaton, the second coming of Christ. The church has enjoyed only a conditional existence, a finite bridge of hope "stretching between the life, death, and resurrection of Jesus Christ and the time when the cries of 'Maranatha,' *come Lord Jesus* will be answered once and for all in the Kingdom of God."[18]

A lot of people do not believe any of this. We are guilty of idolatry if we believe the church is eternal! We are non-believers if we discount these functions of the finite church. The Bible clearly states "there are no temples in the heavenly city, no churches in the New Jerusalem."[19] Since the church itself has no eschatological ultimacy, it can have no claim to ultimate authority and power. So, when we preach and celebrate the sacraments, we lift the story of Jesus as pointing to the end to be expected from God. God grants in the power of his unconditional creativity continuity where there is real created discontinuity. "The *theological*

17 Peters, T. (1993). *God as Trinity: Relationality and Temporality in Divine Life.* Westminster John Knox Press. 176.
18 Schwöbel, C. (2000). The church as a cultural space: eschatology and ecclesiology. In Polkinghorne, J.C (Ed.), *The End of the World and the Ends of God.* Trinity Press International. 114.
19 Ibid.

content of the *Christological* story is the key to its *eschatological* significance."[20]

So then, what does the church do, and what are the members to be about? I believe worship to be the central act. All other things should be as a result of the community of faith coming together and then departing to serve.

There is a powerlessness that is the necessary beginning of spirituality. But if we seek to describe what spirituality is, we must confess it cannot even be defined. It is elusive, ineffable, unbounded and rooted in paradox. We can know what it is not... it is not arrogance or self-sufficiency. It's like humility. If we think we have attained it, guess what! I'm powerless over alcohol, my life is unmanageable. I can only hang out my sign... "Under new management."

Let's do this. Let's take the history of the universe and compress it into one year. So, you got the big bang on January 1st. Our own little galaxy started on May 1st. The Earth (our planet) was formed around September 14th. The oldest life forms were having sex around November 1st. It wasn't until December 1st that we got oxygen atmosphere. The first worms on December 16th; first insects on the 22nd. The very earliest humans come on December 31st to begin a significant New Year's Eve party, which continues to this day. All recorded history occupies the last 10 seconds of December 31st, and the time from the end of the Middle Ages to the present occupies a little more than a second of our cosmic year.

We need not be in a hurry.

The chief purpose of our species would be to glorify God, wouldn't you say? Remember, in the garden of Eden when the first couple could speak to God in the evening, when it wasn't too hot, Adam said, "Who am I?" He could have pondered the interesting one (the Creator) or the naked one (Eve), but his concern was with himself. Wouldn't you have liked to be

20 Ibid. 115.

present at the big popping sound? That would have been Adam's head popping out of his butt. (You can be around when it happens to you!) When one stops long enough to consider it, one is not all that interesting after all, and there is more going on than just one's own little concerns.

That is when sin got going. Sin is the separation of God and humankind. "All have sinned—all fall short of the glory of God."[21] We only know we are brothers when we realize each of us are sinners. All 7.5 billion of us. Remember, God loves each of us as if there were only one of us. God speaks, and it is done. Grace has covered our sins. We are put right again with what God had in mind in the beginning. "God was in Christ reconciling the world unto himself."[22]

The church exists as a people who claim to know something they would not have known if it had not been revealed to them. Apart from God's revelation, we know nothing. What do we know? We know Christ. *"In Him we live and move and have our being" (Acts 17:28).*

God has been faithful (history). God will again be faithful (apocalyptic stuff). God's concern is with right now. This is the moment. This is the day, the only day the church has.

Luke wrote news that stays news. He states it at the beginning of his work in the New Testament. "An accurate and orderly account of all Jesus did and taught." Why?

"That you may know the truth." Luke 1:4

Pilate said, "What is truth?"

And so it goes...

Why could God not just have forgiven Adam and Eve when the trouble started? It would have saved everyone a lot of trouble. Why did God act like that?

Or maybe the problem is not with the original sin. Sin is not all that original after all. I think the problem is with the second sin, not the eating

21 Romans 3:23
22 2 Cor. 5:19 (NLT)

of the fruit, but the blame game which followed. The man blamed the woman. The woman blamed the snake. No humility was to be found. If Adam had just said, “my bad, sorry,” what would have happened?

All we need to know is: God is God and we are not.

Music is music

Music is music. It is "sound in time." There is no such thing as "sacred" music. Nor can music really be profane. If in church, whether choral or instrumental, music is offered up to the very nostrils of God; that is good. I guess. There is good music and there is bad music, but it's not "holy." Well, who gets to decide whether it's good or bad? *I do.* I can always tell. Trust me.

Now, if it's in church and it is well placed on the altar, it may have good effect. God probably accepts most of it. Who can tell? If it's in the concert hall and it's well presented and time-honored, then critics may attend and post a review. Don't do that in church. It has been there offered up and God keeps it, only to make a greater return gift. (On God's celestial refrigerator, the Bach *B minor*, Beethoven's *Missa Solemnis*, and other gifts of his children are held in place.) We can only honor the offering and assume it was sincerely given.

Word precedes tune in church. The word comes first, and it is then set to music. The music then has a purpose. One must be careful when two such powerful forces are joined. For me, the word of God and music together has climbed the very highest mountain in Western culture. "Great" music comes mostly from the church set by great composers from the last few centuries. We don't know what biblical music was like... temple music in King David's time... Those great words with all those voices and instruments and dance. When they sang the hymns in Philippians chapter two, what was that like? We have no idea. In the churches of my experience, it's still, as the New Testament tells us, "Psalms, Hymns, and Spiritual songs" (Colossians 3:16 and Ephesians 5:19). It says in the Bible that the church in Ephesus sang and made melody to the Lord. I've been there, but the church was long gone. I sat on a pillar and preached to our tour group, but we didn't sing that day and the first century church left us no hymnals. Music is an on-the-spot kind of thing as opposed to other art forms. Yes, you can write it down, but what a variety of interpretations are possible! Once music is performed, it is gone. I always liked dress rehearsals more than performance day—you have to give it up once you offer it up. And once it's done, you are on to other things, anyway.

We postmodern people are multicultural. You cannot escape it, nor should you try I suppose, but I like going to a traditional church with good acoustics and an excellent pipe organ with a grand piano on the side. Big choir. Long tenure in the music department. An insistence upon excellence that is *always* hard won over many years. And here's the problem: you can tell if the preacher and the choir director hate each other (you can also tell if they are diddling each other, but that's another matter). They have separate, yet equal functions (like a marriage), and once egos, pride, and other character defects get going, well... The senior minister must call the shots (yeah, I know). Who gets to pick the style? Ideally, most everybody, but worship wars are common. Do you do only what might draw a certain demographic? Do you preach to please and placate? Well, I'm glad to be retired.

Then There's Jesus

Then there's Jesus. Once a newborn babe in a manger, had a navel, took a shit and a piss. Lived in a bag of skin. Must have had a limited shelf life, just like us.

If he hadn't been crucified, what would have happened in the terms of aging and dementia? All of this is a mystery that is revealed in the church, or not. Not all questions can be answered, you know.

Is it true no two of us have the same image of Jesus? The American Jesus is a man nobody hates. 85% of the population claims some kind of personal relationship. Wow! 75% of Americans say they have sensed the presence of Jesus at some time. Nearly half of American non-Christians believe he was born of a virgin and was resurrected from the dead. WOW!

That's really a ridiculous situation. A nation of lip-service. But you must realize the real American religions (football and bombing the hell out of brown people) are only seasonal situations. Nothing must interfere with what we are really about: making and protecting money.

We live in a culture of denial. ("No, we don't!" *Yes, we do.*) Why else do we not learn from our own mistakes? I lived a long time in denial that I was an alcoholic. I knew I was, but admitting would entail doing something about it. So I selfishly went for decades until it quit working for me. No longer was there any pleasure in it, chasing a buzz that was past, over and over, and doing real damage. I hurt myself and a bunch of others.

Now, I have made some half-assed amends, but amendment cannot change the original. Reality is real, after all. The memory remains. I have been forgiven; yet much guilt remains. I am changed, but still hard to live with.

I'll keep on, but it is hard.

the Pulpit...

I preach Sunday at St. John. It's now Friday morning. How is it I can stand in a fellow alcoholic's pulpit? Is it because Bishop John Owen Smith said so long ago, "Take thou authority?" Well, yes, but before that I was called. That night in college, the Lord spoke, and the call to preach has not left me since. There is no other reason for doing the work. Am I worthy? Well, no, but that's beside the point. The point is God called me into the foolishness which is preaching... "*a stumbling block to the Jews and foolishness to the Gentiles" (1 Cor. 1:23).* All of this is true because the Word has pitched his tent among us (Jn 1:14). God has invaded this planet that creation began. We needed it. Thank you, Jesus.

"You alone must do it. But you cannot do it alone."

O. Howbart Mowrer

I think of the Bible work I have done since seminary and it adds up to a lifetime of serious study. If the house were on fire, my old study bible would be the first thing I would grab. It's still amazingly new and fresh every time I turn to that ancient library. I now have a favorable task as one who loves the scripture. There is some work which comes as assignments. There is also ample opportunity to just dive into the deep end of the pool and just look around. No matter where I look, I see lifesaving and changing places in the word. I never tire of it. It all comes from the one who said: "Behold, I make all things new."[23]

23 Rev 21:5

Philosopher of science Karl Popper makes a contribution:

> The empirical basis of objective science has nothing 'absolute' about it. Science does not rest upon solid bedrock. The bold structure of its theories rises, as it were, above a swamp. It is like a building erected on piles. The piles are driven down from above into the swamp, but not down to any natural or 'given' base; and if we stop driving piles deeper, it is not because we have reached firm ground. We simply stop when we are satisfied that the piles are firm enough to carry the structure, at least for the time being.[24]

He wrote those words about science. Empirical, verifiable science should stand any inquiry, but that is not the case. This is why the whole "modern project" has failed, its foundations shaken. It also reminds me of my beloved church.

The modern church never reached firm ground. She simply stopped when the piles were thought firm enough. The institution can no longer carry its freight. The firm middle cannot hold. A whole generation is emerging who cannot even notice an institution it no longer is attracted to. What to do? How to reach out? Perhaps the task is to switch to a more horizontal approach to move out as Jesus did into the world as it is and quit fiddling with the foundation and supporting the old crumble and historic stained glass when those who pass not only don't care; they don't even notice.

The new approach to the problem of epistemology from the point of view of theology and the philosophy of religion has been the recognition of the role of formative texts. There is a story behind it all. It is literary or scriptural texts which create a worldview, not the old foundational approach of building an edifice upon which to stack assurances which no longer ring true. So, when we look at what we think we know on a large enough scale, it all turns out to be the *Word* which was there from the beginning, the interplay between texts and experience. We simply tell the

---

24 Popper, K. (1959). *The Logic of Scientific Discovery*. Routledge. 94.

story of the situations we have faced and when we found nourishment along the trail of happy destiny. The gospel has no unstoried form.

William James identified with chronic sufferers, the "sick souls" he describes in *The Varieties of Religious Experience*. In the late 1860s his diary records a time when he "about touched bottom." After seeing a catatonic patient and realizing an identification with him he wrote: "That shape am I, I felt, potentially. Nothing I possess can defend me against that fate, if the hour for it should strike for me as it struck for him."[25] The experience led James to conclude: "Here is the real core of the religious problem: Help! Help! No prophet can claim to bring a final message unless he says things that will have a sound of reality in the ears of victims such as these."[26]

Edwin "Ebby" Thacher gave Bill Wilson a copy of *Varieties* after he visited Bill and "reached out" to him in the name of religion. Bill wanted nothing to do with any God until his 3rd detox at Towns Hospital. He was desperate enough to cry out *de profundis*, "If there be a God, will He show himself?" God said OK, and Bill had his famous "hot flash." He was to never drink again. He remained a deeply flawed individual but was also the guy who wrote the 12 steps in bed in 30 minutes. Perhaps no greater gift was given to humankind by anyone in the 20th century.

Yesterday in an AA meeting I was thinking of all this, and a wave of grateful peace washed over me. God is so good.

---

25 James, W. (1985). *Varieties of Religious Experience*. Pantianos Classics. (Original work published in 1902). 49.
26 Ibid.

Post Modern...

We are trying to figure out what "postmodern" may mean. Well, I will tell you what it means: the only thing we know for sure is what we meant by the modern world is over, and good riddance.

It started in the latter part of the 20th century; I think. The foundations were shaken; the center could not hold. The whole enlightenment project fell apart. Things are much stranger and more connected than we thought.

I was taught modern things. Nothing prepared me for the changes. They came quickly; they still are coming. We are caught up in a paradigm shift history will likely record as a radical changing. Remember when the world was flat? Could it turn out to be the equal of the transition from the middle ages to the renaissance?

The word postmodern came originally from architecture, of all places. Postmodern is not a very good term, but it is what we have. As I have experienced it, it seems to be a whole sea of changes. Things used to be like this; now they are like that.

Here is my partial list. There "appears" to be a shift involving moves from:

deductive to inductive
rhetoric to poetic
literality to orality
hot to cool
science to art
left brain to right brain
direct to indirect
discussive to aesthetic
theme to event
description to image
authoritarian to democratic
top down to bottom up
truth to meaning
account to experience

The whole modern project did little to advance the cause. Instead, a lot of people died. We built "weapons of mass destruction" and used every one of them and "advanced" to the point when it became possible to destroy this frail planet. Where then would we go?

The policy was mutually assured destruction (MAD).

Wars become cold?

Wilfred Owen—the war poet—writes of Abram, when told by the angel to withhold the knife: "Offer the Ram of Pride instead of him. / But the old man would not so, but slew his son, / And half the seed of Europe, one by one."[27] And we were just getting started. Pol Pot killed 1 or 2 million of his own Cambodians; Stalin killed 10 million; Communist China 72 million; Rwandan Huttus killed 800,000 Tutsis in one hundred days; then there was Hitler! The 20th century. "We bring good things to life!"

Christ is all in all or he is nothing.
And *he is for all.*

"One day at a time." Okay, I buy into that. It reminds us of the manna in the wilderness. It was only good for one day. It turned putrid if one sought to hoard it. God will give it again tomorrow. Be cool. What is needed is to decide once and for all that God is good. Grace trumps all else. God wills for no one to perish. Satan cannot defeat us. He may not even exist. The bible says he was just a piss ant fallen angel at any rate. Fuck the Greeks—duality sucks. There need not be the old 'on the one hand... but on the other...'. There may be just wholeness.

27 Owen, W. "The Parable of the Old Man and the Young"

I've been reading the Qur'an. God is One in there. Hell doesn't exist in our Old Testament. No one is tormented in Sheol. Look it up. Satan doesn't really exist in the Old Testament. There he or she is referred to as "ha-satan." You have to read the book of Job carefully. Fuck John Calvin.

(My advice to my fellow Americans: vote Jesus and remember the poor.)

Particle Physics.

Now we turn to the baryonic. Particle Physics.

A baryon is a subatomic particle made up of 3 quarks. The quarks are elemental particles. Hadrons are formed from quarks. Baryonic dark matter is inferred. We can't see this stuff. It is too small. On the larger scale we know an atom has a nucleus, a collection of protons and neutrons. We cannot measure quarks. They are 10,000 times smaller than the nucleus. We build huge, expensive accelerators and we get particles to go almost to the speed of light and we smash them together. The energy released is equal to a 747 taking off.

I don't understand any of this. *But* something like all of this was the stuff of creation. The creator created the universe out of these small things. The very small became the very large. They made a TV show out of this, *The Big Bang Theory*. Well, anyway, we have interesting stuff going on.

Along came Darwin much later. A lady actually asked me one day did I believe in evolution! I said, "well, it's just a theory." That seemed to satisfy her. She went away at least. Oh well. With such as these, I spent 45 years in ministry. If I had a thousand lives, I would give them all to the Methodist church in ministry. God told me to do it. I did it. I love my retired life.

Worship

It's Wednesday morning, up well before the sun becomes apparent. I'm thinking about worship. The wonderful thing about it for me now is I'm retired. I now go to church to, in fact, worship. I sit with Becky.

Her enthusiasms are equal to mine. We are praising God, praying, singing. It is wonderful. It helps, of course, that this service is excellent. Now, some thoughts.

All folks everywhere are already, in fact, worshiping. Just watch someone: you can tell where their focus is. By the way someone lives, they show their values. They demonstrate their belief. The ultimate object of our gratitude becomes the object of our worship. Alas, the object of our gratitude becomes the object of our service. "What are you grateful for, your life, your family, your stuff, your church, your country?" We tend to serve whatever or whoever we think will meet our needs. If one serves God first, then all else tends to fall into place.

God is number one in my life. From whom all blessings flow is the focus of my worship. I go to the temple and make my best sacrifice there; I worship with joy; then wherever else I go has a Godly and a good purpose. I'm not looking for happy. I believe the search for happiness is the number one reason for unhappiness. The reason is that nothing in the world can offer any lasting satisfaction. We move toward the worship of the living God, not the created order. Then the point of life becomes what we call spiritual. *Spiritual* is not a good word, but it is what we have. We *all* are already "spiritual beings." What we need to become is what God had in mind at creation. Thus, what we need to become is a mature human being living in harmony of purpose within the created order. We need to grow up... to be what God intended us to be.

The principle here is that the object of our worship becomes the master of our behavior. If we worship the American dream, then what happens if we lose it? If we worship the living God, then we will be given what we need when we need it. Saint Augustine said, "our hearts are restless until they find their rest in thee." Who is "thee?" There is only one. If I worship the world, I tend to lose whatever I put in the place of God. This means a radical shift in my life. I become a resident alien. Yes, I live in America, but my home is in the new Jerusalem. The next-to-last chapter of the bible describes it well (Rev 21). It's what will happen when God makes things like they are supposed to be. So, America is great and all that, but I belong in another place (God's Kingdom). See 2 Corinthians 5:1-5. It says if this earthly tent we live in is destroyed, we have a building from God.

I always say, *"It's gonna be alright."*

More about the universe.

More than 80% of its mass is missing. We have known about the dark matter since the 1930s, but we have only recently been able to measure it and the results are amazing. The gravity of unseen mass keeps the galaxies from flying apart. Dark matter pulls things together and ordinary matter (stuff) plus dark matter is only 32% of the universe. The rest? Dark *energy*, which pulls things apart. It represents 68% of the universe and explains why the universe is expanding. Ordinary visible matter is only 5% of the universe. Now this means that stuff is special. God made stuff, and creation required that unseen and mysterious forces take up most of the universe. That is, of course, unless through the wormholes are entrances into other universes. Is God really that clever? Remaining to be seen, even though we can't see it.

By the way, our galaxy (Milky Way) and our nearest neighbor galaxy (Andromeda) are scheduled to collide in the far future. What does this mean in terms of the end to be expected from God?

I don't *understand* any of this. Are we meant to? Maybe our task is to *stand under* it all... We treat the presence of God in far too glib a manner. How many new age girls are walking with God in the cool of the day, even though the Bible (Exod 33:20) says no one can see God's face and live? It's the hiddenness of God we must come to terms with.[28] There are different ways of hiding *from* God, but they are all delusional. Do I gain the presence of the God of my understanding in the monastery or in corporate worship? They haunt me, these lonely questions of mine.

Psalm 27 says in verse 4: *"One thing have I asked of the Lord, that I will seek after: that I may dwell in the house of the Lord all the days of my life, to gaze upon the beauty of the Lord and to inquire in his temple."*

Teach me your way, oh Lord.

---

28 A preposition being a word one should not end a sentence with.

What is Light?

Well, one could "simply" say, light is a name for a range of electromagnetic radiation that can be detected by the human eye. Yea verily, I cannot leave it at that. I have learned to complicate issues 'til I am satisfied...

"Where does light come from, and where does darkness go?"
(Job 38:19, NLT)

I have consulted the dictionary, the encyclopedia, and the internet with the conclusion that no one really knows what light is. One fails to define it in its essence. If the light shines in the darkness, I see it, but I do not comprehend it.

If I consult Genesis, I find this strange thing: not until the fourth day of creation did God create the light givers—sun, moon, and such. Oh, God had said "let there be light," but the specific light givers do not appear until verse 16. The implication is that light from the beginning has deeper import than mere shiny stuff. And we now know electromagnetic radiation has a dual nature as both particle and wave. Whoever wrote Genesis could not have known that. Look to the end of the Word; in Rev. 21, the heavenly city set down by God has no need of light sources because God is its light. Wow! God is not like us.

I think of the bit by Marcel Marceau... there is a clown in a corner of a stage in a circle of the spotlight, looking frantically for something. A cop walks up. "What are you looking for?" asks the cop. "My keys," says the clown. The cop and the clown search the circle of light for a while, then the cop says, "Are you sure you lost them here?" "No, over there," says the clown, pointing to a dark corner of the stage. "Then why are you looking for them here?" asks the cop. "Because there is no light over there," answers the clown.

We are in the same position. Light is mysterious. All we know for sure is somehow God spoke the world into existence. How dark it must have been before the big bang.

A better translation of the first sentence of the book of Genesis, in terms of the original Hebrew, is "In the beginning, when God started to create." God wasn't finished. Creation continues. What God creates is dynamic. The deists were wrong. God did not create the universe as if it were a clock to be flung into space as it winds down. God is still messing with stuff.

We now have a sense from science about the incredible relatedness of things. If a butterfly flaps its wings in Japan, and the weather in New York is thereby impacted (that's a serious joke), then things are rather severely related. So, we belong to one another in word and deed.

Once again, the ancient language—Hebrew—has but one word for both *word* and *deed*. To speak it is to be about it. Then, as language in the bible continues to play itself out, we have a continuing sense in which Hebrew has but one word for activities English expresses as work, service, and worship. I find this rather extraordinary. God's ancient, chosen, stiff-necked people sought to bring us wholeness and unity. The Greeks came along and divided everything up. The light got diffused. We today are so fragmented and torn apart that we join the clown in looking for what's lost in all the wrong places. We deep down know better, but we persist. "O Lord, come to us and bathe us with the son-light of the Spirit that we may see and be seen following in your way."

God creates soul as body, mind, and spirit. It seems as if a certain wholeness was intended. The human was undivided. Creation is *wholistic*! We as individuals are body (*basar*) mind (*leb*), and spirit (*nephesh*).

When God said, *"let us make humankind according to our likeness" (Gen 1:26)*, the Hebrew "in our image" included both the male and the female. But a division between soul and body, or spirit and matter, is a later development in Greek thought and is not to be found in the Old Testament. Again, it needs to be said... Fuck the Greeks!

In Genesis 2 we have a further development. Man (*unity*) becomes a living soul (*nephesh hayah*) when God breathed the breath of life (*ruach*) into man. Man does not have a soul, he *is* soul. We are an ensouled body and an embodied soul.

Prayer and Poetry...

As I look back over my life I am struck with a paradox. The very best of times were when I was employed in utterly useless endeavors. Here is the principle: prayer is that useless time with God. If I take myself seriously, then I am stuck with myself and my efforts. If I am able to rest in God, then I have a non-utilitarian agenda. So, again: prayer is that useless time with God. Each day brings prayer, word, study, and play. This must be expressed poetically. Poets understand they do not know what they mean, and this is the source of their strength. *1 Cor. 1:21* says *"for since, in the wisdom of God, the world did not know God through wisdom, it pleased God through the folly of what we preach to save those who believe."*

This I see as God's good humor. So, what I am called to is useless foolishness. That is why there must be poetry, because the reality of God's good gift outruns all our capacities to speak about it. We have no language to say fully what we know about God's love.

So, let us look for guidance from one in scripture, who is so helpful and sensitive to our need individually and corporately—the great advice-giver Jeremiah. The people said to him, "we are innocent, we have not gone after Baal." Jeremiah says, "Oh Yeah?" then he likens them (Jer. 2:24) to confused camels in heat, "sniffing the wind," a wild ass at home in the desert! Kathleen Norris phrases it nicely: we are like camels "making directionless tracks in the sand."[29] On our own, we are helpless.

Norris also writes: "Liturgical time is essentially poetic time, oriented toward process rather than productivity."[30]

---

29 Norris, K. (1996). *The Cloister Walk*. Riverhead Books. 33.
30 Ibid.

It needs to be done... Some have tried; yet they remain widely ignored. We need new ways of recognition. For example: liberal (mainstream) protestant thought vs. conservative (fundamentalist) thought. We have used the same labels for more than a century, and I find them woefully lacking. The same labels are used, but the products beneath them have changed. Alasdair MacIntyre once defined tradition as "an argument extended through time."[31] Good! Let's talk.

First, I am not a liberal! Of the various positions, that would be my least favorite. Yes, I hold some opinions which are regarded as liberal, but I escape being put in this or that box with enthusiasm. I am extremely within the "tradition" of scripture, the church universal (and yes, apostolic). I am energized by liturgy and enamored of ancient spiritual practices. I am pro-life, which for me extends to capital punishment. I am quite globally minded, yet I celebrate the communitarian theology (see Wendell Berry, a poet, not a theologian). So don't fence me in!

"I believe in the holy catholic church." We say it each Sunday. We cannot then think our little circle of socio-spiritualized folks, just like me, can meet the broad statement of belief meant by the creed. The little 'c' from the apostles' creed can lately then have a capital 'C', as the Roman Catholic outfit added.

I love this new pope. It's been a while since I have been able to say that! We do tend to forget no one has a more "conservative" job description than the pope. This new guy has been able to transcend the usual practice. It's too early to tell if much will come of it, but don't forget much and good change is possible, lest we forget John 23! (the pope, not the gospel). Or, if you like, go ahead and look up John, chapter 23 in the New Testament.

It is really an old idea God is not omnipotent. Aquinas wrote God has power to affect only what is in the nature of things. Leibniz also implied that working within the "possible world" limits God's doings. Or put it this way: if God allows us both to suffer and to sin, it must be because he

---

31 MacIntyre, A. (1988). *Whose Justice? Which Rationality?* Notre Dame Press. 33.

cannot here and now just fix things and make a personal appearance now and then. Maybe we have not evolved enough.

Some theologians—Whitehead's school—rescue the old deductive idea of God by asserting that God possesses all good qualities to an absolute degree, therefore he must be absolutely sensitive, and thus absolutely vulnerable. This to me suggests God is the perfect new-age guy. The whole process of thinking we, with our partial knowledge of God, can sort things out through philosophical inquiry is absurd. So, it's logically a fair question to ask, what then is God's job description? What, if anything, does God do?

God does not give as the world gives. God left god's-self outside the realm of necessity. All this, of course, is why God gave Christians Jesus. It is incredible to consider that Paul Tillich, in a three-volume set on theology, gave us only two paragraphs on prayer. But, in my lifetime, I have known *many* times the power of prayer. Maybe one should simply read Barth instead of Tillich. Or how about this: "Plunge into matter," Teilhard said—and at another time, "plunge into God." And he says this fine thing: "By means of all created things, without exception, the divine assails us, penetrates us and molds us. We imagined it as distant and inaccessible, whereas in fact we live steeped in its burning layers."[32]

(And it is all God, and it is all Good.)

We settled down about 10,000 years ago and began what has been called history. So, what is our history? We are civilized generation number 500 or so. That's not long at all. So history is relatively new. If we look at our species, we are homo sapiens generation number 7,500 (counting from 150,000 years ago when our species presumably arose). If you really want to stretch it, we are something like human generation number 125,000, counting from as far back as possible. I suppose if DNA were to

32 Teilhard de Chardin, P. (1960). *The Divine Milleu*. New York, NY. Harper & Row. 83.

be found from the very earliest of human types, we could trace it up to such as us.

God needs such as us. We matter. Since God is spirit, we must hold the view that we, as matter, derive from spirit. Or I like to look at it this way:

In the beginning, God. God created the Word. The Word was from the beginning God and was with God. Then the Word became flesh and dwelt among us. So there you are.

How about this paradox! The Jews came up with it; I think... God—the God of the universe. This God to whom a galaxy is no more significant than a bacterium is at the same time great enough or loving enough or involved enough that a single human being can be as significant to Him as an entire universe. Now that's stating the case!

In the US of A, for which we stand, only 6,381 of us die each day, but 10,852 of us pop out of our mothers per day. There we are, born between the piss and the shit. Humans are supposed to be the best God can do. We are quite helpless at birth and for some time after. If we don't get a number of things from our parents, we will never get those things. So, if we are not doing so well now, what are we going to do with all these new humans emerging from the womb of their mothers?

And that's just this country. What of these teaming masses yearning to be free? Our country's foreign policy does its best. After all, our country cannot stand to go too long without bombing the hell out of some brown-skinned people somewhere. Once again Congress and the president are dicking around about whether Syria should benefit from some surgical missiles.

God's being imminent, said the rabbi, depends on us. The rabbis, as a whole, say God does nothing except as a result of prayer. They say God needs man. The creator places Himself in our hands. Christians, on the other hand, have Jesus. Remember when they brought the woman caught in adultery to Jesus? He knelt down and wrote something in the sand. We need to know what he wrote. Was it a list of things to do before the crucifixion?

Again, from the Jesuit paleontologist, "In our hands, the hands of all of us, the world and life (*our world, our life*) are placed like a Host, ready to be charged with the divine influence." Then he assured us, "The mystery will be accomplished."[33]

---

33 Ibid. 111.

Science and Theology

In the realm of the very small, the subatomic quantum world, if we ask the scientists to then prove their work, science can only point to the way we seem to "know" the way the world works and quarks *must* exist: we *infer* their existence, though no one has ever seen one. This is not Pascal's wager. It is a different quantum logic, different from the classical logic of Aristotle. The Heisenbergian uncertainty asserts that quarks and electrons can only be known to us on their own terms. We cannot point to them in the lab. Similarly, the divine nature is to be known in the manner God has determined to reveal it.

Theology, of course, cannot point to the logical proof of the existence of the Trinity. Yet science and theology are both concerned with realities. The *what* and the *how* is the meeting place for both disciplines, and much is to be gained from dialogue from each field.

Here is the deal. It seems entities must also be known on their own terms. How entities are known must accord with their own nature; that nature is revealed in what we know of them. No thought escapes this circle! As we search for the *truth* of reality, we can come to the deep intellectual satisfaction we call *understanding*. This is also *standing under*: creation remains mysterious.

The good news is that the modern world is dead. The terrible twentieth century has come and gone. Granted, the world looks little better in these years after 9/11, but there is yet hope. Many bright folks have given up. I'm not all that bright, but I can see a world where even Congress can come together. Well, maybe not Congress, but we must not give up hope. I don't and won't quit. If the people who run the world don't believe in evolution or global warming, I can at least hope they love their children. It remains a bit of a shock that the universe seems to be running out of gas, but there is some time left and the Creator may yet have a game plan.

A universe moving from big bang to hot death or cosmic crunch hardly brings comfort to the human heart, but at the very least we can move away from the concept of mutually assured destruction, the foreign policy of the last century. Many people are opposed to our country bombing Syria. Is that not an opportunity for even republicans and democrats to come together and finally actually accomplish something? The outlook is indeed gloomy, but I cannot abandon all claims about God's continuing care for and involvement in what we call creation or the universe. If I did, the only thing left would be some Tennessee sipping whiskey.

A cultural shift has taken place in the world from the 1980s to the 2010s. The world-wide explosion of TV and internet has resulted in an improved means toward an unimproved end. There has occurred a depreciation of cultural memory. The old canons of value have eroded. A disconnect has occurred in the ways most of us have been trained to think. The news media brings such an enormity of data. Anyone can post anything, and there is no way to judge whether such postings are what we used to call 'true' or not. Some would say, well, 'what is truth?' That wouldn't be a new question, after all. Pontius Pilate asked it in a discussion with the Prince of Peace, and then came crucifixion. Now it's a comfort to the believer that a resurrection came. But I guess you have to believe that something hard to believe is, again, what we call *true*.

The truth is, the postmodern world does not demand deep wisdom, maturity, and informed judgment to function. Children are taught how to make snap decisions using only devices for back-up. What if an elementary teacher somewhere demanded students memorize something? That would cause quite a stir. Memory thereby disappears along with any real cultural significance having been taught or received.

There is nothing in this world that can offer any lasting satisfaction. If we are in the world but not of the world, we can know who God is and who we are. We can learn to worship the living God. *We don't worship creation; we worship the creator*. In fact, we are already at worship. Just watch someone and see what matters to them. If we worship anything other than God, our worship is misdirected. The ultimate object of our gratitude becomes the object of our worship. Also, the object of our gratitude is the object of our service since we serve whatever or whoever we think will meet our needs.

We have an inchoate gratitude, and it is misguided unless it becomes formed on the firm foundation of Jesus Christ. Therefore, worship and service must be joined together, flip sides of the same coin; enter to worship and depart to serve—flip sides of the same sign. The principle here is that the object of our worship always becomes the master of our behavior.

I am more and more drawn to that Stranger of Galilee. What He said and what He did. To be so makes me more and more a kind of resident alien in this place. My primary residence is in the Kingdom of God. And at my age, I've got at least one foot—my only foot—in that place not made with hands (2 Cor 5:1-5). It is declared eternal in the heavens. My desire, as Paul said, is whether in this life or at home with the Lord, my purpose is to always please Him.

I'm starting to lean more into the notion of parallel universes. I don't know how God can pull this off, in terms of what we know from science, but I believe and have faith. 2 Cor. 5:1 says: *"For we know that if the tent that is our earthly home is destroyed, we have a building from God... eternal in the heavens."* And v.5: *"He who has prepared us for this very thing is God, who has given us the Spirit as a guarantee."* Then, in verse 11, one of the great 'therefores' of the New Testament: *"therefore, knowing the fear of the Lord, we persuade others..."*

I'm constantly at work with my curious form of evangelism. I'm not trying to get other folk to be like me, heaven forbid. I'm trying to get the world to be the world. What God has already done is good enough for me. I guess my spirituality is quite orthodox. Saint Augustine said famously, "our hearts are restless until they find their rest in thee." 'Thee' is the God of my understanding, the *Trinity*. The blessed Trinity is the way of looking at the Old and New Testament that they came up with after going through the whole thing after the canon was closed. To me it's this way: the best way to look at God is through the lens provided by the Blessed Trinity. The doctrine not spelled out in the bible is the way it has to be in the church. While we are in, but not of, this world, we experience God as Father, Son, and Holy Spirit. I lift up Jesus because those old bibles have what He said in red. I'm a red-letter Christian. That's the way to live on this planet. To live this way means you are going to get in trouble constantly. (Still in chapter 5), v. 17: *"Therefore, if anyone is in Christ, he is a new creation: everything old has passed; see, everything has become new."* I can certainly remember the old, and I don't want to return. The miracle I experienced was God removed the obsession with drugs and alcohol. It was removed by God because I certainly could not do it. All those times I said, "I'll never do that again..." and then just a little later I was back at it. Over and over that lasted. My families and I went through that for a quarter of a century! The Blessed Trinity did for me what I could not do for myself. I now believe God had a purpose for me. I was chosen to do good work and work I did. As I look back on it all, I am thankful.

"Hope has two beautiful daughters; their names are Anger and Courage. *Anger* at the way things are, and *Courage* to see that they do not remain as they are."
- St. Augustine

Schopenhauer said: "To forgive and forget means to throw away dearly bought experience."

I am not God. If I have truly received forGIVEness, then I have been given a gift from God. Thus, I do not regret the past or wish to close the door on it.

Here's the deal: to be related to any human being is to be both healed and hurt, both wounded and made whole. Bill W. wrote, "pain is the touchstone of all growth."[34]

34 Wilson, B. (1952). *Twelve Steps and Twelve Traditions.* Alcoholics Anonymous World Services Inc.

My favorite graffiti:

"Reality is for those who can't handle drugs."

William James famously used a fearsome German word to describe the inevitable brokenness that is life on life's terms: *Zerrissenheit*. My translation: a veritable shitstorm. It's as if our whole culture was homeless. No one has any place wherein they fit. We find salvation when we find God accepts us, just as we are. Then gradually we learn to accept ourselves. Finally, we are able to accept others. In the hurt, there is the potential for healing.

"All wisdom is plagiarism; only stupidity is original."

- Buddhist Proverb

Hope is a matter of letting one's self go. Hope puts an end to presumption. Hope lies secure in God who cannot be controlled or manipulated. Presumption and despair have to do with our refusal to let ourselves go and to lie back in the everlasting arms of God. Hope is openness to the future of God and as such is far from being a deadening opiate rendering us as passive or immobile in the face of any challenge. Actually, hope is angry for a better world, and it is that which commands and empowers us to trust enough to undertake an exodus out of the present into a future held by God. Hope, in this life, has a temporal quality and is a state of readiness, and like faith and love, is only displayed in action. When we have hope, we are not merely optimists; we are changed into committed persons of faith and love.

I Peter 3:15: *"Be ready to make your defense when anyone challenges you to justify the hope which is in you."*

Christoph Schwöbel wrote:

> If we see the story of Jesus' death and resurrection as the paradigmatic story about God, it becomes clear that this story discloses the faithfulness of God to his

> creation, which grants continuity through the discontinuity of death. The hope of creation to overcome the absolute discontinuity of death is not based on an inherent capacity of creation because death is the end of all created capacities. The disruption of all relationships that can be maintained by a creature. The hope of creation is based on God's maintaining his unconditionally creative relationship to his creation. The continuity that transcends the discontinuity of death is grounded in the constancy of God's love, which brings to expression the unchangeable character of God's being.[35]

This means the gospel story about Jesus has *universal* significance. Jesus' story is God's own story. Our response can only be faith. Faith as the unconditional trust in God is the absolute reliance on the creative relationship of God to his creation. This is the basis for life beyond life. Death simply does not have the last word.

I read recently all good sermons do one of two things: they either start in Jerusalem and proceed to one's own community, or they start in one's own community and proceed to Jerusalem. That means all good sermons have an eschatological thrust. The dwelling place of God is particular, not universal. Revelation 21 tells us God comes to us and brings us home to his home. Jerusalem is a specific symbol of the irresistible Kingdom of God. The earthly city is transformed into the heavenly city. Just think of the music that will be played there.

35 Schwöbel, C. (2000). The church as a cultural space: eschatology and ecclesiology. In Polkinghorne, J.C (Ed.), *The End of the World and the Ends of God*. Trinity Press International. 116.

George Steiner has written of music:

> Music and the metaphysical, in the root sense of that term, music and religious feeling, have been virtually inseparable. It is in and through music that we are most immediately in the presence of the logically, verbally inexpressible but wholly palpable energy in being that communicates to our senses and to our reflection what little we can grasp of the naked wonder of life. I take music to be the naming of life. This is, beyond any liturgical or theological specificity, a sacramental notion.[36]

So, on that day we will be both singers in the eschatological choir and guests at the eschatological banquet. Think of the sacramental dinner talk around the table. (Read Psalms 145-150 for a foretaste of the glory divine.)

36 Steiner, G. (1989). *Real Presences: Is There Anything in What We Say?* London. Faber & Faber. 216-17.

New Testament

Hope so... the word "hope" (*elpis*) is the regular and common word from everyday language (in Greek) and keeps close to that language throughout the New Testament. We who use the New Testament have hope through faith. Faith is not confidence in the things of the world. It is confidence in God. Faith does not rely on the creature; it relies on the creator. The results of scientific research are not directly relevant for religious hope.

Paul seems to be the most helpful writer in the New Testament. *"If in Christ we have hope in this life only, we are of all people most to be pitied"* (1 Cor. 15:19). Hope is relevant for human life only if it is valid as well for human death—the hope for resurrection from the dead which has its evidence in the resurrection of Jesus. Abraham hoped against hope that Yahweh was faithful. He overcame ordinary hope. He had hope based on faithfulness of the promise. Abraham's faith became pure hope as God worked in his life.

The way the new enters into the universe is through the Creator. The nature of God's work is to create things out of nothing. Science always must start no earlier than the first second after the big bang, never before.

Now, as to personal eschatology: if there is life after birth, is there hope for life after death? Well, yes, and hope is what we have, but not just plain old hope, but hope that has been purified. This is done by God, the Creator who brings life out of nothing and who calls the dead unto life. All of which is predicated upon the resurrection of Jesus Christ.

The true faith in the radical creativity of God has the faith that eternal life exists completely in the grace of God. It is a life out of death. That which is described by natural science as a finite being is perceived by faith as a creature. Both aspects are combined in the New Testament use of the word *sarx*, 'flesh'. While the creator is free to create, the creature has been given a definite and vulnerable form like an earthen vessel (2 Cor. 4:7). If worldly experience were not to claim any clues about eternal life, nothing could be said about it; it would remain an empty fantasy. There is continuity in the sense of "seeing" the world to come; there is also discontinuity in that we cannot yet know the qualitative newness of the gift of the creator.

Again, we turn to Paul. The *soma* (body) is sown a natural body, it is raised a spiritual body. The spiritual body survives the gap between time and eternity. In Paul's writing, *soma* does not mean the matter of a human being, but rather the whole person (material body, soul, and spirit). We don't *have* a soul; we *are* a soul. So, when the trumpet shall sound, we shall be raised incorruptible. The naked seed is sown, a dead body is given back to the earth, but the future expression of that body is a peaceful relationship with God which shall persist into the new Jerusalem. "In my beginning is my end, and in my end is my beginning."

ars moriendi: the art of dying

In both the Old Testament and the New Testament our life beyond this life is always spoken of in terms of the divine spirit (*ruach, pneuma*) which gives life to all the living. We do not have the notion of some sort of Platonic soul. The spirit of God gives us eternal life on the basis of a relationship of the whole person to the God of eternity. "Breathe on me, Breath of God, so shall I never die."[37]

According to biblical ideas, this Spirit, who is the giver of life, is in a divine relationship out of which life and the blessing of life proceed. If God is God, his relation to the human form cannot be destroyed. Only God can dissolve the relationship to his creatures into which he has entered, as long as God holds on to this created relationship in his image and our life is in him. Our life in time is transitory, but we have an eternal presence in God. God's memory of us is a healing presence in our lives,

37 Hatch, E. (1878).

whether in time or in eternity. "The one to whom God speaks, whether in wrath or in grace, that one is surely immortal," (Martin Luther). So, although we cannot hold on to anything, everything remains in God. Moltmann has written, "At the end of my life I experience dying but I don't experience my own death, because on this earth I don't survive it. But in the case of the people I love, I experience their death."[38] When death has lost its power over human beings, God is then in charge of his creature, and we can rest secure in God's time. What God has begun, God will carry on.

Now, we are not yet "a soul which has found rest!" The bible says this is *not yet* the kingdom of God. It is not yet "the life of the world to come." It is a state between the life that has died *here* and eternal life *there*. Those we call dead are not lost, but God has more to come which has not as yet been revealed. So, if we are the so-called *living*, we are those who remain in the mystery of the not yet. But we have faith and hope the 'future' is held secure by God.

> ...having accomplished nothing, and being unable to make anything easier than it had already been made... I conceived it as my task everywhere to create difficulties. - S. Kierkegaard[39]

It is instructive that hope is both a noun and a verb. This points to the power of the word and helps posit the problem: do we hope things might somehow get better *or* do we believe and hope in God? The hope that falls into the category of what I want to happen is really a guess as to what I want, a "power of positive thinking." That hope is empty. If our hope begins in God, it is a mystery to be revealed in revelation. In our hoping, we dare not be presumptuous. By hoping we do not become privy to the purposes of God. The path to hope in God is also the way of humility.

38 Moltmann, J. (2004). *In the End-the Beginning: The Life of Hope* (M. Kohl, trans.). Fortress Press. 107.
39 Kierkegaard, S. (2009). *Concluding Unscientific Postscript*. Cambridge University Press. 157.

Gabriel Marcel wrote: "the truth is that there can strictly speaking be no hope except when the temptation to despair exists. Hope is the act by which this temptation is actively or victoriously overcome."[40] So, to *hope* doesn't necessarily mean to *feel* hopeful. What hope does do is to free us from capitulating before a cultural expectation (like the Dow Jones average). There can be no selfishness in hope that proceeds from God. We rise above the future in hope. It is always a biblical hope against hope. We still have a non-acceptance of the present situation in our hoping, yet we are patient and open to that which will be revealed by God. To wait without hope is to be without God. To hope, but not be willing to wait, destroys true hope because we ourselves are tempted to bring about and control the outcome of that which we hope for. Hopeful waiting or a waiting hope is a genuine eschatological hope because what we are *enabled to hope for is already initiated in Christ and will be fulfilled in him.* Hope correlates with the serenity of *being* contrary to the insecurity of *having*. Hope comes only from God. There! That's enough of that.

We have the best congress money can buy. And the one we deserve, since the stupid party is having a tea party at our expense.

Here is an irony: "If people destroy something replaceable made by mankind, they are called vandals; if they destroy something irreplaceable made by god, they are called developers."[41] A congress of developers!

Henry David Thoreau wrote in his journal, "the earth I tread on is not a dead inert mass. It is a body, has a spirit, is organic, and is fluid to the influence of its spirit, and to whatever particle of that spirit is in me..."[42]

Dr. Craddock wrote: "To write for one is not to write for all; to write for all is not to write for one."[43]

---

40 Marcel, G. (1962). *Homo Viator: Introduction to a Metaphysic of Hope.* (E. Craufurd, Trans.). Harper Torchbooks/Cloister Library. 36.

41 Krutch, J.W.

42 Klein, N. (1915). *This Changes Everything: Capitalism vs. the Climate.* Simon & Schuster.

43 Craddock, F.B. (1990). *Luke.* Louisville, Kentucky. John Knox Press. vii.

Writing must have form...

Writing must have form. Form is simply the task of arousing interest and fulfillment of desires. A work has form insofar as one part of it leads a reader to look forward to that which follows and to be glad when that part arrives. Thus, all writing carries sequence. In sermons, ideas do not carry sequence as well as people do. Therefore, put more people in sermons. If the listener is involved in the sermon and gets caught up in the action of the sermon, the sermon is effective. I have come to believe preaching in these times consists of helping people to believe things they already want to believe, but they suspect just aren't true. People desire to come to belief, or they would not come to church. At least this is largely true.

They, of course, don't want the whole faith thing to cost them much. It takes considerable skill to help move folks from that position to the Gospel message (Christ bids us come and die). And yet the innate truth of the message has a power which can help the seeker to remain long enough that they may be found. All great stories have a power that compels human nature to progress to a deeper and nobler place. Why else are people so grateful to finally arrive at a place of true truth? When they arrive, they realize this was the destination they had been looking for without even knowing it. It's all in the journey and the stories encountered along the way.

In many of the churches of my experience, much too much energy has gone into saying who they are not and not nearly enough about who they are. The earliest Christians were known as the people of the way. They were on a shared journey. Their salvation was experienced on the way. It was revealed. So, what did St. Paul contribute to this when he said it is God's will that all men be saved? First, perhaps, our being saved does not have to do with an isolated instant of conversion; and second, its central benefit is not simply our being delivered from hell. The way to salvation is not to gain reward nor escape punishment; rather, it is the way of an evolving relationship. Salvation is an ongoing process of receiving redemption; it is our recovery from chronic separation from God, a recovery that is eternal. It's not so much dying and going to heaven; it's about finally living on both sides of the grave.

Now, again, this is offered to all humankind. I read an account of a wise, old monk in the east who was visited by an evangelical from the west. The monk was asked, but "isn't Jesus your personal Lord and Savior?" "No," the smiling monk said without hesitation. "I like to share him."

It's all in the sharing. We share Christ's body. We are baptized. We acquire our salvation through our being of that body and through our partaking of that body. Thus, when I hear someone say they are spiritual but not religious, I long to see that person undivided. I would hope that person's body could be joined to their spirit. Satan looks for any vessel sailing without a fleet. An individualized, isolated spirituality cannot sustain itself, and faith is not something that can be both solitary and healthy. Even God is in relationship. The One God is said to exist in Three Persons engaged in a single *perichoresis*.

The worst form of idolatry is not carving an image; it is the presumption one has—or any group has—the right to set the terms under which God can be recognized.

Mark 11:28: *"By what authority are you doing these things, or who gave you this authority to do them?"* they asked Jesus.

Today's Christians do not question the state. Jesus engaged in direct attacks on the state in the Holy City at festival time. He was hardly a law and order kind of guy. Nor was there any attempt to rationalize his position; instead, he problematizes their position. Today, the state doesn't say to the church, "by what authority do you say that or do this?" Why? Because we don't question the state. We are safe in our gated communities.

The system works quite well for us. We have given away our authority. Christians have conceded to the State authority over the public sphere in hopes of retaining a modicum of authority over the private sphere. How is this following Jesus?

the Milky Way...

A new study has looked at our little neighborhood. By that, I mean just the stuff in our galaxy we fondly call the Milky Way. It is one of trillions and trillions of galaxies, each with trillions and trillions of stars, as this was a quite 'restrictive' study. They found there are, as our 'closest' neighbors, about 8.8 billion earth-size, just-right planets in our galaxy. By 'just right' they mean planets in the Goldilocks zone—not too hot and not too cold for life, a habitable temperature zone. So, we have more such planets than there are people on earth. Next, we look for atmospheres which would provide further clues. The study sought out planets where water could be liquid. When people complain about the weather I always think "thank God for the weather." It is a quite valuable thing. How self-absorbed we are, and how can we be the only carbon-based life forms 'out there'? *And* did God put all God's redemptive energies into just this little blue planet? What would a Jesus from another planet be like?

Barth would perhaps still hold on to the scandal of particularity, but he is dead and not available for comment. As for me, I can't even grasp the full impact of the Jesus we do have, but I too believe He would suffice for all these 8.8 billion planets in our little galaxy! How's that for bragging on Jesus?

At this time, I'm not ready to speak for other galaxies.

We live in a time, asserted Edward Abbey in his "Writer's Credo," when it is:

> ...not merely heretical but treasonous to question our own government's policies, to doubt the glory of planetary capitalism, to object to the religion of endless economic growth, or to wonder about the ultimate purpose, value, and consequences of our techno-military-industrial empire. Those who persist in raising doubt and question are attacked by defenders of order as the "adversary culture." Very well: let us be adversaries.[44]

Jesus was such an adversary. How can the church do differently?

But every present passes, and what is past never returns. Daily we are given opportunities. How can individuals and the communion of saints learn to step up and serve?

I can do what I can as an example... carefully... as in full of care. I do that to God's glory, not to show others. Then God uses individual contributions for the edification of the community. Is it 'moral man and immoral society' or is it 'moral society and immoral man'? The answer can only be *yes*. By that is meant: individuals and communities are under the influence of the Holy Spirit if good occurs! God uses all the relationships!

It has been interesting for me to realize my primary duty at St. John has been to simply love the folks. Especially I love the blatant conservatives (and most are). I don't stir up stuff because I'm there first to worship and love. Now, they know where I am coming from by inference. There is a certain freedom in being inductive rather than declaratory. One leads the people to the edge of the matter where they are free to form their own judgments. I can simply point to Jesus who is out there ahead of us all, calling us to come and follow him.

44 Abbey, E. (1988). One Life at a Time, Please. New York, NY. Holt. 168.

Theodicy

I'm doing a study on theodicy lately.

It is interesting to find there may not be a "problem of evil" which makes any real sense. Like spirituality, theodicy is a relative latecomer. No question is ever asked in a historical vacuum; a question is asked in a specific time and place by specific persons. If God is loving and at the same time all powerful, then why is there suffering? The assumption is that God could, if God would, simply eliminate suffering. If the question is framed that way, there is perhaps no answer that will suffice.

The fact is, the contradictions of a benevolent divine omnipotence and the existence of evil were not seen by Christian thinkers as an obstacle to belief in the Middle Ages! Only after the 17th century was there a problem. The pre-Enlightenment theologians saw the reality of suffering as a practical challenge for the Christian community (Rom 5:1-5). Now we live in the aftermath of the modern world. Things should be different. Our technology was supposed to fix everything and flatten out the mysteries and bring new things to life. Instead, things got worse. Medicine has failed us, not in a technological sense but in a moral sense. When science became only empirical, the ability to make moral judgments was left by the wayside. How can there be a 'good death' if the damn machine is still plugged in and all concerned employees are only concerned with covering their ass? Of course, the machines do get unplugged. Usually the family has to make the decision while standing by the bedside. The implication is that medicine has failed us once again. What is 'alive'? Are we to last forever? If Jesus had not been killed, would he still be alive? When would I like to die? Am I the one to make that call?

Christians have become caught up in a situation which assumes there is always the ability to explain "the way things are." This 'habit' of mind developed when Christianity became a civilizational religion in the Constantinian aftermath. Christianity was to provide the ethos to sustain an empire rather than a movement that followed Jesus. This means our faith now has a stake in making sure the balance of church and state is sustained in such a way that the goals of the Christian emperor are carried out. In order to do so, we must see history as a sphere of strict cause and effect. Thus the 'good' must ultimately triumph. The "problem of evil" is to show why those with 'right' beliefs must prevail in worldly terms. So, our belief in God is based on being on the winning side of history. A mechanistic metaphysic is combined with a sentimental account of God. Thus, the pagan assumption that the gods are to be judged by how well they ensure our purposes are to be underwritten in the name of Christianity is applied to our faith.

Modern medicine developed as a still young science after the positivistic philosophy of Descartes, who helped establish an unbridgeable gap between the life of the mind and of the body. Modern medicine came along and treated the body as a kind of machine. Thus, illnesses and diseases are regarded as malfunctions of the body's mechanics. The whole person got left out. The life story of the person is discarded. Yet, it is only within a life story that illness has a meaningful place. The patient has become a *what*, not a *who*. We need to understand our story located within God's narrative. God has not abandoned us, even if we are ill or our loved ones are dying.

God created us and gave us moral freedom. We were thus able to choose the good. At first there was only Adam. There he was, alone in the garden of delights. He was created alone so he could experience the fact that even amidst the glory of creation it is not good to be alone. So, he was given a mate, and she was naked and that was good, but the ability to make bad choices was still there. The serpent was not Satan. The serpent was one of God's creatures. The situation was, could the three of them combine their wits to thus exceed their creaturehood? A world of hurt was to then follow. Temptation appears to be given along with creaturehood.

At this point, temptation cannot be separated from God. We were created anxious, and this is the source of our creativity but also of our sin. Now this does not mean sin is intrinsic to our being as creatures. Sin is not *innate* within us. The fall was not inherent in creation. The potential for sin was there in our anxiety, however.

In my anxiety, I chose an artificial remedy: alcohol. It led to a lot of anxiety. I purchased an alleged freedom of or from anxiety at a very high price. Sin was involved, but my first beer was not necessarily a sin. That came later. Suffering was thus there in creation, but not from the hand of God in a direct sense. Life without any kind of suffering would not be what we know as life. The life of the spirit, like the life of the body, depends in a mysterious way upon the struggle to be. So, as a condition necessary to life itself, is the presence of life's antitheses. All of this must mean death is part of God's good creation. Death is still the enemy, but it is a useful enemy.

Creation did not *have to be.* Creation is God's free self-giving. The answer to the question 'why is there something; why not nothing?' is that God wanted things to be.

Our existence makes sense only insofar as we are able to place it within a narrative. We are within the tradition of the Hebrew scriptures; thus, we have a rather grand example of a people who are adept at expressing their pain. The book of Psalms is the prime example. In fact, the Hebrews lifted complaining to a high art form (See Ps. 13, which ends in affirmation, but 35 and 86 don't). Often the Old Testament gives no explanation or attempt to explain the problems of suffering; it is simply acknowledged. The book of Job never answers the question of suffering. Job finally has God speaking out of the whirlwind, not with an explanation, but a "just who do you think you are?"

I think of the contemporary Pastor who ordered the music staff never to play anything in a minor key... just happy thoughts. Positive thinking should chase the devil from the door, right? I wonder if that pastor had ever read the bible. The task instead is to name the silences our suffering has created. It is as if a people unable to shake its fist in God's face would be as well a people incapable of living life as it is given faithfully. The God who created is not merely a God of goodness and power, but also the God who called Israel and gave us the life of Jesus, including the crucifixion and resurrection. This may not be the God we think we want, but it is certainly the God we've got.

So, are we to truly rejoice in our sufferings (Rom. 5)!? Any truthful account of the Christian life cannot leave out suffering. It is, in fact, integral to life. But this is a hard fact. It takes years in a pastor's life before he or she can really be with and comfort the person who can see nothing beyond that hole in the ground where their loved one lies. Then we leave that hole to be filled with dirt and go back to the church for potato salad.

The connection between Christ's suffering and our own suffering is not an easy one to make. Yet in worship the cross is where we turn to when we are being formed by the gospel. This process is nothing other than the working out of our baptism.

The question to ask is, "how do you want to die?" "Well, quickly and painlessly, of course!" (And I don't want to be a burden on someone.)

I've been with many people in such a situation many times in my ministry, and I can think of a few times things worked out just as we had hoped or things worked out as they "should" work out. In the old days, preachers advised folks to go to sleep each night as if they were not to awaken. Their sins confessed, they were always ready: "Now I lay me down to sleep." Children were taught death lurks around and souls would be kept somewhere. Preparation for death was important. We no longer share a vision of a good death. Maybe we can learn a thing or two from the 13th century.

More on Music and Poetry

I'm grateful I can appreciate the genius of Beethoven. If there are heights to be scaled by an artist, Beethoven is at the highest peak. As I listen to the late string quartets over and over, I hear new expressions of his creative genius each time. What a great gift to be able to have this love of music to be stronger now than at any point in my life. I don't 'do' music now, and I don't really miss it, but I appreciate it more than ever.

Singing, conducting, guitar, keyboard, and trumpet. I loved them all, but now I'm learning to listen, just as now in church I learn to worship. It is a good way to do life. People don't get how I can just walk away from performing and not look back. I think part of it is I was always short of the mark of true excellence in all my endeavors. Now, as a lover, there is no critical level to aspire to. I just laugh and love and lift. Anyway, the trajectory of my life revealed my chief gifts had to do with words. Reading, preaching, teaching—those were the things I was called to do. Life is good, and the best is yet to be.

Yes, I do believe that. Up at 5am and at my work. It has taken this long in my life to really feel like I am able to bear the load. Why is it my preaching and teaching is better received at St. John than at other places? I would hope it has to do with the changes God has made in my life. I know not, and it is none of my business. My part is to suit up and show up. Ego adds nothing to the equation.

I still have a strong need (desire) to contribute. That is what keeps me going. If I felt that my church or AA life amounted to nothing much, I would not get out of bed in the morning. It pleases me to be used for good. Thank you, Jesus!

Ran into a poem by Irish poet Monk Gibbon. It's in Stanley Hauerwas' memoir.

The Last Thing

Who'd be afraid of death.
I think only fools
are. For it is not
as though this thing
were given to one man only, but all
receive it. The journey that my
friend makes, I can
make also. If I know
nothing else. I know
this, I go where he is.
O Fools, shrinking from this little door,
Through which so many kind and lovely souls have passed
Before you,
Will you hang back?
Harder in your case than another?
Not so.
And too much silence?
Has there not been enough stir here?
Go bravely, for where so much greatness and gentleness have been
Already, you should be glad to follow.[45]

We must have quite a radical view of Jesus Christ and what he has done and is doing as the 2nd person of the trinity. We need a strong doctrine of the church as the best hope for a correct reading of history, but with a strong emphasis on the eschatological view that God will bring things to the end that is to be expected from Him as creator and sustainer. Mostly we need an intervention of some sort from the Trinity that can

45 Qtd. in *Hannah's Child.* (2010). Eerdmans. 282.

turn history from its 'modern' notions of progress into a view that teaches Christians to act as Christians.

I often feel John Wesley is forgotten not only by the Methodist Church but also by the theologians. That he founded the Methodists is not denied, but his importance to what Christians should be about has been downplayed. His doctrine of grace alone should lift him to the level of Luther or certainly Calvin. Some have said his work in England helped that nation to avoid the kind of revolution suffered in France (*Tale of Two Cities*). His sojourn in America and his later sending pastors to America helped to establish a church which is surely American (although some would say *that* is quite problematic). I think his most often overlooked contribution is he provided ways to help the West appreciate the East. It never quite took hold; yet what a gift if we could overcome that ancient split.

A cartoon shows this new Pope Francis. Subject: how do you expect to run a religion like that? The Pope is holding up a sign that reads "Love, Caring, Justice." The world's response: "You're making exactly the same crazy, impractical mistakes as Jesus."

Repentance is not being sorry, it's being different.

Conditional love is self-gratification.

The beatitude word doesn't mean *happy*. That word falls so far short. It's the Greek word *makarios*. It's a much more joyful word than *happy* (happenstance). It is to happy what agape is to love. It comes from God alone as an undeserved gift. We have *makarios* as we enter the Kingdom. *Makarios* are the meek mourners, the hungry peacemakers, the poor in spirit merciful, the poor persecuted. Why? Well, because they are in the world but not of the world; because they follow in the footsteps of the young and fearless prophet of ancient Galilee, because we now have an eternal home in the heavens. But then you read on in the sermon Jesus gave and fall up against what seems an impossible ethic. Can he mean this literally? All that turning the cheek stuff is not what I advised my son to do on the playground. We've got to live in the US of A. You can't get things done by acting that way. I've been to the self-help section in the bookstore. You can get in trouble by taking Jesus literally.

To whom were those words addressed on the mountain? To America the beautiful... or was he talking to those disciples with whom he had been walking? How do you get a throng of people to be salt and light? Why would Jesus say all that stuff if He didn't mean it? Didn't He know we were not able to live that way? How many times a day do I lust? Well, I lost count. That's not all. If I look at the whole sermon as we have it in Matthew, I can't do any of it. So why did He say it?

Well, of course, we who have studied such matters for a long time can assure you that you needn't worry too much. The economy seems to be recovering, our defense system still works, sometimes we can go for more than a week without someone shooting up a school. It's OK in my neighborhood. Why worry over things we cannot do, anyway? But wait a minute. This is Jesus Christ, the second member of the Trinity talking. When He talks, we listen. Maybe I'm not OK, and I know some of you are not OK.

There is a difference between folks who admire Jesus and those who would be disciples. Jesus sees the crowds, that's what the bible says, but then it says Jesus goes up the mountain and the disciples follow. Then in the rest of Matthew there are those who follow Jesus, and those who don't.

After this, the disciples are sent out to teach repentance to the people. How will this all end? Or has the end not yet come? Today, how do we tell the difference between the disciples and the crowd? The sheep and the goats? The true citizens of the Kingdom of God and those whose allegiance is in the world and what they may gain of the things of the world? Those who follow the Lamb of God and those whose attitudes resemble the scribes and the Pharisees?

Some say these words found in the Sermon on the Mount are fine in the personal lives of Christians, but in the real world, this is no way to run a government. Does Jesus really think we can live without lust? anger? greed? How can one nation turn the other cheek to another nation? Some other folks say since the whole world has been saved by grace, then Christians can live like everyone else. But here is the point, as it seems to be when I read the text. The Sermon on the Mount is the reality of the new age made possible *in time* by Jesus Christ. Thus, we must be careful not to distinguish the sermon from the one who delivers it. This is Jesus talking. The Sermon on the Mount is to be understood as the Word of God who became human. The demands of the Sermon are but ideals if this is not the Son of God. If we abandon these radical demands, we abandon Jesus. This sermon is the constitution of a people. You cannot live by the demands of the sermon on your own, and that is the point! The sermon is not a list of requirements, but rather a description of the life of a people gathered by and around Jesus. To be saved is to be so gathered. The Beatitudes are the interpretative key to the whole of the Sermon—precisely because they are not mere recommendations.

Jesus doesn't suggest everyone in the church will possess all the Beatitudes. As the church formed by Jesus, we learn to act as he acted. We are to have this mind within us as was had by Jesus. We are to follow him and to go where he sends us as the disciples did so long ago. In fact, we are part of the unbroken chain of those who were called apart from the world to live by this new good news that becomes the gospel. (Wherever two or more are gathered in his name.)

Our lives are no longer our own. In baptism we die with Christ in order to be raised with him. We are called apart to follow Jesus as his chosen people.

Spirituality

Words fall short when we turn to spirituality. "Words, as is well known, are the great foes of reality," wrote Joseph Conrad. It's a topic to be lived, not written down. In fact, we turn to the imagination. To imagine. To image. To image-in. A deeper level of language is stories.

Spirituality is a lot like *health*. All have health: good or bad, we still have it. The same is true of spirituality. We are spiritual beings. With what sort of spirituality do we live?

Spirituality is earthy, not ethereal. It is concrete, not abstract. It is now, not later. Earthy spirituality is, in itself, a paradox. The paradox suggests the state of living with imperfection, not lofty ideals. The English essayist G. K. Chesterton (among others) described paradox as "Truth standing on her head to attract attention." The essential paradox of human life is we are always incomplete, imperfect. Paradox is the way we are made. Thus, first to be who we are. For over 1500 years now at the beginning of each monastic gathering to worship is sung from Psalm 70: *"O God, come to my assistance / O Lord, make haste to help me"* (Douay-Rheims). We don't bring our accomplishment; we bring our great need. By ourselves, we are lost.

When we begin the spiritual journey, we start up a path so many have taken; yet we never arrive, we realize the final destination must be beyond this earthly existence. We are not even sure if we are on the right path. Therefore, we join regularly with fellow pilgrims. We recognize them; we share with them where we have found nourishment on the way. We admit that on this journey we have encountered something bigger than our efforts to capture it. We discover a helplessness before the very word, the powerlessness that is the necessary beginning of spirituality itself.

T. S. Eliot described this state quite well in his poem "East Coker:

In order to arrive at what you do not know
  You must go by a way which is the way of ignorance.
In order to possess what you do not possess
  You must go by the way of dispossession.
In order to arrive at what you are not
  You must go through the way in which you are not.
And what you do not know is the only thing you know
And what you own is what you do not own
And where you are is where you are not.[46]

Spirituality is always beyond control. One cannot touch it or hold it, manage it or destroy it. Because spirituality is beyond control, it is also key and possession: one doesn't own it, lock it up, divide it among ourselves, or take it away from others.

Spirituality means "other than material." Obsession with possessions crowds out the spiritual. Beyond the ordinary, beyond material, beyond possession, beyond the confines of self...

Spirituality transcends the ordinary; yet paradoxically can be found only in the ordinary. Spirituality is beyond us, and yet it is everything we do. *Agi quod agis*. "Do what you are doing." Just do it!

The words *human*, *humor*, and *humility* all have the same root—the ancient Indo-European word *ghon*, best translated by the English word *humus*. We all know what *humus* is: "worm shit" (a brown or black substance resulting from the decay of plant or animal matter). The alcoholic's problem is not that he thinks "I am very special." Nor is the alcoholic's problem that he thinks "I am a worm." The alcoholic's problem is, he is convinced: "I am a very special worm."

46 Eliot, T.S. (1968). Four Quartets. Mariner Books. 17.

Humility involves learning how to live in (and rejoice in) the reality of our own mixed-upedness, our being both saint and sinner, both beast and angel. Humor, it has been said, is "the juxtaposition of incongruities," the placing together of two things that do not "belong" together. That is our reality. Laugh or cry, comedy and tragedy, fighting ourselves or laughing at ourselves.

When I came 'home' to AA, I could both laugh and cry. I found a very special place of serenity amidst all the confusion and chaos of the world. I was to be both accepted and admonished. AA is the place where I belong, precisely because I do not "fit in." Ironically, AA is the place where I also learned I am just an ordinary human being.

The word *sin* is not found in the 12 steps of AA. Bill Wilson knew how loaded up that word was. "Defects of character" has the sense of all the human failings we are heir to, all our "falling shorts." AA is a screwy place because we are all screwy. The point of an eventual humility is we find some balance. We become a sober alcoholic. But, saints or sinners, we all still have the *ism*! To be human is, after all, to be other than God. We will struggle all our days, and in the journey that is AA we shall become whole again. Only those who brave known darkness can truly appreciate light; only those who acknowledge darkness can even *see* the light.

"Wholeness," then, doesn't signify that there has ever not been brokenness. In fact, the way to true spirituality means that we, broken ones, have been *made* whole, a gift of grace that has been given on the journey. Both within each person *and* within the community as a whole, both good *and* evil, strength *and* weakness, coexisted and continue to exist.

Spirituality is, above all, a way of life. We don't just think about it, nor do we search for a sense of it or a feeling of it. Spirituality involves a daily walk in the sunshine (*son*shine) of the Spirit. We share our experience; we fit together seeing, feeling, and willingness on the way to wholeness.

Early in May 1935, Bill Wilson was in the lobby of the Mayflower Hotel in Akron, Ohio, on a bad business trip. His deal had failed, and he was lonely and defeated and rather newly sober. He could hear the ice tinkling in glasses from the bar calling to him. This stood for the lie told to him for many years, but Bill W. said, "I don't need a drink, I need another alcoholic."

In the old days, a church directory hung on the walls of hotel lobbies; he called, and the clergyman he talked to knew a drunk. Bill was to meet Bob, and a tradition was established which enabled AA to be a community of unconditional love, and a mutuality of acceptance that transforms people by opening them up. I was a tangled web in a closed system when I came to AA. It was to become the first place I ever felt I belonged. But if I had not met the one who would reach out and save me at my very first meeting, I would not have returned to another experience of folks sitting in a circle quoting bumper stickers. I inquired of Bob, where are the meetings for special folks with advanced degrees of academic achievements? He explained the difference between my brain and my butt and which one to leave in the parking place and which to take into the rooms of AA. No one had ever spoken to me like that before. (I came to love it.) Somehow, God told me through Bob to shut up and to learn to listen to others.

By now I have heard thousands of others. They tell me my own story and I am forgiven, and as I am, I can experience the presence of God in AA and take it into all the world. That includes church. The community of faith is just as important to me as AA. After all, church is the place where the God of my understanding is worshiped and glorified. So, my chief allegiance remains: Jesus Christ, my risen Lord and Savior, is my all in all, but I could lose all if I drink alcohol again.

Someone once said, "honesty gets us sober, but tolerance keeps us sober." One of the very best gifts of AA has been for me the great diversity of people I have met in the last three decades. I just would not have run into this variety of souls had I stayed merely in the church. It all has to do with acceptance. I drew closer to God as I drew closer to others. First, I had to accept myself and God's acceptance of me. Then I started to learn to accept others. This is a daily task that will last 'til I die, of course, and I improve the longer I "trudge the path to happy (joyful) destiny."

What great people I have met through the years, both in AA and in church. If my ox was seriously in the ditch, and I needed help right now, the first 10 people I would call would be drunks, not deacons or elders. But that is because I have been honest and tolerant with the drunks. If only church were more like a meeting. In a meeting we admit and name who we are, and we are given the freedom to choose the God of our understanding. In church we are assigned one. I have come to see the value of both approaches. AA split off from the Oxford group over this very thing. You can 'tell' a drunk, but you cannot tell them much. Folks who have been operating as the God of their understanding of themselves are not quick to join in someone else's conception. But the thing wouldn't work unless people early on can sense there is a higher power at work in the rooms of AA. That higher power works through people who can clearly witness to that which they can and do and have experienced in their own reality. This is the ultimate pragmatic concept of God. The alcoholic cannot do this on her or his own power. So, if only they will keep coming, they will be surprised by joy.

For me, church and AA are essential activities. Both call for long-term hard work.

Does anal-retentive require a hyphen?
"No, but a colon would be helpful."

Thoughts

Write a 1 minute, 30 second telegram about Jesus to someone who has never heard of him.

In Jesus we have the power to be born again. We must take that phrase back from the religious right.

Are metaphors more powerful than literal language?

Craddock said the longest journey for the preacher is from the head to the heart.

In sermons we are not writing an essay, we are making a movie. How does TV hold us? How can sermons hold us?

Theater is not worship, but worship can be theater.

Bodying forth reality is preaching.

I am what I am 'cause I ain't what I used to be.

Wendell Berry has written this Prayer After Eating[47] :

> I have taken in the light
> that quickened eye and leaf.
> May my brain be bright with praise
> of what I eat, in the brief blaze
> of motion and of thought.
> May I be worthy of my meat.

A better way to say *grace* I think.

"O God, do not let go of me, for I simply can't make it on my own."
—my main prayer

---

47 Copyright © 1971, 1972, 1973 by Wendell Berry, from *The Country of Marriage*. Reprinted by permission of Counterpoint Press.

Journals Volume Two

Worship as Joy

Retirement has taught me more and more to abolish utilitarian purpose. For years and years, I produced. Sunday after Sunday there was assigned work; now I play. I am in the community of faith playing with the scriptures. 1 Timothy 6:17b says, our hopes are set *"on God, who richly provides us with everything to enjoy."* If there is a purpose or a goal, it is expressed on the final part of verse 19: *"So that they may take hold of the life that really is life."*

Not work, but play.

Play is purposeless and non-utilitarian, yet meaningful. There is no *reason* to play except because play is fun. All worship can be fun. There is not product, but process. If it is not fun, God is not in it. I have come to believe that the best thing Becky and I can offer to the people at St. John is to thoroughly enjoy ourselves, as in to be filled with joy!

One of the woes of the church is: woe to those who have taken away the joy of meaning. I was taught in seminary that proper exegesis was a complex series of tasks. Therefore, I would pick up a commentary (the heavier the better) *before* I sat with the scripture passage for a while in prayer and meditation. The church today needs to recover *Lectio divina*. Folks have been taught to think there is only one meaning to a text. The people must recover the joy of meaning. We have operated top down. For too many years I operated as a kind of middleman between the pew and the experts.

A person's regular life precedes the "meaning" of any text. Lay people tend to bring their life to a text quicker than trained clergy folk. A preacher often seems to think "he" has found the right answer to a text, which is dropped down on the heads of the pew people from a lofty pulpit.

The preacher often does this apart from participation with anyone else. The problem is, no one is good enough to do it alone. The scriptures were not written to individuals anyway. The bible is the church's book; if the pastor is the only reader of scripture in the church, then the whole project is over before it is begun.

The church must develop a relationship with the Word. This is really the whole point. There can be such a thing as community exegesis, and it can be a joyful thing. The scriptures are the church's constitution, undergirding everything the church is about. It is not top down; it is bottom up. The church learns together how to read. There is no such thing as a "right" reading of the text. There is only a responsible reading of the text. The whole church prepares for Sunday. They know what's coming up. The lectionary is the guide for worship, and the preacher and the rest of the church have prayerfully prepared; they each are responsible to the text. Everyone gets caught up in the rhythm of Sunday to Sunday. All find themselves in the texts of the day.

The stories of scripture get the people "caught up." People find their own stories there, and they cannot help but apply their lives to the texts. If they approach the process with anticipation, they will share their excitement with others and the Holy Spirit will bless all concerned. All, then, move forward together. *The people become church by acting like church.* Many people who attend church already have a lifetime of experience with the bible. The planners of worship tap into that. Rather than the sermon being an objective searching for the "meaning" of the text, the collaborative congregational reading produces a subjective understanding of the text. This is not new. It is actually *midrash*. Lead with questions; stay away from answers.

In a situation like this, stuff gets sorted out. Group process will automatically emerge if there is a genuine looking forward to each time of worship. Leaders of groups will be easily identified. Governance is, after all, a gift of the Spirit. All that is needed has already been provided. The body of Christ simply has to come together. Once assembled, it becomes what the scriptures have always talked about. It's all about wisdom. There will always be differing gifts of the Spirit. Those gifts can always be discovered. The Giver of these gifts can guide this discovery, and the Giver's people can then bring this new giving to each gathering. In corporate exegesis, the people learn to rightly discern the Word by building up the church, the body of Christ. The spiritual disciplines will emerge in such a church. Since sharing in the body is practical; people will find their own interests in praying, meditation, silence, fasting, and all the rest. As people grow older, they develop the ability to share their stories. The elders sit around the campfire and tell the old stories. The young ones are excited to hear the old accounts of how things came to be. Stories pile up and the community is established. The truth will out! Things will change; lives will be thus transformed. All of this is from the Creator of all there is. It is pure gift: we don't deserve it; we didn't earn it.

First, came a garden of delight; yet we disobeyed. Instead of worshiping God, we sought to *be* God. Thus, all of creation is fallen. All of creation was meant to praise and glorify God; yet as a result of sin it became fallen. If all of creation is fallen, it cannot praise God adequately. Therefore God, in Christ, gave us a way out. As in the Old Testament when the high priest would offer a sacrifice on behalf of the entire nation, so Christ came to offer the acceptable way to worship. No detailed instructions were left us; yet we have sufficient biblical materials upon which to build.

Now, with Christ as our great high priest, our worship can become, through the Holy Spirit, our participation in Christ's high priestly life. In our worship, Jesus takes what we offer to Him (our sacrifice, our sins and brokenness, plus our very best), then sanctifies our offering. He offers all we offer back to the Father, who in turn gives all back to us, every good and perfect gift, all we could possibly need. This, then, is the Trinitarian nature of all true worship.

The common movements in all of this are sacrifice and offering. The church must find a way to lift up 'the offering' as the high point of the worship service. It is not a sacrament: a sacrament is something God does in worship. The offering is something we do. We must allow the great high priest to bless the event of offering and have it be sacrificial, not the blood of bulls or lambs, but the absolute best of all we are, through Christ, on the altar. The practice of giving our very best music at this time is one good way of celebrating this time of offering. In this way, we 'feed' upon our Lord in praise and thanksgiving as we (all present) make this sacrificial offering. This biblical pattern must be restored in our contemporary worship.

This also restores a proper understanding of money. Money is a medium of exchange. It is simply something we *use* as we make a life in this world. Everything belongs to God already. We just get to use certain things (to God's glory) as we pass through. That which we place on the altar is *all* we have been given. The offering is the time in worship when God is most present. In praise we *play* to God, in Word we teach in the presence of God, but in the offering, we give, and God blesses. It is a direct interchange. We must restore this in our worship.

When God's people worship, they are being formed by the spirit into the church. The community gathered in worship is being and becoming defined and shaped by the liturgy, by everything that happens from the time we leave our homes until the time we come back from church. This is what we mean by 'going to church.' Christ is always present; we don't conjure him up through the incantations of worship. He gets there before we do. In worship, the liturgy is a human action which opens the community to knowing God in Christ through God's own self-revelation. Liturgy is humanly orchestrated, yet divinely directed. It is human words; yet it is God's Word.

We worship as a community of distinct individuals for the sake of all creation. Worship centers our lives and communities. It draws us to God, and as we grow closer to God, we become closer to each other. Our individualism and egoism slip away, and the mission God has for creation becomes focused. Corporate worship is unique, irreplaceable, and essential for the Christian life.

How to do it? Worship is a communal activity. Planning for it is also. The trend today is to have a worship 'team'. The team concept has been borrowed from the world of commerce. It's OK if it truly works, but I wouldn't use that term. We want a bottom up process where all have a say. There simply must be a consensus in what is done on Sunday morning. If there is a worship war going on, then move on to a church where something can actually happen. Once we know who we are, we can begin. "Form follows function," Frank Lloyd Wright said, not to mention all those who said it before him. A formed function has been established. In many churches people think they already know what to do. There is a lot of diversity going on today. We are in a state of flux and face a great paradigm shift in these times. This upheaval is as great as any other time in our history. It's the modern-postmodern thing. The only way out is to prayerfully wait and see. The only thing for sure is that the modern world is over and done. Since this is so obviously true, the first thing to do is to rejoice. Church ought to be able to help with that.

People pick churches today. It's no longer a thing of going to the closest one. There is huge diversity in the culture and currently some diversity in the church. Diversity is implicit in creation, so there is scarce need to oppose it. In worship we have at our disposal thousands of languages; why not find a way to use that diversity to God's glory? We always do offer a wide variety in worship with wise balance. Worship involves compromise; thus, some blending is necessary. Authentic worship has to do with wise blending over the space of a whole church year, according to spiritual purposes. Decisions are made wisely, and all come together. For what purpose do we come? Well, foremost to praise, pray and participate, as has been discussed.

What is our human need as we come?

We come to cleanse our lenses and tune our instruments. We are to allow the gifts of seeing and hearing to be given in such a way that we realize we all belong to each other through the Spirit. We belong to each other really, originally, and ultimately. We each see and hear together with the mind and the heart. All our senses should be combined with our best offering as we learn how to worship.

What place shall we give to excellence in worship? What are the standards? Who picks what as we plan for worship? Well, that is the interesting thing, and I'm glad to be retired and to not have to do this difficult thing anymore. All I know for sure is that sometimes in my past, through God's grace, we somehow managed to make it look easy. This is where artistry comes into play.

Life

Life is difficult. Well, yes, but at the end it is so glorious. They say *old age* is not for the young; they couldn't handle it. So true, not because they couldn't stand the pain, but because their little brains have not yet developed sufficiently, and mostly because they have not yet learned enough from life. Not that they come to me seeking the great wisdom I have gained by long living and wealth of knowledge. Instead of trying to elevate them, I get with them. I show them that I really do like them just as they are. After all, they have qualities most of us tend to lose as we "grow up." They are silly and outrageous, wondrous qualities that adults tend to lose. I like to get young people to have fun. I think back on wonderful choir tours. Kids having fun, and yet, they are as disciplined as any group I have ever worked with.

I am very peaceful with where life has left me now, but sometimes I wonder, "what if?" If I had not been such a fearful, sorry ass drunk, would it have been different? Well, sure, but God gave me what was given. God did not appoint me to be an alcoholic, but I am certain I was given the gift of recovery. Dare I say I was chosen? Yes, I think so.

The first AA meeting I went to was no inspiration to return; yet I said to the one leading the group, "What's this sponsor shit?" She said, "Wait right there," and went to fetch Bob. It was as if he could see deep inside me from the beginning.[1] He told me what was what from the very beginning. The miracle was, I listened! How did I know I wanted what he had? That's the point and the mystery. I couldn't have known; I was just out of trying and lying and hiding. It was a time of ego deflation. I was ready and didn't even know it. It was God doing for me what I couldn't do for myself. That's how I know I was chosen.

Thank you, Jesus.

---

1 Later I learned that I was just like everybody else.

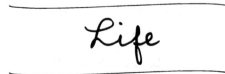

Caught in the Act

Aidan Kavanagh said, "in liturgy the church is 'caught in the act' of being most overtly itself as it stands faithfully in the presence of the One who is both the object and the source of faith."[2]

How is it that God is both the audience and the director of worship? As we worship, we praise God, and when we worship well, we are lifted higher than we can go. How is that possible? Well, I think it's why the early church had to come up with the Trinity as a doctrine. We sing, pray, and listen, all directed to God. He is an unseen prompter in this "service." He is the object to whom we witness in worship, and He is the source of the strength we draw on as we do those things with excellence which are part of our worship.

Well, how do we renew worship? The identity and integrity of the church call for the church to *be* the church. If we stand faithfully in the presence of the One who is both the object and source of faith, we will move to the center of worship—the praise of God. This praise is a vocal thing. All are to use their bodies in this offering to the God of their understanding. The preacher does vocal things, the scriptures are read by voice. The choir sings. There is a lot of listening going on. There is a focus of attention not usually found in group gatherings in our culture. There are also silences. We listen, for what? The still, small voice. The sound of silence.

There is also a lot to see. That's why we use colors. Whether cathedral or chapel, we have a sense of space. There is often a sense of "holy." We are now using mind, heart, gut, awe, and adoration. Things deep within come to the surface of our awareness. Emotions of all sorts are employed. Often, we even use our minds. It is indeed possible to learn something in church. The ears are tuned to truly hear the gospel as revealed in the

2 Keck, L.E. (1992). *Caught in the act: praise and renewal in the church*. Religion Online. https://www.religion-online.org/article/caught-in-the-act-praise-and-renewal-in-the-church/

scriptures of the Old and New Testaments. The full range of intellectual abilities are employed in the congregational consciousness. All are caught up in the act of the church being church. When praise acknowledges, it proclaims the truth. Both the one praised and the one doing the praising are brought into the reality of the light of the truth always shining, thus the candles. Therefore, the first thing which happens is the lighting of the candles, and the last thing is the light being carried out into the often-dark world.

Praise of the people of God... this praise reveals a glorious response to the God who is praised. The object of this praise reveals what we believe to be praiseworthy and draws the worshipers closer to the object. Since the object we praise is the Trinity, the church gets formed in this transaction of praise. *If anyone present in this process does not value excellence, that person will not strive for it in their personal life.* The wonder of praise is that the church itself gets lifted up in the act of praise, and the commonplace is transcended and glory rains down.

Schleiermacher spoke of this in psychological terms: *Gefühl*—an immediate sense of dependence; but it is much more than that. H. Richard Niebuhr got it right when he said: "We are in the grip of a power that neither asks our consent before it brings us into existence nor asks our agreement to continue us in being beyond our physical death."[3] To praise our God is to realize that God is not waiting for the time we might get it right. God is to be praised because God is God. We come with gratitude because of what God establishes in this act of praise. The God we worship is the Creator of all there is; God is worthy of praise inherently.

But there is such darkness and suffering in this world. How do we sing and offer praise if our mouths are in the dust? In true praise, we bring all of scripture into play. Are the psalms all happy? If we look, we find most aren't. That is what I recoil against in "contemporary" worship which sings seven words eleven times (7/11 worship)—words of vapid uplift, when there are those who are suffering and cannot bear to stand, lifting their arms for thirty minutes of silly choruses given only in the major keys.

---

3 Coalter, et al. (1996). *Vital Signs: The Promise of Mainstream Protestantism.* Grand Haven. FaithWalk.

The God we praise did not make this world disaster-proof. The God we praise did not protect us from the consequence of our sins. There is much brokenness brought to the altar in this sacrifice of praise. When we are beaten down and yet still bring our offering, we do so not under our own strength, but because we have been formed by the body of Christ. We cannot "explain" our suffering, nor can we explain the good that can gradually heal us, we simply dare to bring it all to the altar. The church understands why we praise the God who let Jesus suffer on the cross. We learn how to dare to do this by being formed by that same cross. God let our Lord suffer. We can share our suffering as Jesus shares his. All can be brought to the altar. If God honored this Son who brought his primal scream to the cross, we can be assured our own agonies need not alienate us from God. Jesus brought his last cry to God directly. We can also. That is why some silence is good in worship. We can bring it all to the foot of the cross.

I understand that, today, there are some contemporary churches which have removed the cross from their worship centers lest folks find it offensive. To me, those are simply no longer churches. They have people arranged in theater seating while the 9, 10, and 11 o'clock show happens on a stage. Much "praise" in our time reveals how much our churches have become secularized. The only antidote to this is *genuine* praise. Market oriented churches are using the techniques of the culture to get good numbers of dollars and bodies. People and their gifts are obviously essential, but we must not make the byproduct the main product. The utilitarian mind should not be a member of the worship "team." The worship of Almighty God is an end in itself. What we need to have is *purposeless* praise. We don't seek to make worship useful. Maybe reform of our praise could actually make *us* useful in following our risen Lord. I believe it can.

If a congregation sings well and with good spirit, that in itself is an indication that good worship is going on. Hymn singing expresses the community's faith and belief. When we sing, we state who we are theologically. Word and music combine. The most powerful emotive forces join in such a way that our efforts are lifted higher than either word or music could alone. The poetry of the text and the musical setting of the tune, brought together, carry the meaning and belief at a deeper and higher level than the preacher could ever achieve.

The old saying, "those who sing, pray twice," comes to mind here. Again, we are using our bodies in a complete way. We stand, breathe in, produce sound, enjoy, follow word and tune, lean on a good choir for guidance, respond to the leader of music, listen to the organ or the piano or whatever. We make mistakes, but through it all a body memory of faith is established. It is so important that this experience starts early in our lives. So much is going on when we sing the great hymns of faith. I can tell you *all* about a church just from watching and listening to them sing hymns.

All of this is no mystery. It is such a part of our wide experience that there is little debate about this, *unless*. Unless someone comes in and announces they are going to change things around. *Then* debate occurs. Again, if this produces a worship war, change churches! The point here is that "style" is not the critical ingredient in looking at what is done in our worship. There are much deeper aspects we need to realize. We look at the broad sweep of history, back to the Hebrew and early Christian worship. For two thousand years, Christian Worship has always had certain common elements. It has also been done in *many* styles, cultures, languages, and phases of history. Think of how many musics have been employed in the celebration of word and sacrament. One can see how God has guided this whole process because certain things have remained true in all ages. The broad history reveals how song and scripture and sacrament have reflected their times, and yet how the Gospel has been carried through it all. If this has been true for some time now, it is probably the case that God will press on with us in these times of ours. What shall be has not yet been revealed. All we know for sure is times are changing.

The Christian faith is simple. A small child can understand it; yet authentic simplicity is rich and complex with many layers. It takes the best a church has to wisely plan a Sunday morning. At worship, we are all gathered about pulpit, font, and table. We are still in the world, worldly; yet we do not come together in celebration of the world's brokenness. The church has another vision to embody. All are brought to a vision which lifts and leads each person beyond their current place. When the church has lost that gift, she is like salt devoid of saltiness.

End Times

How are we to "make sense" of the universe? If it is, as science clearly shows, winding down like a clock, what are we to do with Christian hope or the end to be expected from God? Earlier, I wrote a lot about the lack of a truly unified theory to hold together the very large (relativity) and the very small (quantum mechanics). As regards quantum theory, the *quark*—which can only be inferred, not seen—is said to exist because it must be so. In like manner, the doctrine of the Trinity (not found in the bible) must be true because it explains so many things. This may be a stretch, but at least one with credentials both in science and theology, John Polkinghorne, has stated that the theory of everything may be revealed through something like the continuity/discontinuity of the Christian resurrection hope. St. Paul said, *"flesh and blood cannot inherit the kingdom of God"* (1 Cor. 15:50). (Do we here read *carbon-based life forms?*) Are we to be changed in the twinkling of an eye to that new eternal form, wherein there is a balance between order and disorder? If the world to come is to be free from suffering and death, its "matter-energy" will have to be given a whole different character. There will have to be a discontinuous change of physical law!

It is surely significant that the empty tomb implies the Lord's risen body is the transmutation and glorification of his dead body. In Christ, there is therefore a hope for matter as well as for humanity. The theological motivation for entertaining this hope lies in the resurrection of Jesus and the faithfulness of the Creator.

But the matter of the new creation will be divinely transmuted matter. I believe it is indeed possible that the Creator of the Universe could take the human creation and hold it in the divine mind, to await its re-embodiment within the life of the world to come. And not only this, but if the Creator likes the patterns and realities of "this" created world, could it not be the case that some of the created dimensions could continue? If space, time, and matter all belong together in this creation, perhaps the new created creature will be in its 'space' and be situated in its 'time.' If we think of it this way, the continuity of human nature will be more interesting than just some timeless experience of eternity. On this side of the grave, we have experience of the unfolding nature of life, a dynamic concept of being, and the growth toward a full flowering of being. Maybe the new creation carries with it some "change". Change does not imply imperfection. If the dead are waiting for the "general" resurrection when Christ returns to this creation to bring his sheep safely home, then all manner of things are possible. We cannot prepare our minds to even approach understanding what being in the eternal presence of God would be like. If we have sacraments now, the new creation would be wholly sacramental. Although the bible says there won't be "church" in heaven, we won't need it if everything is wholly sacramental. God will be all in all (1 Cor. 15:28). I don't know what place judgment has in all this. (The scriptures say plenty about it.)

When Paul wrote 1 Corinthians, he feared that those who denied the resurrection of the dead had abandoned the most fundamental conviction of the faith and that the Corinthians' believing was in vain (1 Cor 15:12ff). This is a life and death issue, and this 15th chapter has some of the most forceful and lofty writing in all of the New Testament. Paul, as well as others in the New Testament, make it clear that the risen Lord is no ghost or apparition, but neither is he merely a resuscitated corpse. Resurrected life is embodied life (Luke 24:36-49). The resurrected body of Christ was *soma pneumatikos*—a new, strange, reworked body, but it was a *body*. No modern neo-platonic assertions of a "spiritual" body will do here. These Corinthians who inspired this magnificent 15th chapter of 1 Cor. were not unbelievers: in fact, they were hyper-spiritual; they just could not get their heads around this bodily resurrection. These were the educated, sophisticated Corinthians, who claimed a higher *gnōsis*. Paul says Christian hope affirms the body. It does not reject the body. This chapter goes so far as to say the whole cosmos will be redeemed. All of this because of the resurrection of Jesus.

The Beginning of Wisdom

There is a God-set limit to human knowledge. The bible is quite clear about this. "Adam and Eve, you stay clear of that one tree." "You Tower of Babel-ers, guess what?"

God seems to demand this limit, because God cares for his creation and the human creatures especially. Moses cannot see God's face on Sinai, "for no one will see me and live." Then, yesterday, I preached two different sermons on the Transfiguration. We human types can stand just so much wonder. Knowledge of God seems to be a dangerous thing. Thomas Merton, who spent a lifetime approaching God, wrote, "God approaches our minds by receding from them,"[4] and then Merton added this: "We know Him better after our 'minds' have let Him go." Even those who get to go up the mountain with Jesus reach a time when they lay prostrate with awe having sealed their eyes, and even Peter was speechless. They lay face down and only were able to get up when Jesus touched them. Is the point that what we have is a relationship based on obedience? I think so.

The poet knows that he does not know. That is what gives poems power over prose. It is one of God's gifts we are kept in the dark about, the things which most matter. What we need to attain is a satisfactory philosophy of ignorance. *To know that we do not know is the beginning of wisdom.*

4 Merton, T. (1955). *No Man is an Island.* Boston. Shambhala.

Consciousness

Albert Einstein said, "science without religion is lame, religion without science is blind."[5] I guess that is why I have such an interest in science after all these years of reading novels, studying theology, preaching, and learning music, along with poetry and the other liberal arts. If the question, "Is there a God?" may be beyond science, the question "Why do I believe in God?" calls for the best of all the disciplines. I'm not trained in science, so some study of the neurobiology of consciousness and spirituality would be helpful, I suppose. This brings us to self-transcendence, which is consciousness altered by a blurring of the normal distinction between the self and the other. If there is a God gene, the place to start is with monoamines such as serotonin and dopamine. The key role of monoamines is to link objects and experiences with emotions and values. Science has begun to look at these things with brain scanning techniques and drug interactions.

Religion, unlike spirituality, is transmitted primarily not by genes, but by memes:[6] self-replicating units of culture, ideas which get passed on through writing, speech, ritual, etc. Thus, genes open us up to spirituality and faith, but memes carry religion and make distinctions in our cultures. If these things are looked at scientifically, we are confined to why we believe, not whether those beliefs are true. So, we are really dealing with the firing of electro-chemical currents through networks of brain cells. How boring, you say. Well, it's just science, and a young science at that.

Self-transcendent people tend to see everything, including themselves, as part of one great totality. Non-self-transcendent people have a more self-centered viewpoint. This all has to do with 'feelings', as William James pointed out in *The Varieties of Religious Experience*. Since we don't possess mechanical devices which can read feelings, we are stuck with asking questions. As usual, the key thing is, which questions?

5 Einstein, A. (1941). *Science, Philosophy, and Religion: A Symposium*. University of Michigan.
6 Richard Dawkins made up this term.

Ironically, one of the helpful analysts of all this was an avowed atheist, Abraham Maslow. His interest was the good side of our mental life, rather than the usual disease model. In his work, he called people who had realized their human potential "self-actualizers". There were certain similarities in such people. They were spontaneous, ethical, empathetic, such good things, but imagine Maslow's surprise when he found another key feature: these people also shared spiritual experiences. Since Maslow was an unbeliever, he called these events peak experiences. The key feature of these experiences is a sense of wholeness and unity with the universe, a letting go of the ego. As Albert Einstein wrote:

> The most beautiful and most profound religious emotion that we can experience is the sensation of the mystical. And this mysticality is the power of all true science. If there is any such concept as a God, it is a subtle spirit, not an image of a man that so many have fixed in their minds. In essence, my religion consists of a humble admiration for this illimitable superior spirit that reveals itself in the slight details that we are able to perceive with our frail and feeble minds.[7]

Science seems to strongly state that spirituality and religiousness are fundamentally different. Spirituality, as measured by self-transcendence, is innate. It comes from within, not from without. It has to be developed, just like any other talent, but the evidence suggests the predisposition is there from the beginning.

So, let's explore DNA. If one needs to look at it, there is a recipe. Get a tablespoon of spit, add some shampoo. Remove the proteins by adding table salt until a large cloudy precipitate appears; pour this through a coffee filter. Then add four parts of vodka and place in the freezer. After an hour, the DNA will appear as a web of silky white threads. These can be twirled into a glass rod, such as a martini stirrer, dried with a hair dryer, and dissolved in a glass of water. Then drink the remaining vodka.

---

7 Bucky, P.A. and Weakland, A. G. (1992). *The Private Albert Einstein*. Andrews and McMeel.

That's your DNA, and all this time I wondered what they did in all those labs!

The result of all this is just a clear liquid when it's in solution. Within it lies the code which makes you human rather than a chicken or a roundworm or a duck-billed platypus. It has the blueprint for your liver and your pancreas, your eyes and hair. It has the instructions for the development of your brain from a few cells to the most complex biological structure in existence, and at least in part, the instructions for your sense of spirituality.

DNA is important. James Watson and Francis Crick discovered this double helix in 1952. After identifying these strands and allowing for the interplay of amino acids, proteins, enzymes, hormones, and such, we have that which makes us who we are. Our DNA has about 35,000 different genes, each of which codes for its own distinct protein. Dogs and mice have about the same number. There is a type of weed which has a full 25,000. Each person has about the same 35,000 genes. Since each human contains a total of 3 billion bases of DNA, there are about 3 million differences between my DNA and my neighbor's. We have no idea what one third of our human genes are up to. It remains a mystery. So we don't know much about which gene may be the God gene. However, someone in some lab is working on this, if they can secure a government grant.

Humans are possessed with consciousness. This is a rare gift in the universe. We seem to be the only ones who have it. Consciousness is selective. Although our brains can process a vast amount of material, they seem to do it only one topic at a time. Consciousness is continuous. It connects each moment to the one before and the one after. Also, consciousness is personal. Each event is yours alone. Now, can consciousness be explained scientifically? The answer perhaps is: if we could do this, we probably would not understand the data! I'm going to leave it as a gift from God. Although again, someone, somewhere, is working on it (if they can get a grant).

Spirituality Once More

Spirituality: there is so much searching for it today. Many claim to have it; yet if you ask them what it is, they cannot really tell you. Most run around looking for it, searching for the spiritual place, if only they could find it. Those with some experience say to them, the reason you cannot see the red X that marks the spot is because you are standing on it. Everyone already is spiritual. All we lack is the willingness to imagine we already have everything we need. The only thing missing is our consent to be where we are. Or as my recent prayer asks, *"Lord, help me to keep my feet and my head in the same place."* Spirit has been placed inside us in creation. It is part of a human nature or being which has changed little during the whole history of homo sapiens. This inner essence, this vital energy, is the stuff of spirituality. What we search for is really the experience of being more human, more whole. Spirituality consists of engaging our ordinary lives with the most exquisite attention we can muster. *There is no way to God apart from real life in the real world.* We are not trying to think of things in a certain way. We are trying to live our lives in a certain way. Spirituality is a way of life. If one is a human, one lives in a world awaiting the recognition of the holiness of it. We have everything we need to begin.

There is need to avoid the self-help section of the bookstore or the check-out lines at the grocery. The surrounding spiritual culture of self-help and self-sovereignty goods is not helpful. When simple truths of the life of the Spirit are reduced or when God is interpreted through fragments of ecstasy or strategies for happiness, no real good can emerge. The very term, spirituality, is not helpful, but it is what we have.

Now, since I am a Christian, which is the whole point of my life, then my spirituality must be seen through the lens Christ provides. The way spirituality as a term is used in our culture is very vague. The culture searches for *that which provides some transcendence intermingled with intimacy*. That is good. I want that also, but as a Christian I have a specific frame of reference. I have a powerful particular to deal with: Christ! *To me, it's all about Jesus.* Thus, spirituality is never a "thing" I can attend to as a thing in itself. It is always spoken of in terms of a living relationship with the Lord of Life. Now, it is easy to get caught up in projects or ideas about God and find we have wandered from the vital presence of God. Spirituality often gets trivialized in our church lives, and certainly from the culture. Thus, we need to focus on Jesus as the name which keeps us attentive to the real life with God. Jesus is the way we see God. He is God's revelation. Jesus places before us what we never could have found on our own. We are saved in his acts in our real lives, in this real world. By accepting Jesus as the final, definitive revelation of God, the Christian Church makes it impossible for us to then develop our own little spiritualities and get away with it. We know too much about *his* life, *his* spirituality. Jesus enables us to take seriously who and where we are. We are saved from being swept away by intimidating lies and illusions which tempt us to be someone else or someplace else. Again, *"Lord, help me to keep my feet and my head in the same place."*

Preaching

Preaching is the concerted engagement of one's faculties of body, mind, and spirit. It is, then, a skilled activity. Preaching must be nourished, informed, disciplined, and authorized by Scripture. In the texts, there is no single form of speech which qualifies as a sermon. Both parts of the Bible amply demonstrate the variety of shapes the proclamation may take. Whoever goes to the Bible in search of what to preach but does not linger long enough to learn how to preach has left its pages too soon. Preaching is necessarily defined not only by speaking but also by what is spoken. And since the basic content is not a creation of, but a gift to, the speaker, preaching is both learned and given. Preaching then takes a lifetime to learn and is a complex activity.

When you lead praise, you are the lead bird. Ever seen a flock of them in formation? The lead bird is a piece of work. We inspire celebration. If we don't lead it, it won't happen. You won't get anything out of it if you don't bring anything to it. All of this must start with prayerful preparation. And the best we can ever do is foolishness before God, but it is also the ordained way. God uses it all, somehow. What a miracle!

Of course, it's all there in the Psalms. It starts with the voice and the great gift of language. Out of the language of the Bible comes the instructions. Call the baptized together, sing and praise. Use instruments and dance; all the gifts are worthy of praise. We are to shout and lift up our hands. When we lift them up, it is the image of a little child lifting its arms to a loving parent. "Pick me up, Daddy. I need you."

"Take thou authority!" Indeed, what an incredible power! And I'm aware as a lead bird, it won't happen unless I lead it. God says, "Chuck, take point," and I must lead the patrol into some unexpected places and take some great chances. I get to lead the procession from church to "under the bridge," and then we learn to kiss the culture in ways we never thought would happen. The homeless and helpless follow us back to church and we sit next to each other and God gets church going.

It seems to me the Bible talks a lot about kissing. Kissing and touching are powerful things. I believe in the New Testament it was Jesus who got all this going. Some 23 times in the New Testament, it says greet each other with a holy kiss. Try it sometime. Reach out and touch someone. A drunk slumped against a wall in the city. Someone in church you can't stand. Some co-worker who's always kissing up to the boss. Your spouse and children. Kissing and touching is powerful. Kiss the culture. How would you greet it with a holy kiss? How to kiss the culture without encouraging some of the players? How to do it in the name of Jesus Christ?

Judas betrayed Jesus with a kiss. Jesus said to Mary after the resurrection, "don't touch me yet." What does that mean? (*How do we touch Jesus* in the Spirit? *How do we get in touch* with Jesus? *Keep coming back.*)

Or even in church as usual. The point bird says, please make an effort to greet someone. How do you do that? With a holy kiss, with a handshake? Why do we have to be asked to do it in the first place? It's like the 7th inning stretch thing we do in "passing the peace." (It interrupts the whole flow!) Do it at the right time.

Prayer changes things. Oh, really? Then why are you not more excited about it? Seek and ye shall find?

Hang in there. Be persistent. Beat a shameless path to God's door. "I'll fly away!" Sure, there is a celestial home, but we have our marching orders while we are yet alive.

Barth

In re-reading *With the Grain of the Universe, Hauerwas' Gifford Lectures,* I realize how Barthian I have become, and what a debt I owe to Stan the Man Hauerwas. He is old and retired now like me, but as long as he draws breath he will be at it each day.

God is Trinity. God has never not been Trinity, but *only through the struggle to make its own existence intelligible did the church discover God's Trinitarian nature.* The God who moves the sun and the stars is the same God who was incarnate in Jesus. The God we worship and the world God created cannot be truthfully known without the cross. God would rule all of creation from Christ's cross.

Barth rightly refused to separate our knowledge of God from how we are to live if God is properly acknowledged. Barth's theology is to make the reader a more adequate knower of God.

Barth wrote of the Bible:

> The Bible tells us not how we should talk with God but what he says to us; not how we find the way to him, but how he has sought and found the way to us; not the right relation in which we must place ourselves to him, but the covenant which he has made with all who are Abraham's spiritual children and which he has sealed once and for all in Jesus Christ. It is this which is within the Bible. The word of God is within the Bible.[8]

In his commentary on the Epistle to the Romans, Barth was doing no more than reminding us that what is wrong with the world is its failure to acknowledge that God is God. *God is God and we are not;* it's all but variations on that theme. All of it.

---

8 Barth, K. (1957). *The Word of God and the Word of Man.* (D. Horton, trans.). New York. Harper & Brothers. (Original work published 1924). 43.

Of course, if I really want to encounter Barth, I need to read *him*, not just about him. I pick up again his commentary on Romans. This book rocked the world and is still rocking. He had concluded that the world was literally godless. Christendom had replaced the Christian worship of God (Protestant liberalism). This is the Karl Barth who wrote the Barmen Declaration. This is the Barth of whom Flannery O'Connor said: "I like old Barth; he throws the furniture around."[9]

As an old Methodist preacher, I must be aware of how different my theology and "experiences" are from Barth, however if any theologian in modern times has quickened my pulse, it would be Barth. Of course, he called his massive (14 volumes) Dogmatics no more than the beginning of a new reflection on the Word of God. But, what a reflection! Nothing else compares!

Barth learned from Kierkegaard that Christianity is an invasion, an event whereby the Eternal sweeps into time, disrupting all. The Revealed God demands an either/or decision from us. This insight and Barth's ten years as a pastor meant the theological liberalism he had been taught would no longer do. He was a disruptive preacher in Safenwil. He wrote, "My calling is to speak and to speak clearly... If I wanted to be liked, I would keep quiet."[10]

As I look back upon my years of preaching, I know much of it was a waste. Yet I know in my heart, if given another chance, I would be bolder. Barth said the church was a place of crisis and disturbance, not refuge. "You cannot go in and come out peacefully."[11] He thought the Bible to be a ticking time bomb which made the church dangerous. And it is! Yet we can also tame or ignore the book if we choose. And in my experience, we have so chosen.

Barth, as a pastor, began to read the Bible closely. Early on, he began to encounter the "strange new world within the Bible." We are given new questions, much better ones than the ones we had formerly asked; yet the

---

9 Stephens, R. (Ed.). (2008). *The Correspondence of Flannery O'Connor and the Brainard Cheneys.* University Press of Mississippi.
10 Willimon, W.H. (2006). *Conversations with Barth on Preaching*. Abingdon. 13.
11 Ibid.

Bible answers few questions but rather negates our questions by raising before us the question we had been avoiding: *the question of God!* Barth said, "the Bible offers us not at all what we first seek in it."[12] If God is God, our theological probings are about to get turned upside down. The Bible is not about how we might climb up to God, Barth explained; scripture is about how God has miraculously, triumphantly descended to us. Kierkegaard had taught that faith cannot be communicated from one human being to another; it can only be revealed by God. Luther had claimed that Romans 3:22-24 is the core of all scripture: "For there is *no distinction*, for *all* have sinned and fall short of the glory of God; they are justified by his grace as a gift, through the redemption that is in Christ Jesus." With Luther and Kierkegaard, Barth proclaimed, the righteousness of God is displayed by the absolute separation between God and humanity, including especially those attempts by which humanity tries to attain God by evading him, namely what Barth labels as "religion." Dostoevsky strengthens Barth's contempt for "religion," seeing it as a false human attempt (represented by Dostoevsky's Grand Inquisitor) to set up some idol in the name of the living God, which gives people what they desire—mystery, authority, security, and miracle—rather than the world-shattering freedom which is theirs in Christ. Throughout his life, Barth was criticized for caring more about those who were outside the church than for those within. From his earliest days, Barth cultivated a thin differentiation between the "insiders" of the faith and the "outsiders." He really believed Paul when he said that "there is *no distinction,*" except the religious tend to delude themselves into thinking their "religion" is a faith in the living God rather than a substitute for faith.

Barth's conviction was, "either God speaks or He does not." This was his premise as he moved from being a pastor and began his dogmatic work. He believed "Truth that really goes back to God cannot be a particle of truth. It is either the whole truth or it does not go back to God and is not revelation at all."[13] According to Willimon, "Barth was attracted to Zwingli's teaching that *we can receive God's grace only through God's*

12 Barth, K. (1957). *The Word of God and the Word of Man*. (D. Horton, trans.). New York. Harper & Brothers. (Original work published 1924). 39.

13 Willimon, W.H. (2006). *Conversations with Barth on Preaching*. Abingdon. 19.

grace."[14] Barth thought that many in the reformed tradition moved away from receiving grace as pure gifts when they engaged in apologetics, and he began a lifelong opposition to apologetics. When he studied Anselm, he began to rid his thought of philosophical or anthropological foundations. Anselm taught Barth that all theology is a practice of prayer. Grace comes as a momentary gift over which God has sole control.

Barth now began to make his theological work rigorously Christological. Everything begins and ends with the Word made flesh. Barth's opposition to the Nazis was basically homiletical in form. As a preacher of the scriptures, how could one not be opposed, but he was fired from his position in Bonn and spent the rest of his life in Basel because he would not sign a loyalty oath to Hitler. All this was from the word within the Bible.

> Preaching must be exposition of holy scripture. I have not to talk *about* scripture but *from* it. I have not to say something, but merely repeat something… Our task is simply to follow the distinctive movement of thought in the text, to stay with this, and not with a plan that arises out of it.[15]

His great conviction was simply, "He speaks for Himself whenever He is spoken of and His story is told and heard."[16]

Barth (reflecting on Anselm) was attempting to explore the grammar of what it means to say only God can act without loss. (Only God exists in a manner such that nonexistence is unthinkable.) (Aquinas' claim that only in God are existence and essence one.) Barth put it, "the name of God demands that his existence, even if it is denied, cannot… be conceived merely as an existence in fact, but only as one that is necessary."[17] We know God exists through revelation. Thus, because God wills, there is not only God, there is a Word of God and a work of God. God is to be sought and found in His Word and work, not elsewhere. Our lives are not fated, and we are not trapped in a closed universe. Barth has theology

---

14 Ibid.
15 Ibid. 25.
16 Barth, Karl. (1956). *Church Dogmatics Vol. 4.1: The Doctrine of Reconcilliation*. Bloomsbury.
17 Hauerwas, S. (2001). *With the Grain of the Universe: The Church's Witness and Natural Theology*. Baker Academic. 186.

overcoming metaphysics. He had a single concern: to use every resource at his disposal to show that our existence and the existence of the universe are unintelligible if the God found in Jesus Christ is not God! Of course, we can never be sure God will make our speech God's speech. When we participate in revelation, we find ourselves involved in a story.

Barth rightly saw that the truthfulness of Christian speech about God is a matter of truthful witness. He wrote, "God is known in the world thanks to the ministry of Christianity."[18] We no longer live under the law, now we live under the Gospel. "Witness" is one of Barth's ways of displaying what it means for us to participate in the life of the Trinity.

Barth did not think Christians could be witnesses as individuals. He wrote, if he were not in the church, he would not be in Christ. Individuals as witnesses are always part of the larger witness of the church, and the church, as this witness, must be visible.

If one tells a story or uses the storied forms of the Gospel in Scripture, one can be both truthful and entertaining. Most philosophers and theologians think stories can do the work of argument. But "narrating," exactly because narration is the science of the particular, is a more basic category than either explanation or understanding. Creation and redemption constitute the story necessary for us to know who we are. Such knowledge comes only through the telling of this story. Thus, the necessity of witness again. For Christians, "witness" names the condition necessary to begin argument. Witness, for Christians, is all about God and God's relation to all that is. Witness must exist if Christians are to be intelligible to themselves and hopefully to those who are not Christians, just as the intelligibility of science depends on the success of experiments.

When Christians get this theology wrong, they cannot help but get their lives and their accounts of the world wrong as well. Or, often, Christians get their theology wrong because they have gotten their lives wrong. Barth understood that to get our theology right, we must get our lives in order. For Barth, Christianity is not a "position," or another

18 Ibid. 195.

set of beliefs, but a story, at once simple and complex, which encompasses all that is.

When Christians express the truth of the faith to the world, there will be inevitable difficulties, for this proclamation cannot help but be countercultural. The gospel cannot be at home in the world. There will always be resistance when the truth of the cross and resurrection is told *and* lived out by the church, and when the church realizes it is not at home in the world. God has chosen not to be without us. God has chosen us to be the presence, the body of Christ in the world to redeem the world. As God is in the world, so Christians are in the world. The relationship between the obedience of God's people and the triumph of God's cause is not a relationship of cause and effect, but one of cross and resurrection.

What the church owes the world is to be and say the truth, which is nothing less than *Jesus is the Christ*. Faith is a lived knowledge of Christ, a living remembrance of his commandments, and a truth to be lived out. When Christians accept the "culture of death"—abortion, suicide, capital punishment, war—then the truth of Christian witness is compromised.

Poetry

Someone said prose writers tame language, and it's up to poetry to set it free again. How can the said cut into the unsaid? Poetry insists that resolution must not come too quickly. It flies in the face of the rational. Many poets have sought to *explain* poetry. Many have refused. There is a thirst to "communicate," but the poem insists on being rather than explaining.

I love to read poetry, to collect and write about poetry. I read poetry too quickly, trying to *get* it. Poets tend to know we are doing that and insist on slowing down language. Again, the poem insists on being before meaning. So, we allow ourselves to open ourselves up to the experience of poetry, to the sound of it. We become enthusiasts. We search out poems we like. We keep trying to read the poems. Poems move and inspire us.

All verbal events—prose, poetry, essays, novels, reporting, sermons, and speeches—move horizontally through time. There is a certain progression along the lines of cause and effect. Poetry, among the verbal efforts, tends to leap and surprise; it desires rapture and astonishment. Poetry seeks to go to the abyss and transcend the rational sense of loss, and to dance at the edge.

I use language of all types. In AA and in church, very different ones are used. To *be* in each group requires the learning of each of the languages. I strive for the "pure clear word," as James Wright put it. Those are the words which can carry the most freight.

Dark Matter

At the center of things in our own little neighborhood lies an unseen monster. It lies there quietly now, though in the past it has risen up with great violence to utterly consume anything which came near its hiding place.

I speak of the black hole in the center of our Milky Way. There are other ones in other galaxies. Ours is almost completely inert now. It only becomes ferocious when any outside stuff (anything it can eat) comes near it. We cannot "see" it because it's black on black. We see its effect when there is something to eat. Then it wakes up and gobbles up the stars and anything else which comes around what scientists call its event horizon (or its mouth). Then, incredible forces act like a waterfall and whatever falls over the edge goes into oblivion, cut off from the rest of the universe. We can only see a group of stars racing around madly for no obvious reason, except that the monster must be awake.

Of course, when we observe this, we are not talking about real time. It's 26,000 light-years away from us. When it did act up, the luminosity of the original event shone like a million stars. The mouth of the thing is what has in the "popular" world been called a worm hole. Some conjecture that this may be a door to an alternate universe. Why are they there in the first place? Well, to hold the galaxy together. All of this is theory based on observation of what we really cannot see.

In the beginning, the Bible says, "Let there be light." This is not a theory because it is not science. Science is a young thing as we know of it today. It's self-limited by what can be tested and proven. We know very little about the creation from science. Much of what is most fascinating about the cosmos is what must be true, because of secondary experiments and such. No one has seen a black hole, dark matter, dark energy, and those things which make up the vast majority of the universe. Ordinary matter constitutes a tiny part of the observable universe, and we know only a little about it as well, even though we learn more on a daily basis. This causes scientists to come to the same deep humility theologians have always found necessary. Our common lives are shrouded in mystery.

Back to Preaching

Much of the preaching in our day is, as Phillip Brooks said, like lecturing to sick people about medicine. Certainly the biggest fault in worship today is we act as if God is not in the room. It's the way I felt in my son's Unitarian Universalist church in Arizona—it seems care was taken not to mention God at all. Of course, I can also sense that situation in many of the churches in my experience. As the Bible puts it, "It is a fearful thing to fall into the hands of the living God."[19]

Now, it's not the goal of joyful worship to be dangled over the pit of hell while suspended on the single strand of a spider's web, although that remains America's most famous sermon (Jonathan Edwards). We remain 'sinners in the hand of an angry God,' but the goal of worship today, in my mind, at least, is: how do we make God real? If the sermon is to be God's salvation breaking into the world, then the sermon is what salvation *sounds* like. The sermon is made up of things like challenge, experience, invitation, response. Its content is those things which make of the sermon an event. The event of worship should cause the people to go out of church with their relationship to God restored and renewed, and the people, having entered to worship, now depart to serve.

The sermon, having reported on revelation, now participates in the event of revelation. The preacher, in the study before preaching, is told by Christ, "the one who hears you hears me!"[20] Armed with this awesome thought, the preacher climbs into the pulpit and the work is done. The deed becomes word. To speak it is to do it.

Barth has the preacher merely as a conduit of the word. Can we move beyond Barth? Can we have a joyful, living, embodied word with a pulse? Every time we speak, the people are establishing a relationship with us as well as with God. They at least get a sense of who we are that week. If

---

19 Hebrews 10:31
20 Luke 10:16

preaching is truth through personality, this cannot be avoided or denied. Does the preacher stand in the way, beside the way, out of the way of the word, or what? Where in the word stands the preacher? The reality is, if the preacher says well, but does poor, they are not gospel, and they say not gospel!

What is the need of the congregation, and when is it better to ignore the expressed need and to remind them what God needs? There are so many needs unrelated to the congregation's needs, wishes, and desires. The preacher needs to sort all of this out.

When the preacher approaches a text, the first question is, what is God doing in or behind this word? We begin with the action of God in the word, then we can move toward what the people think they need. The text says the gospel has the power to save us. Who has the power, the speaker, the hearers? No, the *gospel* has the power. Jesus accomplished all this in the crucifixion and the resurrection, but Jesus is the one who was, who is, and also the one who will come to close the time.

In the meantime, we can only hear the word in our time. The One with power is not trapped in time, but is all in all. What God says was true, is true, and will be true. Now, we can only see dimly, later we will see face to face. We have only mere words, but words are what we have. Can our words become the Word? We must broaden the word. Preachers are trained in the word, but then we tend to think in terms of the page. "Where shall the word be found, where will the word Resound?"[21] Not in a closed book, but in the air. The word is *ruach*, *pneuma*, breath. The word is preceded by "God says." What follows cannot be dry, empty, abstract. What follows must have life. Engraved in the pulpit must be "we would see Jesus." God's word is event. The word is *dahbar*, both word and deed! *Indeed.*

How can the word become alive, even in the midst of our mere words? In Genesis, God creates through the word. How to preach to the incredible thing God created called the *mind*? When the mind hears living words, the mind sees. The brain creates pictures when it hears a good sermon. If one can see a sermon, then it is not too abstract. If one cannot see it, it *is*

21 Eliot, T.S. (1930). *Ash Wednesday*. Faber & Faber.

too abstract. We are thus speaking a movie! The Bible has words like creating, eating, seeing, smelling. Preaching can create a vibrant word, a dynamic, coming alive word. This is a word of hope. It is audacious.

The word makes life, abundant life.

The problem with the Bible is almost no one is into it. Conservatives say they are, liberals are less vocal about it, but almost nobody even reads it. This creates problems for the preacher. The church cannot pay the preacher to read the Bible for them. Daily bread, as mentioned in scripture, cannot be stored up. Manna is given daily. You can only come daily to the Word for spiritual nourishment. The amazing thing to me is that as 21st century people, we are still a biblical people. Even the president can occasionally quote scripture. It is not too late! God created people in the beginning because God loves a good story. We can still tell the old, old story in a new way which can come alive, and even create life. We can tell the story in such a way that when people hear it, they are *in* the story. People leave worship declaring *I once was blind, but now I see.*

What do they see? They see a mission field. They see, in what has been termed a post-modern world, how the realities are different than what we were trained to do. Ambiguity is everywhere. Such things as objective and subjective were easily discerned in the modern world; now, not so much. We go out into a culture of cascading catastrophes with the sure and certain, pure word of the gospel. We tell the old, old story with gusto and hyperbole. It is always fresh, and it is always a surprise. Cultures can always be redeemed. The church is a culture. It is in the world and, in our day, largely of the world. The church uses the tricks and strategies of the world to reach out to the world (see the problem?). Our evangelism conferences resemble sales conferences. Where are the churches where God can actually do something?

In our day, the church becomes less important and more important at the same time. Less important because the power to truly speak and influence the culture has been lost. The church has become more marginalized. If the council of bishops petition the White House today, will there be a rapid and urgent reply? Seventy years ago there would have been. The church is better off now from the marginal stance to really speak the fresh, clear word of gospel power to the power structures and to the individual persons on the street. The church alone offers the invitation to a saving relationship to God through Jesus Christ. When people come to church, they want God.

Self, Selflessness, and Others

Agi quod agis. "Do what you are doing." It's 6am, and I am at play. Play, for me, is doing the ordinary while being absorbed in it completely and utterly. I write and am learning to write. Easily distracted, I just keep trying and that is the key. This is something I have always done—at least I have always said this is what I do. I'm learning to keep things to myself. Paradox and ambiguity are fixed at the heart of the human condition, and to grow up involves a lot of acceptance. If there is an answer to this dilemma, I shall not be the one who finds it. The goal is to give up my fixation on *self.* To become selfless is to find freedom in Christ. Spirituality is that which allows us to get beyond the narrow confines of self. Yet we learn to embrace our true selves in the process.

I am learning not to fuss over myself too much. I do believe I am probably right where God wants me to be. At least I seem to be on the right path.

Paying attention is most important. It calls for a focus and a clarity which are quite rare. What does it take to truly see what is before us? First, the big popping sound must occur! When our heads finally emerge from our butts, we can look around and register what can be perceived. Novelists must be able to watch human nature very closely. If human cognition and behavior and self-awareness are so similar throughout history, then to write characters into a story must be done accurately. Falseness would be detected quickly. There is a clear sameness among humans of all stripes; yet, at the same time, there is an amazing diversity, culturally and historically. The storyteller must be able to sort all of this out. So it is necessary first of all to be other-directed, as opposed to being entrapped in one's own stuff and not able to see the horizon.

I'm able, late in life, to become more and more interested in others and what makes up life. As I grow closer to God, I draw closer to other homo sapiens on our little planet. We are all along for the same ride, so we should stick together for safety's sake.

Things We Take on Faith

When they first circled the moon, an amazing view was given as they emerged from the dark side. They were able to get some color film loaded quickly enough to picture our little blue planet as it rose into sight. It became a famous photo and fostered among earthlings a new perception of our special particularity. We are blue! Mostly salt water. A place to stand is rare. Many people had a moment of reflection, perhaps realizing how precious are so many good gifts we take for granted. Then, most people looked down and re-applied their nose to the grindstone. Business as usual. How can we take the universe so lightly? Do we really think the stars are there purely for decoration? Do we take for granted that we are alone in the universe? Did God do all this just for us? How do we gain a galactic perspective? Why bother?

The more we learn, the more we get the sense that we are indeed privileged in the largest realm of things. We come from the stars—stardust if you will—adhering, because of gravity, into matter with some basic elements which were probably present in the beginning. We are carbon-based life forms. That is the membership requirement to be alive hereabouts. Does this mean all life everywhere must be carbon based? If one takes the best of physics in one hand and in the other hand the best of scripture, what have you? Well, two hands! I have become enchanted with the dialectical relationship between the two. I think the best path is to keep them separate, yet to learn from each.

There seems to be a God-set limit to our human knowledge. There seems also to be such a thing as wisdom, as in the wisdom to know the difference. There are amazing things yet to be discovered, even in our lifetimes. There are many other things we think we shall never know. Both theology and science can make contributions to the now known and the vast unknown. I'm interested in such things.

(How do we know we exist? Because our dogs recognize us, and dog is God spelled backward.)

Of the two realms, religion and science, it is the latter which seems more remote, esoteric, and unapproachable to me. It even has a language (mathematics) which I certainly never learned and saw no use for. I never had a math teacher who knew what it was for either; so I said, well, I'll just not learn it. If I had life to do over, I would have learned math, Latin, German, French, Italian, Greek, and a little Hebrew. It is too late now and thus the problem. If you want a scientist to listen to you, you must either know the language or be a grant bestower. Thus, there is little discussion between the various disciplines. In this manner, science came up with the atomic bomb and there was never an ethics review board involved. Today, science says global warming will gradually destroy the planet and the tea partiers haven't a clue what's involved. They say, well it's been cool around here.

Religion, on the other hand, never in dialogue with science for the most part, is still living in a pre-Einstein and pre-quantum mechanics world, or in some instances in a pre-Newtonian world. The fact of the business is, *all* have a great part in what science has recovered or in what remains a mystery. For example, are we alone in the universe? We have instruments continually aimed at the sky, but it seems likely we are stuck on the small land areas on this pleasant little earth. We know nothing of planets beyond our solar system and the technology to get there is so far, far away. What about tending and weeding this little garden of Eden? That's an ethical call which scientists are not trained to make.

The word "universe" comes from the Latin *unus*, meaning one, combined with *versus*, which is the past participle of *vertere*, meaning "to turn." Thus, the original and literal meaning of "universe" was "everything turned into one." It was in the 5th century BC, when the philosopher Democritus proposed that all matter was made of tiny and indivisible atoms, and we were off and running. This started a long period which led to modern science. This period may be ending now, when many cosmologists are proposing that our universe may be one of an enormous number of universes. It is, perhaps, impossible to say how far apart these universes may be or even whether they exist simultaneously in time, but they almost certainly have different properties. The new word for all this is *multiverse*. The physicist Alan Guth said, "the multiple-universe idea severely limits our hopes to understand the world from fundamental principles."[22] If there are multiverses and this notion is correct, the style of basic physics will be radically changed.

Theoretical physics is the deepest and purest branch of science. It is the outpost of science closest to philosophy and religion. Experimental scientists occupy themselves with observing and measuring the cosmos. Theoretical physicists, on the other hand, are interested in the *how*. They want to know *why*.

Two theories in physics have caused this change in fundamental principles. They are "eternal inflation" and "string theory." These branches of physics have forced many scientists today to admit they cannot *see* or *measure* these things, but that they must be true. We must take them on faith. Like what theologians have been doing all this time.

If our science and religion can come together in the realm of faith, then we have a good place to meet. All can participate in the discussion. We begin by naming the mysteries. What do we not yet understand? With this long list considered, we start with a genuine humility. Life, death, faith, hope, healing. What does our faith yield?

---

22 Lightman, A. (2011, December). *The accidental universe: science's crisis of faith*. Harper's Magazine. https://harpers.org/archive/2011/12/the-accidental-universe/2/

Addiction

Addiction is, in its own way, just as insidious as cancer. In fact, taken as a whole, cancer has a higher cure rate than addiction. Many forms of cancer respond quite well to treatment. The odds are only one out of three that the full-blown alcoholic or addict will make it even if they try. Factor in the person who comes back from the depths of the disease to not only recover but to be a person of great worth and witness, and it is clear that the recovering addict was given the greatest gift of healing. I, at least, will always believe this.

In treatment, the memorable object-lesson is this: each person is asked to glance to their right and then to their left. Then the therapist says, "Of the three of you, only one will make it." Pretty scary, but the one who truly hears and turns their will and lives over, and then changes everything, that one might *get* it. The getting it comes as a gift. To reactivate the disease, one has only to drink or drug again. The disease comes roaring back, as if no progress were ever made. In this sense, addiction is worse than cancer. How many times have we heard, "the cancer is in remission?" Well, where does cancer go when it's in a state of remission? Does it hide behind the liver? Maybe so, but through the years I have come up with a more likely answer. Where does it go? God holds it. I can think of no better answer to the riddle of spontaneous remission. God also gives the gift of recovery. It cannot be done under one's own will power.

Hope, Despair, and the Virtual

Hope is a mystery. In our hoping, we dare not be presumptuous. When we hope, it doesn't mean God reveals special knowledge to us. I return to Gabriel Marcel, who wrote in *Homo Viator*: "The truth is that there can strictly speaking be no hope except when the temptation to despair exists. Hope is the act by which this temptation is actively or victoriously overcome."[23] Thus, to hope doesn't necessarily mean to "feel" hopeful. We, as St. Paul said, 'hope against hope.' This is not stoicism, because stoicism is inward turned. Hope is nurtured within the community of hope. The solitary, standalone Christian cannot sustain hope. One needs help. To wait without hope is to be without God. To hope, but not be willing to wait, dismantles true hoping because we try ourselves to bring about what we hope for. But hopeful waiting or a waiting hope is genuine eschatological hope—enabling us to wait, because what we hope for is already initiated in Christ and will be fulfilled by Him.

The despair so apparent in our society today produces the sense that time is a prison, that it's closed in; hope appears, then, as piercing through time. Hope, then, liberates us. Marcel doesn't think such liberation is available to many. Most people are "destined to remain entangled in the inextricable meshes of Having."[24] Escape is possible, but rare.

Not only entangled but buried and bombarded by confusions of context-less information. Jacques Ellul, in *Technological Bluff*, particularly emphasized that "people... deluged by information become incapable of making decisions. An excess of information... results in total paralysis of decision[-making]."[25] Does the daily news really help us in understanding and serving our world better? Do we ask, "what am I to do

---

23 Dawn, M. J. (2003). *Unfettered Hope: A Call to Faithful Living in an Unfettered Society*. Louisville. Westminster John Knox Press. 184.
24 Ibid. 187.
25 Ibid. 6.

with all these disconnected facts?" We have what Neil Postman calls a "Low-Information-Action Ratio" in *Amusing Ourselves to Death.*[26] The acronym LIAR reminds us that a TV soundbyte about world poverty with no response or action from us, makes "liars" of us. TV is bad enough, then add the internet and the new glut of electronic social interactions, and we have what should be called disinformation. It is misleading, misplaced, irrelevant, fragmented, or superficial information which creates the illusion that we know something. This is what happens when news is packaged as entertainment. We lose our ability to hold on to that which is necessary. We are rendered "unfit to remember." "We vault ourselves into a continuous incoherent present."[27] Consequentially, information keeps us from thinking.

If we are constantly in the noise, we cannot ponder over the deep issues. Even worse, we lose the still, small voice which is everything.

When I tell folks my hobby is collecting monasteries, they cannot believe I can actually go "unplugged" for days at a time. No electronics, no media, no entertaining events! How does one do it? Well, I just got used to it. That's the real world, not this infested life we live in the culture. Getting quiet is not only desirable; it is essential. This is true not only for monks, but also for CEOs and housewives.

What does the word *virtual* mean anymore? It used to mean, something missing, a false note, the not-really, half-assed, not-ness. Now this is, I guess, an apt definition, since our new reality *is* a virtual one. We have become virtualized creatures, floating somewhere in cyberspace. We are like the birds sent down into the mines to see if the air was toxic. Look into windows at night. People sitting in front of monitors fiddling with their mouse, while the rest of the family is watching "reality TV." Meanwhile, reality has actually lost its meaning. Reality, the really real, is becoming rare and unrecognizable. Remember back when we had "institutions"? They were for folks who had lost touch with reality as I recall. So, what is real? Or, as Pilate asked the Lord, "What is the truth?" What is truly real? What is true?"

---

26 Ibid. 7.
27 Ibid. 8.

In the time of a virtual reality, we turn once again to the vital truth of Christianity. Christians cannot be pessimists because of the eschatological nature of our hope. We know the future and its connections to the character of God. We believe the future aeon has already broken into this present age, and God's kingly reign has already begun.

Christians cannot really be optimists either, because it is clear we are in a world of hurt. We are still trapped in a time of sinfulness, brokenness, evil, idolatry, and despair.

What we are can be called hopeful realists, not virtual realists, but those who can see, diagnose, and understand the truth of our realities. We can have a deep and abiding hope. We are able, as Jacques Ellul says in *The Ethics of Freedom*, to get outside ourselves through faith and thus to have objectivity in studying the cultural forces which alienate us. Christian freedom allows us to be "able to hold at arm's length these powers which condition and crush me... [and to] view them with an objective eye that freezes and externalizes and measures them."[28] Because of resurrection hope, our realism does not leave us in despair.

28 Ibid. 80.

Preaching and Progress

The task of preaching is to show that the way things are is not the way things have to be. The job is not to explain the text; it is to proclaim the text. I need not get all caught up in the "original setting" or to bring out the "meaning" of what most assume to be a dead text. The text is very much alive. Some preachers not only know this, but are so caught up into liveliness that the scripture gets up and dances around the church. If we can learn to encounter the text in this way, new life can emerge. We do not liberate the text. It brings us to abundant life. God, after all, has already gifted us with the means by which the Gospel word can be understood by the congregation. The name of that gift is Holy Spirit. The church can be taught to expect that if preaching is faithfully done in this way Sunday after Sunday, God will show up in a powerful way. God's presence is an awesome thing.

If we have been taught to take God seriously, we will embrace the Old Testament teaching to properly fear God. If we do this, we will want God to be the audience for all we do at worship time. When the church and those who plan worship are merely trying to sign up new members, we only get low expectations, because the bar was set too low in the first place. If we expect to actually fall into the hands of the living God, I believe God will bring folks with him when he actually finds a church where he is truly worshiped and glorified. All will be well. Either that or all will be what was intended in Creation.

Our trouble is that we believe none of this. Either that or we have not been paying attention. After all, the Cross and the resurrection have happened; God sent Jesus, who was with him from the beginning, into the world to redeem the world. We have been saved on the cross, given eternal life in the resurrection, and not only this, we may now walk daily in new life with our Lord and Savior. Wow! If we believe in these things,

God will bless our gatherings and give us new life. God is more real than we are. Don't you get it sisters and brothers in Christ? This is all good because God said it was. My life depends on learning to worship God.

Here is a staggering statistic: 45 million of the 70 million martyrs who have died for their faith in Christian history were persecuted in the 20th century.

Trinity
Pater – father

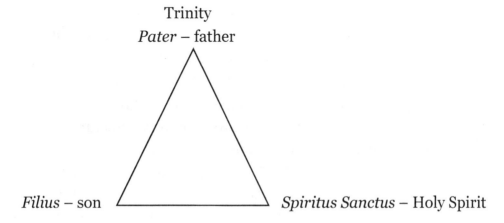

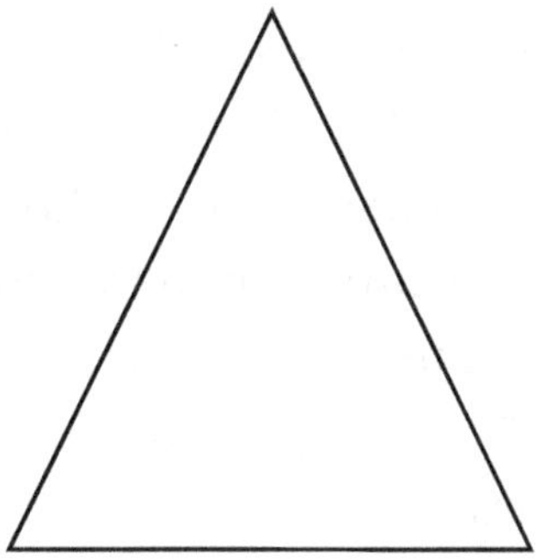

Filius – son   *Spiritus Sanctus* – Holy Spirit

I was trained in the modern era of seminary education. There were already some forward-looking folks around thinking, "This must be the last gasp of doing church in this culture." Most kept doing what they were taught anyway. Therefore, in preaching we thought we had made great strides, because we, at least, had *progressed* (note that word!) beyond the old 3 points and a poem form (although there were still some of them around). Modern worship in the 60s had us blowing up balloons while the text was being atomized. We used form, source, historical-critical and redaction criticisms. We took the text apart, dissected it as if in a lab. It was 'Eleanor Rigby' time; the priest fell, and no one was saved. We so wanted to be relevant. Then along came Fred Craddock and others. Inductive method, narrative preaching—what does the text actually say? Where is the story? "Oh, it's all story!" Now things are better, but we lost what we had been trained to do. I'm glad I didn't pay much attention in my seminary days, anyway. I just read and concentrated on music. I was enamored over worship as a kind of onlooker. I got by.

Now I'm retired. Now that I have started to learn what to do, I'm too old and tired to do it. But that's all right. I still need to get some things straight in my own head, *and* I still go to church! Now I believe we must have literary, narrative, and canonical approaches to scripture, a people-forming, community-forming process that helps people to learn the genuine story of our faith, not the lame spiritualities of our culture. I still preach when asked, but must be driven wherever I go and can hardly mount the damn pulpit. The point is, I am learning how to worship.

Now, what do Christians do in this post-modern age? We agree the modern notion of progress almost killed us all. It was a myth. Also, we list the technologies that have run amok, the scientific, political, and economic failures of the modern culture. We are aware of these structures which no longer work to bring "progress" to humankind. Where are we today, as one era fades into a different time? Is it what Hegel noticed in his pendulum analogy? The change first tends to swing too far in the other direction. Christians cannot accept the total rejection of objectivity and the un-critical celebration of perspectival understanding. Post-modernism would also reject the Christian meta-narrative, which tells what still must be called truth. Christians must be careful not to throw out the baby with the baptism water, so to speak. The modern world looked at the book of Joshua and said, "look how violent this God is and the people he directs." Then went on to defend just-war scenarios. What Christians must come to is the politics of Jesus, a holy war must be the most horrid of oxymorons. What does the Bible really say about war? [29]

Well then: how does the church in our time teach "the royal waste of time, profound meditation, awe-ful silence, reflection on meaty doctrines, musical depth, memorization of extensive texts, steadfast intimacy with the true God, the continuity of the Church, genuine community, earnest repentance, grieving lament, disciplined cross-bearing, timeless truth, the beauty of holiness, and faithful goodness?"[30]

---

29 According to Hauerwas, organized murder wrapped in idolatry

30 Dawn, M. J. (1999). *A Royal "Waste" of Time: The Splendor of Worshiping God and Being Church for the World.* Grand Rapids. Eerdmans.

Jaroslav Pelikan famously said, “traditionalism is the dead faith of the living, whereas tradition is the living faith of the dead.”[31] In the worship wars, we have traditional and contemporary. How stupid can that be? If these are the polarities, I want the absolute best from both perspectives. The church has a great treasure of new and old. It cannot be new vs. old, an either/or situation, but it is probably impossible to do what is called “blended” in a really creative way. Each church will develop a certain way, a style, if you will. If it works, it will mean staff and congregation will come together around a way of worship, so the “way” can get out of the way and the triune God can be worshiped in spirit and in truth. If truth be told, yes, that’s it! If the *truth* be told, if the total message is the truth, the mediums will likely sort themselves out. If the church out in the ‘burbs worships only to attract new members, the clamor of evangelism will trump worship. If the “traditional” church only exhibits pride, snobbery, and exclusivity, then the Trinity will not be allowed in the building. To worship authentically is not easy. 2 Timothy 3:14-17 invites us to be trained in the Holy Scriptures, to *know* them and be *formed* by them, not to just believe. Here’s a good question: what kind of people are our worship services forming? Are we offering that which is needful or are we catering to neediness?

Marva Dawn gives us this wonderful paragraph as a description of worship:

> ...that by God’s gracious invitation and Christ’s intercession and the Spirit’s enabling we are welcomed to learn of the Trinity through the biblical narratives passed on by faithful witnesses. Gathered in the community of saints, we are formed by the truth taught in worship’s music and word to be Church so that out of our Christian character will flow the witness of our words and deeds for the sake of the world. [32]

Now that’s a mission statement!

---

31 Ibid. 66.
32 Ibid. 69.

How to Practice Safe TV

Since 98.3% of U.S. homes have televisions, with an average of 2.2 sets per household, and the individual dwellers watch re: 4.5 hours daily with the set turned on 7 hours per day, the situation may well be hopeless. When a kid graduates from high school, she has spent more hours before the tube than she has spent in school. 80% of discretionary time has been spent watching TV. This is, in my thinking, *the* issue before us in the culture *and* in the church, if we care about how we are being formed as people. The church, when I was a child (way back in the days *before* TV), was the major way people were formed. Parents and schools and churches taught values. The question in the days of yore was, how will this formation in values affect people? Now, in the age of TV, the question is: will this make a profit?

Today, the fortunate church gets a person one hour per week. The average person watches TV 28 hours per week. What do we gain if churches are using only the tricks and devices which may be learned from TV in their worship?

Reading has decreased by half since the 60s. TV stifles the imagination. Trivialization is inevitable in the world of the technological era, with its emphasis upon utilitarian means rather than truthful ends. We become less motivated to think. Need we say any more than to simply list the issues of violence and sexual immorality? What about greed and the muddled perception of reality? What TV has given us is a whole new and very successful religion. It even has a liturgical year. Rose Bowl parade, World Series, Superbowl, etc. What gets the highest ratings? How to practice safe TV? Pull a giant condom down over the set.

The God's-Eye View

Faith, hope, love—*abide*, because each of these is a gift of grace: a spiritual gift, if you will. (He lives and He gives.) We are, then, perhaps to employ these gifts on the journey toward wholeness. They say these gifts survive even death. We still employee them in eternity because they are given by and directed toward God. They transcend time.

If we say we try to see things with a God's-eye view, then we get to the heart of things, for if we know anything about a God's-eye view, it is that only God can have it. We get carried away by the *imago dei* picture from Genesis and Psalm 8 and go right on to heresy. In thinking we are totally in control (while learning we are not), we stand at a hopeless period in our current time in history. We had such confidence in our progress and control in the modern era. Now we come to a full realization that our greed and mismanagement has resulted in a time without hope in seeing a clear way forward. Therefore, it becomes clearer that it is not that God is dead. It may be that man is dead. The idea that man is large and in charge (the fully autonomous and rational agent of classical science), *that* man is dead. From a God's-eye view of things, that is good-riddance. But thank God *we* are not God. Hope, then, is a matter of letting ourselves go. We are to die to presumption. God is God, and we are not. Therefore, we are not hopeless, and there seems to still be enough time. Hope is not a feeling; it is a readiness to act.

The kingdom of Jesus proclaims a reality which breaks in on the cusp of past, present, and future—when one's world is overturned by news of God. We are called to discern that the world *has been, is being,* and *will be* made new (Rev. 21:5) in ways which involve our participation and responsibility. In any case, it is clear enough that God loved this pale, blue dot enough to give his only son, or invest the very God-self into this particular place to stand in the universe. That is the God's-eye view we can believe.

Brueggemann

Walter Brueggemann writes a lot about preaching, and I always learn from it. Here is a quote: "I understand the moment of preaching, in the designated place of preaching, to be a freeing and primitive act that flies in the face of all our accepted certitudes, conservative and liberal."[33]

So, preaching should be unsettlingly provocative. All should be disarmed. Well, of course it should! Nothing new here. All ages and stages of preaching should be prophetic. It should also be wearing the long hair of the Hebrews, and it is most un-Latin-like (and not Greek, either). I dig it. *And* there must be some "Finally comes the Poet" parts.

My point is, this is truly a wonderful time to preach. Most sermons from the pre-Enlightenment times don't move me. If all in the house are of the same mind, what a bore. What would you say that would stir shit up? The long modern period presents some interesting preaching tasks of course. The obvious opportunities of this period are what I was trained for. I can pick apart a text and leave the chancel with scripture fragments cluttering the floor of the sanctuary, but that never really was "it" for me. Then along came what we have learned to call post-modern. What a paradigm shift! This new time was as different in its context as the shift from medieval to modern. All the rules changed, and we were given a new set of possibilities. Now, my thought is... *this is the best of worlds.* I would rather preach now as compared to any other time. Perhaps it is because I'm old and have only a handful of sermons left.

Brueggemann writes of preaching his ass off on the way to prophecy, but then realizing "they" just didn't get it, other than he quoted a lot of scripture. If you do that, folks will think you did good no matter what you thought you were saying. He presents preaching as a "sub-version." I like that. Congregants will after say of a particular preacher, "She really

---

33 Brueggemann, W. (2000). *Deep Memory, Exuberant Hope: Contested Truth in a Post-Christian World.* Augsburg For-tress. 2.

preaches the Bible!" And I was listening as well, but didn't hear any of that! All I heard was "please like me for I know not what I do, but let's do it together." If preaching is sub-version, it means it is on a level beneath the dominant version. The dominant version of reality *is* the problem. The preacher undermines all that, for it is part of the current culture. Our hearers are still deeply rooted in the modern world of consumerism, capitalism, militarism, and technology. They are quite self-satisfied, despite that they deeply understand when something is bad or wrong. They are too addicted to the society to know how to break free of that which is slowly killing them; they long for spiritual nourishment, but at the same time, they don't have a clue.

Then as Brueggemann says, finally comes a poet. Someone from outside the circle. Someone not a part of, but subversive to the common cause. It's a lonely job, but someone has to do it. The God-called preachers of the gospel have as a subject, Jesus of Nazareth, sent by the God of Israel to show the kingdom purposes which are the blueprints of a new church.[34] Jesus brings that which is needful. Brueggeman says the situation should be a subversive offer of another version to be embraced by subversives. We bring peace to enormous violence. Sexual abuse, racial violence, school shootings, road rage, endless 24-7 violence piped into our homes by TV, and severe economic violence, which is scarcely realized, as long as the consumption is vigorous. We have a ridiculous myth of scarcity in a world, an isolated and insulated world, a world of me and mine. As we exist in our little armed camps, we are so cut off from reality that the 3/4ths of the world which truly experiences scarcity cannot even be acknowledged. We just want to keep what we have as we focus on what we lack, and don't impinge on our little world for we will shoot your ass if you do. We are cut off from our neighbor and there is a violent breakdown of connections. We are alone and lonely. We are powerless and what we need is *power*! That power is not violence, but a peace that passes understanding. It is always power from God, and it breaks forth as an everlasting light which overcomes our little world. The gospel gets preached and new subversives are made.

---

34 New in any age

Alcoholism

Four of the six Americans who have won the Nobel Prize for literature were alcoholics. About half of our alcoholic writers end up killing themselves. Alcoholism is not easy to define *definitively*. (Impaired control over drinking, preoccupation with alcohol, continued use despite adverse consequences, and distortions in thinking, most notably *denial*.) In the 20th century, the *what* of alcoholism made huge changes. From a moral dilemma to a lack of willpower to a disease, then the terms became alcohol abuse and dependence. The medical people keep on theorizing, yet some would say the cause of alcoholism is unknown. We in AA know the cause is swallowing alcohol, but what do we know? Personality traits, early life experiences, societal influences, genetic predisposition, abnormal brain chemistry, you can get a grant for any of these things. The question remains, why do one in ten become so affected?

Discussing Poe, Baudelaire once commented that alcohol had become a weapon "to kill something inside himself, a worm that would not die."[35] To me, the best part of John Berryman's "novel" *Recovery* was the introduction written by Saul Bellow. He said inspiration contained a death threat and, as the poet wrote, he just waited for things to fall apart. Bellow wrote, "Drink was a stabilizer. It somewhat reduced the fatal intensity."[36] Could it be that the poet can see and sense and taste and feel so deeply that the beautiful gifts of existence simply overwhelm her and she dies of inspiration, dies of breathing in reality? Who knows? Of course, the thing about writing alcoholics is, writing is what they do. Obviously *they* can be counted upon to explain the mysteries. Why do they not get it that the alcohol was destroying what they were getting at? If writers could describe the affliction best, why did most persist into death and oblivion?

---

35 Laing, O. (2013). *The Trip to Echo Spring: On Writers and Drinking*. Picador. 8.
36 Ibid.

Were the commonalities generally true? A weak father and an overbearing mother, torments of self-hatred and inadequacy, sexually conflicted and voracious, hard, and hectic living, a tragic wreckage of broken relationships—these are some of the things in common. I guess. Again, I think of the thousands of AA meetings I've attended. There certainly are things we share.

At first it works. All agree. It is a wonderful thing. That for which we had long searched. Ethanol is both an intoxicant and a central nervous system depressant with an immensely complex effect upon the brain. It messes with neurotransmitters. It activates dopamine and serotonin, which is a good thing, but it also has a related downside: after a while, the negative forces emerge and the drinker strives for the right balance. Of course, the alcoholic just keeps drinking as long as there's any left, then she pukes on her shoes and passes out. The ups and downs of ethanol make it a marvelous drug for many. Its allure is perfect for every gathering. It goes great with any feast or party. It works until it quits working. The problem is, over time the brain begins to adjust to the presence of alcohol, compensating for its effects on the central nervous system.

There isn't an alcoholic personality per se, but the brain becomes affected after a while, and alcoholism takes on a life of its own.

Hauerwas

Hauerwas wrote, "If we are to be human, we are in the business of learning to die."[37] His contention is, in this lies the essence of Christianity. Our faith is training in how to be human. Therefore, theology aside, what we have to say should be interesting to all, not just those who are "of the faith." We can learn from those outside the faith as well, however. Such as yesterday, in an AA meeting: the wonderful image of "stumblin' over mouse turds" was brought up. How well that suggests not sweating the small stuff. What percent of stuff we sweat is large stuff? Well, then, in the words of Stanley Hauerwas: "Jesus is Lord, everything else is bullshit."

Remember: spiritual is not always good. There are certainly bad spirits. I've come to use the word "spiritual" as those energies that all peoples, places, and things give off. Sometimes these "spirits" are good and sometimes not. We must always pray for discernment, because this is a gift of the Spirit. We do not receive this ability from our standard equipment; this is a dearly won option. Such discerning prayer will make us necessarily counter-cultural. We must be trained in the church!

There are spiritual energies everywhere—in people, institutions, governments, schools, churches, prisons, bars, gyms, barracks, and neighborhoods—whatever and wherever. We need vigilance, lest we fall prey to the devil's lure to "be like God" (Gen. 2:5). Or to fall under the influence of principalities, powers, or anything which is not Christ.

In short, we need Jesus! In the Christian church there is nothing vague about life. We see spirituality as an operation of God in Christ. This movement of God in our lives allows us to be pulled into and made participants in the life of God. The Christian community is interested in spirituality because it is interested in living. Life is a gift. Your own life is a gift. Rejoice and accept. God is good; life is good.

---

37 Hauerwas, S. (2013). *Approaching the End: Eschatological Reflections on Church, Politics, and Life.* Eerdmans. XVII.

Jesus is the name which keeps us attentive to the God-defined, God-revealed life. Jesus is the central and defining figure in the spiritual life. It is Jesus who comes to us. We don't seek him out; he comes to us, often in surprising and unanticipated ways. It is Jesus who reveals what we never could have figured out for ourselves.

Jesus is God among us. He is God speaking, acting, healing, helping in our daily lives. Salvation is the word into which all the above words fit.

The Trinity solves so many dilemmas for us. If we tend to stray into heresy, we can be pulled back into "the one holy, apostolic church" and be given our marching orders once again. Hauerwas has taught me so much about theology, ethics, and life (through his own life). I thrill to think of it all.

Spirit, Matter, and Stuff

Scientists come in two packages. There is the active one, measuring things and sticking to those things which seem to be the laws of the universe. Then, there are the theoretical physicists sitting around thinking and writing shit I don't understand on the board. I like the latter group because, except for the math, I'm drawn to the way they practice their craft. I aspire to be a theoretical theologian, sitting, thinking about God and stuff.

Here is some stuff.

Spirit is regarded popularly as an entity floating around and yet able to do some stuff. It is not thought of as *matter*; we know matter with our measuring and sensing devices, etc. C.S. Lewis once told an audience that, for the Christian, "spirit" is not lighter than matter, but heavier. Spirit is the "real" substance of God, acting in creation and redemption and in reconciliation. Scripture links spirit to the material. Now, old Clive spent most of his life at Oxford among all the intellectual disciplines and such. I wonder if someone called him on that. How could spirit-fused matter be heavier than regular matter? I know what he meant, but I fancy that, if one could measure things Jesus touched, one could quantify the spirit within them. The loaves and the fishes, the wine in Cana, the nails and wood from the cross? At the very beginning of his ministry, *things*—ordinary things—seemed supra-real. In the beginning, at the river Jordan and beyond, we find the very Spirit busy in real, heavy, earthly things. Real water, real bread, real wine, clothing from camels, diet from bugs, sandals, birds descending bringing the actual presence of God into the lives of God's people. It is Jesus, 100% God and 100% man, who speaks and acts in these very real situations.

The four gospel writers, in light of the context of Israel's prophets and poets, tell us all we need to know about Jesus. This is the treasure of the church universal. As we read, study, ponder, believe, and pray these gospels, we find both the entire scriptures and the entirety of the spiritual life accessible and in focus before us in the inviting presence of Jesus of Nazareth, the Word made flesh.

Abundance and the Myth of Scarcity

In the real world, our world, we belong together at least in the sense that this is the only place we can live. On this little blue planet, third out from a diminishing middle-aged sun, in a corner of a neighborhood called the Milky Way, here we are. We are the species of life currently in charge of this world. We are alone, as far as we know. The universe is so vast, we cannot even wrap our little minds around such vastness and what this really means for humankind.

A few things are clear. Here is one of them; I can understand the following: I exist here as a male member of the human race, in the south of a country called the US of A. I worked, got tired, retired, now I write. On this globe, ¾ of the humans lack and go hungry often. I am fat. We go to the store and get whatever we want and do not even give it a thought. I believe we ought to share, but for many reasons we don't. We have limited resources on our planet, we believe, and we want to get what we can while the getting is good. We work for what we get, and we want to keep it, not to share it. This is just the way we naturally are, right? So, it must be the right way. Well...

Most of the world's resources pour into the United States. Money and *stuff* have become a drug for us; we must have it and we do. We get richer and richer. We are blind to our own prosperity and certainly to the poverty of so many others. As we gain more and more, we become less generous. *Countless studies have demonstrated this!* In the churches I know about, it's not that we mean for this to be. Preachers preach good stewardship. We are well-intentioned. But folks just do not get it. We have invested our lives in consumerism until it is the ruling force in our culture. We have a craving for more, and *more* is never enough. Consumerism has become the most powerful spiritual power in our culture.

All I know to do is to preach about this. If we are up against a demonic spiritual power, what then does the Bible say? Scripture starts out with a garden of abundance. Everything is provided, even a naked lady. Genesis is a song of praise for God's generosity, and the refrain is, "It is good, it is good, it is good." Damned good!

As far as the universe is concerned, this is the best garden in existence (we think). God's presence insures the incredible vitality of humans, plants, animals, fish, and birds, all of life. The only instruction is "be fruitful and multiply." This goes on until God says, we need a Sabbath. Let's step back and look at all of this. Enough is enough. It does not get any better than this. This is all we need. Let's rest. The people of Israel, God's own people, celebrated God's abundance. We know the story and things were not always a garden of delight. The point is, the old, old story is basically a story of abundance. God is good.

Way later came Psalm 104. (We do not use this hymn book of the bible enough.) It is a creation Psalm. It serves as a commentary on Genesis 1. It is quite long. In it, the psalmist names all the good stuff that is part of God's creation. In words equal to the poetry of any age, a complete picture of God's abundant goodness is given great expression. Not only has God created, God also sustains. It says, in effect, "If you give your breath, the world will live; if you ever stop breathing, the world will die." It is directed, directly to the Creator. A great hymn of praise for all that is. The incredible abundance of creation is guaranteed!

Now it seems to me, the problem is, we have ignored the promise of abundance and have developed a myth of scarcity. In history, it is clear that whenever more has not been enough, the trouble begins. We see it again and again. Greed becomes obsession; it breeds violence, wars are waged, time passes, new power emerges, war again, and so on and so on. The myth of scarcity breeds greed. It causes an addiction for more. It is sinful. The operative element in this sin is the little word *fear*. It is fear which fuels the flames of greed. It is fear that fuels the myth of scarcity as well. What if we run out? How much do we need to be sure we will always have enough stuff? When, in fact, there is never enough if you are filled with fear. It is fear which causes us to live in an armed camp. We can feed the world; we just don't want to. After all, "we worked for what we have. God helps those who help themselves. Jesus said we would always have poor folks, so as long as me and mine are not poor, things are as they should be. God bless the USA." This is bullshit.

We should learn from what God has done. When the children of Israel finally got free of Egypt, they kept looking back. They were free; yet they were worried about running out of bread and water. They were fearful and faithless. Then God's love came to them from above. God gave bread. They say "Manhue?"—Hebrew for "What is that?"—and we get the word *manna*. Now there is a great lesson in God's generous gift (Exodus 16). It was "daily bread." Later, Jesus taught his followers to ask for daily bread as they prayed.

Now this gift God provided, this manna, was not what His children were used to. They had no control over the product. It just was there every day. Again, the Liturgy of abundance. God's faithfulness. Everybody had enough to eat every day, but in Egypt the children had been taught the myth of scarcity. The lesson for us is that God's abundance transcends the market economy. The children soon tried to hoard the bread. When they tried to bank it, to invest it, it turned bad. It was no good if you didn't just gladly receive it day by day. You cannot store up God's generosity. Walter Bruggemann has written:

> We who are now the richest nation are today's main coveters. We never feel that we have enough; we have to have more and more, and this insatiable desire destroys us. Whether we are liberal or conservative Christians, we must confess that the central problem of our lives is that we are torn apart by the conflict between our attraction to the good news of God's abundance and the power of our belief in scarcity—a belief that makes us greedy, mean, and unneighborly. We spend our lives trying to sort out this ambiguity.[38]

---

38 Brueggemann, W. (1999). *The liturgy of abundance, the myth of scarcity*. Religion Online. https://www.religion-online.org/article/the-liturgy-of-abundance-the-myth-of-scarcity/

That states the case rather well. Which will we select: abundance or scarcity? Which one leads us to God? What did Jesus say about all this? He said we must decide. You cannot serve God and Mammon. You cannot serve God and then do what you please with your resources. Jesus says, "Don't be anxious, because everything you need will be given to you."

Do not fear. Look around you; there is abundance everywhere. But we must decide. Do we really believe what scripture says? Christians in my experience have reduced Jesus. They have removed him from public life and made of him a private little Savior—that which we honor at Christmas and Easter, and largely ignore the rest of the time. To do this is to clearly ignore what scripture says. If we look at what Jesus said in red, we find a radical, new way of living. If we seek to follow Jesus, we start by paying attention to what he said. If we actually start to believe what he said, we will find a new way. We will start to live our lives into the purposes of the Kingdom of God.

The real issue confronting us is whether the good news of God's abundance can overwhelm the myth of scarcity in our lives, minds, and in our culture. The great question now facing the church is whether our faith allows us to live in a new way. If we choose the story of death, we will lose the land. In Joshua chapter 24, the choice is put before us. Joshua begins by reciting the story of God's generosity, and concludes by saying, "I don't know about you, but I and my house will choose the Lord." It does not get any clearer than that.

Jesus tells us clearly, if we have money we are in trouble when it comes to getting into the Kingdom of Heaven. That is what the man said and there is just no way around it. So, what do we do? Well, we just ignore and deny. He can't mean us; we are not rich! (Republicans are rich; he must be talking about them.) It gets worse. Not only was he talking about you and me being rich, he also implies or declares it to be dishonest wealth. The problem is we have inherited practices of injustice. The truth is, all wealth is the result of murder! For example, Columbus discovered the US of A in 1492, right? And there were no people already here? This is not our land originally; we had to kill a whole lot of "savages" first. In Hegel's words, history is a "slaughter-bench."[39] Jesus is saying we live in a world in which we cannot help but be possessed by dishonest habits and unjust systems. "No slave can serve two masters." Does this mean we have a choice between being a slave and not being a slave? No, Jesus presumes we are enslaved.

Perhaps few in history have been as enslaved as Americans are today. We think we are the land of the free. What an irony. We are so caught up in the system, we cannot see beyond the confines of our consumeristic society. Yet, we are also Christians. Confession is the place to start. We can become more generous, but even this will not save us. That God is generous is our hope. That forgiveness can come as we become consumed, consumed by God's generosity and abundance. We can become free, free in the sense that we need no longer pass on systems of injustice. We can even begin to understand we are wealthy and what to do about this great burden.

39 Hegel, G.W.F. (1988). *Introduction to the Philosophy of History*. (L. Rauch, Trans.). Indianapolis. Hackett. 24.

Economics

This kid from France is the new guru of economics. Thomas Pickety wrote a 685-page tome which is all the rage. Number one on Amazon's best-seller list. *Capital in the 21st Century*. Named THE economic book of the decade, and the decade is not even half finished, and guess what? The 1% is getting richer. Not only that, their wealth doesn't trickle down. It defies gravity and trickles up (who knew?). He says inequality will likely continue for many more years, or at least until the peasants rise up. World wars or huge government interventions can move things around, but when the rich get entrenched (the "natural" order of things) the poor just get poorer. So, the golden age of the average American may be over. Just look to the current congress: any hope or help there? Don't look for any New Deals, Marshall Plans, tax reform, or minimum wage raising there. Since the rate of return on capital is naturally greater than the rate of growth in the economy as a whole, the rich look to their investments and those who get paid in salaries get smaller fixed wages. The gap grows. Here's the rub: the CEOs get up to 30% of their "wages" in stock options, so what incentive to change rests there?

So, all this is supposed to be *new* news? I don't know much about money, but I knew all this.

I believe no one really knows what economics is really all about. It simply is not a science, but a study of greed and power. I believe that behind it all lurks a Creator capable of predicting some of the vagaries and who is unchanged in attitudes about widows and orphans and such. The bible is as good an economic indicator as the latest book on the subject. I'm embarrassed to be one of the rich. We seem to be in pretty good shape. What is my witness? Little to none. It takes too much courage to tell the truth. What a coward I am.

Salvation, and God *Pro Nobis*

Now to soteriology (*soter*, to save). Salvation is a word theologians use to speak of the Christian life as a whole; a good definition of salvation (there are many) is: *Jesus Christ in all that he is and all that he does.* When Paul is arming the Christians in Ephesians, he finally says, put on the "helmet of salvation" (Eph. 6:17). That way you won't forget your baptism when the world hits you on your head. All of this helps us remember who we are when confronted with the wiles of the devil.

Salvation is primarily about God. This world teaches us to narrate our lives without God; salvation implies there is that from which we need to be saved. Maybe we are not doing as well as we thought. Maybe it's not us who have the whole world in our hands. So, we first get over the notion that our salvation is about dying and going to heaven, although this is a happy thing. Salvation is not destination; it is our vocation. When I was baptized, I began a life-long journey. God is with me all the way. It's not about death; it's about life.

The Bible says a lot about all this. Luke-Acts uses the 's word' a lot, Matthew and Mark almost never. That's not the point. In the Psalms, we find God's job description, *"working salvation in the midst of the earth"* (Ps. 74:12). God is *"the God of our salvation"* (Ps. 65:5). In scripture, salvation is what God does. Karl Barth taught salvation was the whole point of Creation.

The Hebrew verb root *ya sha* ("save") is found 354 times in the Old Testament, usually with God as subject. It is telling that *salvation* appears most frequently in Psalms and in Isaiah. We need to take John 4:22 seriously: *"Salvation is from the Jews."*

Salvation is not only what God does in Jesus Christ (grace). It is also who we are, in that converting awareness that God is not only God but also God "for us and for our salvation" (justification and sanctification). When the God who was presumed by us to be an enemy against us is known as God the friend, *pro nobis*, this is salvation in its fullness. To be saved is the fitting human response to the stunning divine move on us. Though we are not the agents of salvation, God's salvation is meant to be received, embraced, and enjoyed.

What then is gospel? Karl Barth says when we say "gospel," *good news*, we are talking about salvation, about the mighty acts God has worked *pro nobis*. This is not religious experience, not something personal and subjective. Salvation is the mighty acts of God in history for the liberation of the cosmos. A Christian is one who lives in the light of this story.

As Wendell Berry has pointed out, God has provided across the earth, at several places, a good ten inches of topsoil. This can and does feed the world; yet we are to be the stewards of this gift. How are we doing? This principle exists through all of God's creation: God has given us a garden, we get afraid we will run out, and the trouble begins. Christians are those who are called to break the chain of greed and violence. If we try, we *will* get into trouble *but* be not afraid. God has provided, God is providing, God will provide. Our part is essential, *but* we are not alone. God will give us courage, protection, and strength. it's a done deal. Be not afraid!

God has determined to be God *pro nobis*, the God *for us*. God could just zap us, and we would do whatever, but God works through us. God loves us characters. Moses, Abraham, Job, Jeremiah, characters like them. God gets so mad at the Israelites he thinks, well, I will just zap them. Moses begs for pardon, and God changes God's mind (Exodus 33:10-14). The God of scripture does not work alone. God is not remote and unresponsive. God is God *pro nobis*. God is determined to be the God of our salvation. The Cross demonstrates this once and for all. What is closer to us than Jesus giving his all as he comes to us to save us? The

Creator of all that is, comes to us in a personal, direct way. This is so amazing we can barely conceive of it; yet this is the clear message of scripture. When asked, "where were you saved?" Karl Barth replied, "In Golgotha."

I have done funerals for close to 50 years. They are all the same in a general way. I am called to preside, almost always someone who I didn't know well enough to adequately sum up his or her life. This is why you meet with the family. You have to learn the story from them. I became skilled enough to be able to "do" funerals; yet I have rarely felt equal to the task. It is quite a task, to preside as one passes from life to what we call death. What do you say? Well, a few platitudes which are so common and regular, you could basically use the same "service" over and over. *But* what gets lost? Each person was and is a particular being, with a story common to only them. Who can sum all that up? You say what scripture says and try to address the particularity of a person for whom Christ died. Every time it's different, and every time it's the same. We usually turn to Paul, but everybody is thinking Plato. Greeks have won the day philosophically, with the view that there is some imperishable spark of soul which goes on and on, even past death. That's what most people believe and thus, it must provide some comfort. *It's just that it's not what scripture says*. Christians believe when we die, we die. There is no veiled metaphysical state to it. Whereas we came from dirt, to dirt we shall return. Tears and wailings are appropriate. Death stings. It is the final enemy. And yet, as a marvelous victory of God, the same God who raised Jesus from the dead, God somehow reaches out and intervenes. Death gets defeated and a journey is assured which does indeed continue beyond death. Jesus said, "because I live, you also will live."[40] Here is the key: "Immortality is attractive because it acts as if eternality is something we possess as human beings. Resurrection is humbling because it is pure gift to utterly mortal beings like us."[41]

I continuously choose resurrection over immortality. Rather than be an angel in eternal choir practice, I will take my chances in a resurrected

---

40 John 14:19
41 Willimon, W.H. (2008). *Who Will be Saved?* Abingdon. 27.

life in a whole new world, a radical discontinuity from this tired old place, a place where we are healed and near to the heart of God. So we look to the end to be expected from God. We get a new body. That's why Becky and I are comfortable with cremation. At the last trumpet, we will be raised incorruptible. We *shall* be changed. God can find an atom which can become me in God's future. This old bod—what's left of it, anyway—can be burned to save a bit of land.

God may be *pro nobis*, for us, but God is also *extra nos*, outside us. In Jesus Christ as a member of the Trinity, God has accomplished things far beyond human thoughts. We dare not make the cross and Resurrection contingent on any human responsiveness. Redemption is *pro nobis*, but God is not done with us yet. There is a continuation of creation. If salvation is God's job description, God will then bring the end when He is finished with us and creation. So, even though there is a finished and completed quality about God's work on the cross, there is also an ongoing dimension to the creation-salvation work of God in Jesus Christ. All we can do is say yes when we get the chance. God is not finished with me, as long as I draw breath (and perhaps beyond my earthly days). We can get "surprised by joy" many times. We grow in our ability to receive God's Great Gift. Don't give me any of this once and for all crap. "Once saved, always saved" is a smug and arrogant misunderstanding of God's ongoing grace! "I'm saved, how's about you" is North American evangelical Christianity at its worst. It turns God's grace into some subjective psychological experience rather than a work which God does. Barth said our reconciliation to God is an ever-present actuality, a fact which has been established by God's work, not an occasion we think we have experienced. The church is not here to produce a product—to *make* disciples, *produce* converts, or *win* people to Christ; those are capitalist metaphors. God in Christ handles all that. The church tells the story of what it was like, what happened and what it is like now. What does the world look like when it's been invaded by the reality of Christ? The Church is to demonstrate and embody this. We are those who have been baptized. *Baptism is God's word in water that saves.* Baptism gathers up all the meanings of Christian salvation and demonstrates those in word and water. You can't save yourself. Baptism is a gift offered to you. Baptism is a sign God works through the church to do for you what you cannot do for yourself. This corporate, ecclesial gift they call salvation. Baptism begins a life, thus what takes minutes to begin takes a lifetime to complete. Baptism is a great comfort in life and in death. Baptism is a sacrament: God has done in us what we never could do for ourselves.

Jesus, in his stories and sayings, reveals a God who is no discrete minimalist. Abundance is in the nature of God. There is a pervasive nihilism at the heart of modernity, a sense of scarcity. Freud, who did much to form the modern mind, spoke of "obscure, unfeeling and unloving powers" which determines our fate, reviving the early Greek view that we are, in Homer's words, mere "toys of the gods." Modernity tends to think, if there are gods in the heavens above, they are hidden and have no benevolent intent for us here on earth. When we look to scripture, we find that Jesus' stories are all about God. If we need a general interpretive principle for reading the Bible, it is this: Scripture always and everywhere speaks primarily about God, and only secondarily, and then only derivatively, about us. God starts the story; God sustains the story, intervening from time to time, making a way when there is no way, nudging forward despite twists and turns, subplots, and diversions, holding to the overall intent of the story, calling in a surprising cast of characters, all the while remaining the author and the chief actor in the story. The name of the story is salvation.

We must always remember Christian salvation is inextricably linked to the story of Israel's salvation. Paul wrote, *"all Israel will be saved"* (Rom. 11:26). Then Paul expands "all" to include even Gentiles.

Of course, who is saved is God's call (John 15:16). Jesus said, "You did not choose me, but I choose you." Nothing about us contributes to our own salvation. John Wesley would add, salvation is not simply about heaven. Salvation is here, now, whenever we get caught up in the divine life.

Rev. 5:11-13 describes salvation completed: *"myriads of myriads and thousands of thousands"* in a massive crowd before the throne, not just us, even *"every created thing which is in the heaven, and on the earth, and under the earth, and on the sea."* Whales get saved? Does this mean ALL? 1 Timothy 2:4 declares God desires *"all people to be saved and to come to the knowledge of the truth."* (*All.*)

See also: Eph. 1: 7-10; Col. 1:15-20; John 10:16; 1 Cor. 15:28.

The Acts of the Apostles recounts Peter preaching of a "universal restoration" (*apokatastasis*) that God announced through his holy prophets (Acts 3:21). The fourth century Cappadocian Gregory of Nyssa taught that the Resurrection will finally restore human beings to their original state before the Fall. *This universalism has never been fully orthodox.* The Augustinian-Lutheran-Calvinist counterview (some will, and some won't make it) has tended to prevail.

But God is not done with us yet.

The great Jewish theologian, Franz Rosenzweig, who described Christianity as a "perpetual journey of salvation,"[42] said Islam and Christianity could never get along because Islam had no theological means of comprehending how "the failings of human beings 'arouse divine love more powerfully than their merits.'"[43] God loves us. Jesus told us to pray for our enemies. I take this to mean, "out loud" of a Sunday morning in worship. For those we call terrorists, tower bombers and such. How are we doing with that? If we pray, "thy will be done on earth as it is in heaven" we should consider God's will to love all, ALL. Here is the radical stuff. If we are forced to decide who and what best suits our national interest, then do we really love those brown people we keep bombing? Are we as Jesus to them? Is the government our most cherished hope for security, that we must defend it with murderous intensity? Have we radically personalized salvation so that it applies only to me and mine, and have we radically nationalized it as well? Read Romans 5:12-21. The word "all," *ALL* is repeated five times. Read it! Does "*all*" mean some or

---

42 Willimon, W.H. (2008). *Who Will be Saved?* Abingdon. 55.
43 Ibid.

most? Martin Luther and John Wesley affirmed the universality and all-inclusiveness of the electing and reconciling work of God. Calvin taught limited atonement; it's all grace, but grace is not for all. Calvin even taught double-predestination (God predetermines some for salvation, some for damnation), although that's not in our scriptures (nor is having someone killed as Calvin did to Michael Servetus). Read Eph. 1:3-6. I don't get "some" out of that. Or Rom. 8:39 or Matt. 28:20—no "some" there.

Our church today needs to work on its mediocre soteriology. What we have to say to the world has been reduced into technique. Our salvation is in Jesus Christ, God was reconciling the whole world to himself. Eph. 2:8 adds, "this is not your own doing." It's the gift of God. When modern evangelicals beg folks to "make a decision for Christ," it's not unlike anything else in our consumeristic North American capitalism. Our culture is a vast supermarket. Folks dash around grabbing all they can before we run out. We think we are who we decide to be. We make up our own individual minds about everything. Our lives, however, are not the sum of our choices, but rather the results of the impact of God's grace upon us. Willimon has written:

> Does affirmation of the ultimate triumph of God in Jesus Christ, and the possibility that all might be saved, mean that human beings are rendered irresponsible, that grace is ultimately irresistible? Our salvation is a gift, and yet it is a gift that is offered along with God's gift of human freedom. If God loves us in freedom, then the very nature of grace entails the possibility of refusal and rejection. If grace is automatic or assumed, it tends to be neither gracious nor grace. John Wesley (along with Paul) taught that even our receptivity to the gift of grace is also a sign of the working of grace.[44]

Wesleyans believe salvation in Jesus Christ need not be a single, momentous, all at once affair. In the Eucharist, we acclaim Jesus Christ

---

44 Ibid. 61.

has come, has overcome, and is yet to come and will overcome. Our peace, rest, security, salvation, and destiny rests there, in Jesus.

Well *hell.* Yes, the New Testament speaks of it far too much to ignore. It must be possible to look up Hitler in the afterlife, so what about hell? Hell is the opposite of heaven. In Hell, as C.S. Lewis said, the door is locked from the inside. Hell is getting what you think you wanted. Hell has been much more artfully depicted through the years than has heaven. It is, on the face of it, a more interesting place than the bland insipid portrayals of eternal choir practice. But I certainly want to be in the herd of sheep, and not among the goats at the last judgment. Willimon says we should speak of hell with the same enthusiasm as did Jesus. Augustine's insights on hell made their way into the Athanasian Creed. Luther and Calvin, as usual, joined right in. There are 200 references to hell in the New Testament. Origen, who pushed for some final restoration, agreed that hell was real, but disagreed that it was eternal. He thought hell to be more educative than retributive.

We turn to Jesus. Luke 16:19-31: rich guy goes to Hades and a poor man goes to be with Abraham. A great gap of retribution separates them; yet the rich guy calls out to Abraham who says simply that the tables have been turned. End of discussion.

The horror of life without God has been lost in our imagination. We are not afraid enough of hell to worry about it overmuch. We are the modern one capable of figuring out all these matters. What can we possibly know about eternity? If we turn to Barth again, we get a refusal to give a clear answer. He refused to get God to say all are saved, or all are not saved. We know what he hoped for, based on Jesus' work for the salvation of all (how could it not be completed?). Still, sin has always been rampant. God is a deliverer not because we deserve deliverance. According to Scripture, we sinners can never escape judgment. When we look to scripture, we are given hope, yet we have no way to escape the judgment. It shall come to all (Rom. 12:19).

So how much time do we have or need?

We have, in Christian history, reduced the great gift of Atonement. By the Middle Ages, the church had made a firm link between salvation and sin. Anselm's 1098 *Cur Deus Homo* argued Jesus' death was needed to satisfy an angry God who had been violated. Our need was atonement—at-one-ment with God. To do this, an elaborate penitential system was devised. The church offers a way out. Salvation, once corporate and social, was made private and personal. The Protestant Reformation stressed even more strongly the penal, substitutionary model of atonement. Our sin merits death: there is nothing we can do to repay God what is due. Therefore, a loving God sent the Son to undergo the punishment that should be ours. This is our salvation. The substitutionary model has been predominate in the Western Church. But, in it, salvation is separated from ethics. Jesus pays our debt, so we are saved from hell. This vale of tears is of our making, so if we accept Jesus as our personal Lord and Savior, we can escape our just desserts. Isn't it better to say Jesus was not some helpless pawn in a cosmic game, but he was put to death for bringing the kingdom of God uncomfortably close, in a way which threatened our alliances with the power of evil? Jesus says, "today salvation has come to this house."[45] Eternity can begin in this life, and so can our response to the goodness of God in Christ. Salvation is not only about God's response to the problem of our personal sin, but also to the sins of the whole world (cosmos).

The church wisely never fixed one exclusive doctrine of Atonement as *the* one. We can, however, learn of a saving work of God in a way more consistent with what Jesus said and did. Just as there was bad theology in the old revivalistic hymns, there is bad theology in the new ones. "From the earth to the cross, my debt to pay. From the cross to the grave, from the grave to the sky."[46] Compare this to Romans 8 or Colossians 1. What sort of Christians are formed from such music?

The hard part about Christian salvation is not earning it, but in receiving it as God gives it.

---

45 Luke 19:9
46 Founds, R. (1989). Lord I lift your name on high [Recorded by MercyMe]. On *Traces of Rain Vol. 1* [CD]. MercyMe (1997).

Kant said the human condition was a search for answers to three questions: *What can I know? What ought I do? For what may I hope?* The church is the focus for such questions. This salvation for which we seek happens in the church. *Extra ecclesian nulla salus* ("apart from the church, there is no salvation"). If salvation in Jesus Christ is corporate, even cosmic, then salvation is not an individual matter but a communal one. We go to church to practice salvation, not only to be prepared for an eternity with God, but to follow Jesus in this life for the purposes of the Kingdom. The church is Christ's means to save the world. The church is saved for the world, not out of it. The church is where the risen Christ graciously takes his place. Our salvation being a gift also implies a summons. In salvation we are enlisted by God to work with God for the salvation of the world.

The End, and Getting Ready

People always want to look back to moments in their lives, occasions of epiphany when they uncovered the latest gift from God, something they can celebrate the anniversary of. I like the ongoing journey metaphor—not a climb, but a cruise in which one seeks day by day to live life creatively while focusing on the so-called 'spiritual' aspects. There is not a thing wrong with the word *spiritual*. It is what we have, and it points in a general way to a reality. It's just that the word has suffered nowadays like few words ever have. There is little I can do about it. When I try, people look at me funny, and I will continue to use the word as a 'new pair of glasses'. When I look at it that way, I am reminded of what God has done for me. I remember clearly what it was once like, and that I do not ever have to go back to a life of fear and addiction. All I must do to keep the great gift is to do with joy the things which are saving my life right now. I no longer have to make huge, difficult changes. There is such freedom and joy in all of this that I hope I have a few more viable years to go. To continue to write and travel would be a good end. If Hauerwas is right, and I do not doubt he is, then *being a Christian is preparing for a good death*. This no longer seems depressing to me. It is clear the task looms large. They speak of the fear of the unknown. Of course, it is unknown. A river cruise of the Danube is unknown to me, but I would love to make a trip like that. The metaphor of a journey returns. One can generally gain an anticipation of the unknown as easily as a fear of it. The preparation for the journey is to banish as much fear as possible in every area of our lives. The good news is we have a risen savior who goes before us to prepare the way.

One of the gifts of ministry is, you get to do enough funerals that you begin to believe what is spoken before the hole in the ground. You stand there with blessed assurance and fears are resolved; at least one can hope for that reality. It all has to do with the grace of God, and I am so grateful to be a Wesleyan. As we pass through the ongoing gifts of grace, we start to get a sense of the sanctification phase and what is meant by it. So few speak of it, it must be rare, but if one knows their redeemer lives, how could one ever lack again? To be joined to Jesus in the wonders of this world is also to be beloved in a world beyond, equally full of wonder.

My fascination with science in the last few years is a part of all of this. What is the end to be expected of God? The restoration of eschatology to a proper place in theology gives us a glimpse of what the full message entails. How dreadful it must be to find oneself trapped in a fundamentalist mindset which is not open to things which are clearly true.

Who cares if the sun will let us down five billion years from now? That does not diminish one whit the truth of our gracious reality with God. If God could construct us out of stardust in the first place, can we not count on the creator to continue to be creative? Well, certainly that must be the case. At the end, all we have is our story. Who could ask for anything more? I guess that is what I am doing. In longhand, with a fountain pen, on good quality paper, in a journal which can be saved and preserved and placed in an archive where future generations of scholars can come with gloved hands to view the wisdom of the ages. I'm sure this will get tossed with the trash as will many cherished treasures; it remains, however, that if this is truly an offering to God, then God will use it if it is needful. "God goes to us when we are sore distressed. Men go to God when He is sore distressed" (Bonhoeffer). If God is having a bad day and she gets a kick out of these scribblings, then it was all worthwhile. It is all some kind of soul-crafting, and it is what I do. It is what makes my toenails twinkle (Dylan Thomas). It is what is saving my life right now. At least that is some of what is saving my life right now.

God is Dog spelled backward. There can be little mystery thereunto. It cannot be a coincidence.

At the end, is there a tunnel with a light? Does one's soul separate and float above the operating theatre while a doctor records the time of death? I have rejected (as if I were capable of such) the notion that one sits in on some sort of eternal choir practice in the beyond. What would a spiritual body really be like (Jesus)? At the end of 1 Cor. 15, what can be said? Well, Paul said (I am not making this up), "Would the ushers please come forward" (Chapter 16!). That should serve as a good reminder not to take ourselves too seriously at least. The heavenly is certainly tied to the *earth* reality. You gotta love it.

I have learned much through the years because I have kept the study thing going. I know other retired pastors still work at it. I just don't know them personally. I have always worked alone with my personal drummer banging away. It's too late to change (or is it?). Yet here, late in life, I am convinced of the radical nature of Christ and of his church and that the community is the key. By going to both church and AA and by having friends I can be deeply immersed in communicable process; yet I yearn for more. I still want to communicate.

Preaching, teaching, and going to meetings has helped a lot, but there could still be more.

I'm reading Yoder, *The Politics of Jesus*. It's really a commentary on Luke as he plucks the seeds of non-violence from the gospel. Fine by me. I never tire of bible stuff. It's just that to try to be a pacifist in this reality is an impossible task, akin to the challenge of Jesus' own ministry. Jesus had at least three opportunities to have the crowds at his back if he had wanted leadership as it plays out in the real world. And then what!? He leads a rebellion? Would he then become a political leader in the sense of all the examples of history? We must go back to the temptations in the desert to get a sense of the gospel narrative. Satan would have him large and in charge. If he took a role at the front of a mob, what would the outcome be? We know the answer; it's just we never learn the lesson. Jesus knew what he was called to and for, and as he sets his face toward Jerusalem, his message is to non-violence. God has called us to the kingdom. We must remain faithful.

When I was ordained, the bishop asked: "Are you going on to perfection?" John Wesley put it there (only clergy profess it), I said, under my breath, "Yeah, sure!" Also, smoking and drinking were prohibited in those days; I flat out lied! Wesley was not content with any belief which did not result in a changed life. I (we) did not take ordination seriously, and we were to be the leaders. No wonder Wesley is listed among the last and the least of the "reformers". Wesley used the unfortunate word "perfect" to characterize the progress toward perfect love. He said, "When God has circumcised your hearts, and enabled you to love him with all your heart and with all your soul, think not of resting there. That is impossible. You cannot stand still; you must either rise or fall; rise higher or fall lower."[47] "Go forward," was Wesley's command. We disobey and that weakens the faith. Sanctification is but a movement of God's grace in our hearts. Wesley was correct to place it in the center of the faith. In this world, a world which was just beginning to be born in Wesley's time, we would rather think of ourselves as troubled sinners, and certainly not as righteous saints. Wesley was certainly aware of the hypocrisy of being a halfway Christian. He lived in an age when what it meant to be a "better sort of person" was assumed to be equivalent to being a Christian.

We can turn to Alastair MacIntyre, who lifts the virtue of constancy from the novels of Jane Austen. Constancy is the quality which allows us to reaffirm the unity of the self across and through our many loyalties and actions. It is akin to the Christian virtue of patience and the Aristotelian virtue of courage. The notion of constancy results from the recognition of a certain kind of threat presented in the modern world. Constancy requires a sense of self-knowledge based on the necessity of repentance, since the constant person is acutely aware that the generally agreed upon manner of behavior, quite right in itself, can also be a snare which only gives the illusion of constancy. Novelists and theologians are those who can explore the difference between those who only appear moral and those who are genuinely moral.

---

47 Wesley, J. (1872). Sermon 106 "On Faith" in *The Works of John Wesley* (T. Jackson, Ed.). Via wordsofwesley.com.

Wesley wished to remain loyal to the Reformation doctrines of justification, yet he needed to characterize perfection in reference to the wholeness of a human life. In Wesley's sense of 'going on' to perfection, the Christian life is a journey, a 'process' in which God's grace transforms a sinner into a saint. Progress is an essential element of the Christian life. For Wesley, 'love' is the central virtue—love that loves all as God loves (*agape* love).

My life is now centered in these stacks of books. The result is my continuing education. It is, in part, a thing I have always done, but it is also "more" somehow in retirement. The work I put in is hard work. The books and study I do are more difficult and more intense than from past years. I finish books I only began before, and I am a more careful writer now.

Only a few folks I know would comprehend or care about my interests and passions. These things are part of my prayer life. They are part of my daily walk with God.

Iris Murdoch and Anthony Trollope, my new favorites. I had completely missed these two until I read Hauerwas recommending them. Coetzee as well. I just finished his philosophical treatise, *Elizabeth Costello.* It is in the form of a novel, and it is so powerful. One doesn't mind his using the form of a novel to do philosophy because he does it so well. Hauerwas uses all the above in his wonderful essays. One also doesn't mind that Hauerwas doesn't really write books, although he is prolific. He just throws together essays loosely held together and gives them a title. His one exception is *The Peaceable Kingdom,* a textbook, if you will, on ethics. He does so because he doesn't trust "systems." Whatever he does is fine by me, because I have read most of what he has written carefully. It is clear Stanley Hauerwas has been the major influence on my life in theology (except for Barth). To him I owe my newfound attempt to be a pacifist, even though I am a closet pacifist in the sense that I don't preach it. It is simply clear if one seeks to follow Jesus, one must be a peace-seeker. I lack courage.

After considerable grounding, study, and long, good work, when one has an insight—the 'eureka' of Archimedes—that is a thing to relish. One turns the 'vision' into a statement, joins it to others of what we can be said 'to know', as well as to test the veracity of the given idea. (Religious epistemology is the center of modern philosophy of religion.) I have had these serendipitous moments. Everything seemed to click into place. I got it. I've had them in my daily life, in the program, and in the church. I'm reminded that religious life cannot be reduced to religious beliefs. These moments were not sprung from doctrine anyway but were given from the community. *The epistemologist will seek to find the conditions wherein a person can be said to know*. The problem is, a bunch of contingent factors (mostly social ones) help or hinder the person from getting in position to know. The modern separation of "epistemic" from "moral" or "prudential" issues is more than misguided. *I know as I do*. Ethics comes into play immediately.

It brings things alive.

The Binding of Isaac

Akedah—the binding of Isaac. We have this horrid story as the climax of the Abrahamic saga. The sacrifice of the promised. God had said according to Abraham's faithfulness would his offspring be as the stars. Since this was a time before modern astronomy, he accepted the possibility. Isaac was not his firstborn, may not have even been his personal favorite, but Isaac was the promised one, the one named after the laughter of his mother.

Since the wind calls out "Moriah" (2 Chron. 3:1), they took off on a journey. All the "mono" religions agree the hill in Jerusalem was the destination, but this is after the fact of the story. (I find myself looking at all the projections of this E-source material.) Ishmael had already been banished in chapter 21 (Sarah had insisted, Abe had acquiesced). They get to the place; Abraham told his servants to wait. He said, Laughter (Isaac) and I (we) are going up the mountain to worship, and (we) will be back after we're done. That (we)—does it mean Abraham knew they both would return? Some traditions suggest instead of God testing Abraham, Abraham could have been testing God's faithfulness. Many interesting questions emerge: how old was Isaac? How much therapy would he require after an incident such as this? When did God put the ram in the bush? What about the angel? Have the great Classical paintings of the event influenced our interpretations? What have the Jews believed about all this across the ages? What about the Muslims? On and on. There are many traditions which have insisted Abraham did sacrifice Isaac! I prefer to stick to the traditional story as it comes to us. More questions could be asked. There is, of course, a sense in which we do sacrifice our offspring as in offering them up to the Lord. The mother who prays that God will take her child and use her for the Lord's purpose, for example. How unlike this story is that? There are many examples of parents sincerely giving their kids to the Lord. What of the missionary family hauling little ones off to desolate and dangerous places? My own Momma laid great expectations on me. I was to be “special”. (I turned out special alright!) I think it is important to take ancient stories and bring them into our own accounts of reality. It would be good (as I have tried to do) to bring into our current worship the old idea of sacrifice. We really offer so little back to God’s great grace.

Child sacrifice is, of course, an absolute horror. We must realize, part of the background of this ancient story is that child sacrifice was common enough in the ancient cultures. Scripture takes note of this, and the overwhelming impact of the biblical witness is that child sacrifice is an abomination. That is, until we get to the end of the four gospels. God brings up the idea of child sacrifice once and for all. The traditional message has been that the Akedah is the prototype for the crucifixion and the resurrection.

At least we learn that to sanitize scripture according to our modern sensibilities and to thus remove any notion of sacrifice from our worship is certainly at least misguided, but also outside the clear witness of scripture from beginning to end.

Writing and U-tube

To be a writer, as I have often noted, involves sitting down and writing. It seems to be the thing everything was propelling me to. All the study, reading, preaching, AA, not to mention a lifetime of musical effort. All has led me to words in the end. So, the end can be the beginning. For that to be, I must live and laugh and love and lift. It requires an enormous energy to do this latest work of mine. How to concentrate the mind and extend the time of effort. Today is Tuesday, my "study day". The only difference between this day and any other day is I don't go to AA today. I generally go from one book to another and write notes or reflections in these volumes. The books chosen are arbitrary; I just grab one off the shelf. The good thing now is I finish the volumes I grab. In the old days, I was a poor finisher. Stay the course and all that. It is certainly progress and that is good.

I am hooked on U-tube lately. It is great to scroll from one category to another. Lectures, debates, stand-up routines, music of all kinds. I love to put on some chant and other early church music while these pages get themselves written. I have thrilled to the trumpet stuff.

Again, how can I have just quit all the applied stuff in music when I retired? I have always said if I could not aspire to a certain level, I would retire. Mostly true. But the old thrill comes back in my first love (trumpet). It is strange how one's life plays out. There were many loves lost, and I mostly walked away, pretending my heart was not broken. Perhaps all must endure some of this. To come to a point of acceptance is key. How to bring doxology to all the ages and stages is something I am able to do in my end times.

I try to figure out how to die like a Christian while sorting out my own "grand unifying theory." If the universe is winding down, and it is! After all, science is accepted with enthusiasm, even though almost no one really understands the realities of the cosmos, and the whole world of quantum physics is to be taken as presented. Even though no one has seen a quark, they "must" be there, right? My faith about the end to be expected from God is stronger than ever, and I get no real impulse to avoid any science I read or hear of. I'm perhaps too dumb to weigh the conflicts, but I keep at it. Constancy.

'Tis a Gift to be Simple

"Tis a gift to be simple." I find whenever I'm able to find true simplicity, I'm closer to true spirituality. In AA, we say the brain is no real help. My way of going about the program keeps all this in mind, and in meetings we are closer to the mark when we "Keep it simple stupid." For it *is* stupid to try to complicate the basic message of *don't* drink and *do* go to meetings. In fact, the reason alcoholics need help with the steps is we tend to complicate things, and insist on doing things our way instead of following instructions. We hook up with a sponsor to be reminded of the ways to the way. The traditions are emphasized to keep us from wandering off on our own. We are a community of people saving our lives day by day as we share with one another our stories and practice a radical acceptance. In short, here toward the end of my story I have come to realize my vision of the program has helped me to understand what church is all about. There is a sameness and constancy common to both communities which blesses my life greatly. I even find lately I am no longer burdened with the responsibility of straightening out peoples' theology and views of spirituality. Being strongly centered in myself is the only real witness I have to share. I can take myself and others lightly and avoid many deadly forms of seriousness. No matter how advanced a person in AA may ever become, if he or she begins a sentence with, "I've been thinking..." it's time to clear the room and leave them alone with their thoughts! No real good will come of it anyway.

What is it I am drawn to about what I do, in point of fact, each day at my desk nowadays? Well, thinking is a large part of it. It is thinking in search of practical ways of living and understanding. It is thinking, but like Pascal's *Penses*, it is thought which yields results and helps to advance epistemology, as applied to the interpretation of various forms of literature. It results in breaking out of endless circles of debate toward clarity and strength in speaking to the current culture. It is no longer mental masturbation. We know we cannot escape the metaphors of old, which speak of those matters of the heart which seem timeless. Brain, mind, heart, gut, whatever, if the image serves to advance the truth, then it is apt. We seek to get to the place Steven Colbert calls truth-i-ness; that is the goal. We need not know—what is truth?—we need to be on the road to that which shall be supplied like manna in the wilderness. It means not taking ourselves too seriously as we accept the gracious fact others do not take us seriously anyway. There is freedom there, and peace and being comfortable in the old wrinkled bag of skin we were issued in the beginning.

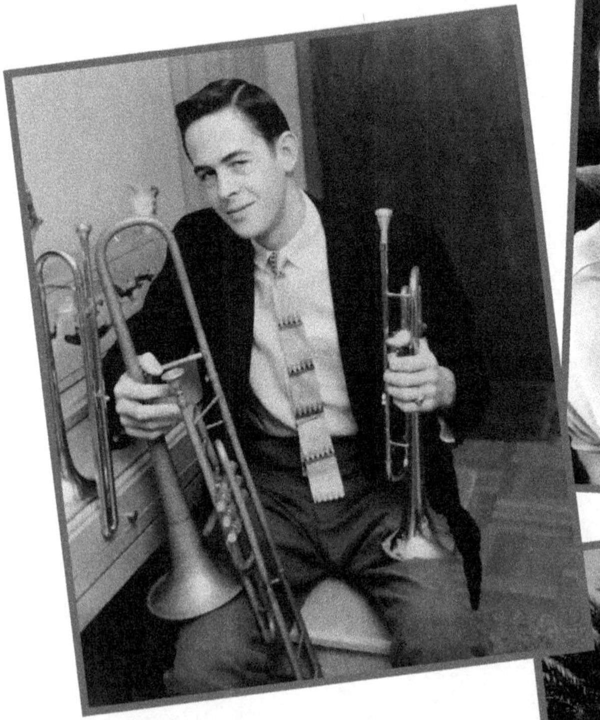

Journals Volume Three

Preface

I am a retired United Methodist minister. Born and raised as a Presbyterian, I went over to the Methodists while in high school because they had a better music department. I had always had a great attraction to the church, but this was Mississippi in the 1950s, so what model for what I now believe was to be found in those days? I was to become a musician; that was my goal. Now I know I was always called to the pulpit (but only after much else took place). Music did me no harm; it was to be in college that I 'heard the voice' so to speak. I still spent a decade and a half in church music before finally coming to the life I was meant for. How was I to know until I arrived?

Today the denomination I worked in for half a century is in shambles. Wesley had no idea what was to happen in the colonies. American Methodism is, incidentally, related to Christianity, but it is a very American activity. We became an accommodated organization in the country and, instead of prophecy, we have 'played' church almost from the beginning. One of the reasons Wesley is not among the names like Luther and Calvin is he is perhaps blamed for what would happen in the colonies.

Nowadays we are considering a split. The issue is homosexuality. We have seen no problem with war and poverty, etc., but what someone might do with his penis is a matter of grave concern. All during my ministry all we could talk about was sex.

I do not desire a split. I desire a church. It is never too late because of the Lordship of Jesus Christ! First, we must recognize who Jesus really is, and then we are to persevere in celebrating the Lamb's lordship and in building the community shaped by that celebration. If we see Jesus at the right hand of God, if we actually believe the creeds of the church, we accept Jesus' role in the cosmic victory and that he is now in charge of history. He reigns over the principalities and powers, and he will return in the end to set *all* things according to God's will.

I was a great coward during the 50 years I was given to preach. I was afraid to speak out about the things I deeply knew to be wrong. I'm still afraid. (They might mess with my pension.) God may or may not forgive me the great sin of cowardice. So, I just write these things down, though no one will ever read them. I write every day starting before dawn. I see the sunrise. Life is so good I can only live out of gratitude.

Idolatry and Witness

The blessings of the life I now live are great. I read deeply and daily in theology, science, and great literature. My two communities of AA and church sustain me. I can grow in these two necessary groups daily. I never get bored; it's always a great journey and adventure. Becky and I get to travel about this little planet. Thank God I can still get around a bit. I hope for a few more volumes at least.

Augustine is said to have said to a group of people: "We are talking about God. What wonder is it that you do not understand? If you do understand, then it is not God." The wonder of God is so great, we lurk about this tiny blue planet without a clue. But it's OK. In fact, it's the way it was meant to be. "To create, God did not extend himself but withdrew himself; he humbled and obliterated himself, and left outside himself the domain of necessity in which he does not intervene"[1] (except rarely). Even in the domain of souls, he intervenes only "under certain circumstances." I am no deist, and I'm only beginning to understand the construct of the mystery of the Trinity. The church had to name Trinity. How could they proceed if not? And it is not a construct. It is a name, chief in the cosmos: Creator, Redeemer, Sustainer.

In the beginning, God flicked his finger and started the big bang. Scientists theorize this particular universe began with that flick. Physics is my recent interest. It is a dandy endeavor. If I had a do-over I would take math, but I can at least read the popular explanations and enjoy without the equations. In fact, I can even imagine the advantages if physics could be restored and returned to its rightful place among the liberal arts. In bringing together theology and science, great benefits could emerge. The great realities could be given light; new understandings could enrich all. We could then begin to address the things which must be

1 Dillard, A. (2000). *For the Time Being*. Alfred A. Knopf. 166.

done to avoid the results our current ignorance warrants. It's only been a short time in cosmological terms since God flicked his finger and caused the creation—the big bang, if you will.

In the beginning, God! Only 13.8 billion years ago, God wanted light, and like a match igniting in total darkness, light happened. First, what is light? Well, we don't really know. Just try to define it. We can only speak of it in terms of its properties. How does it originate and travel through space? How does it emerge from and enter into matter? Is it substance, vibration, pure energy? We do know the quest to understand light has given rise to the two great revolutions of physics in the last century: relativity and quantum theory. In a profound sense, Genesis has great significance and also simplicity; God simply demanded it and there it was. And he only created the light-givers 16 verses later! See, it's already getting good.

The universe consists of trillions of island galaxies, each containing hundreds of billions of stars. The distances are expressible, but incomprehensible. Our sun is nearly a million miles in diameter and is 24 trillion miles from the nearest star in our little neighborhood called the Milky Way. The galaxies are so distant from each other, we find it hard to express in any intelligible linguistic sense.

I'm just starting to read a book which seriously suggests we may be alone. That we exist is such an improbable thing, maybe it is true God did all this just for us. It is hard to believe, but a lot of things are. In the book, the author restricts himself to just this galaxy, but he makes a good case.

We know most of the universe does not have light. Most of it seems to be empty space. Lately they find there is a lot going on in the darkness.

Dark matter and dark energy are things we cannot see. The vessel called Kepler, launched in March 2009, has ascertained that in the observable universe, the fraction of stuff which exists is one millionth of one billionth of one percent. A place to *be* is quite rare. The universe, for all intents and purposes, is mostly empty.

On this lovely little blue planet, mostly salt water after all, the totality of *living* matter (all life: humans and plants and animals, etc.) makes up about 0.00000001% of the mass of the planet. We are special, are we not? Or at least we like to think of ourselves this way.

What we are, after all, is idol-makers. After a while, we forget we ourselves have created the idols we follow. After a while we forget our part, and the idol becomes a god who takes on powers far beyond the human beings who actually invented them. How does this come about? We cannot think and believe on any kind of cosmic scale. So, we set up little gods in our back yards, where we are comfortable, and ignore the truths which exist in quite large and infinitely small ways, and which posit deep truths and great significance. The idolatries of money, power, control—these are the gods of today. Thus, young Christians train for war and just because someone across the globe might be trying to become like us, we rush over to kill them in order to keep the peace. The notion of sacrificing them to the god of the nation state is considered a glorious thing. Let's kill in the name of democracy and rampant capitalism. Keep the dollar strong. Screw the environment; there's more oil down there somewhere. And a lot of this is done in the name of the Prince of Peace.

I have come to believe, at this advanced age, that non-violence and pacifism is the only way a Christian may go. Reading Yoder and Hauerwas finally did it for me, but it was there all along. If one is to take Jesus seriously, what else is there but pacifism? The key issue is that the very way God triumphed over the powers and principalities was by suffering rather than strength. The lamb reigns from the cross. This is so counter-intuitive, we must be reminded again and again. The Eucharist is the best occasion for this memory, and this is why frequent celebration of the sacrament is so important. I never had the nerve to insist on a weekly celebration. Cowardice again.

We take so many things today in exactly the same way as the ancients treated their golden calves. We tend to worship those things we have, after all, created ourselves. We must have control! All should be about *me*.

What is also clear is we forget to take seriously that all scientific theories, together with the whole system and rationale of the so-called scientific method, clearly originated in the human mind. This 'building' of science is not really foundational; they simply dug deep enough to hope the foundation would hold. We have yet to really get to the bottom of anything scientific or in theology. The astonishing view of the natural world we call 'science' is the product of human imagination, thought, and genius. Even the modern notion of empirical method is like a vast board game whose rules, playing board, and pieces were all created by human beings for their own purposes.

The Old Testament prophets gave us what we needed to diagnose idolatry. We just need to turn to Amos and the boys for insight to see how things are for us today. That which science has given us today is a view of the cosmos declaring there is no meaning or purpose; we are not at home on this planet. We are supposed to content ourselves with a pathological detachment. If our creation myth is so bleak that we understand ourselves to be just dropped off by a meteor and waiting for the sun to run out of gas, we are in a world of hurt. We are given no view of a nurturing, participatory universe. We are just an old clock, running down and flung into emptiness for no certain purpose. No wonder we trash the planet. Why not grab off the gusto as we may?

In the rain forests are perhaps answers to many things which speak of the graciousness of creation; yet we look to them for quick profit. We have wedded scientific technology with a political system dressed with domination and control. Science has become a sort of state religion. I saw on TV a segment which said if you ever had anything to do with the development of the nuclear bomb, you can send off and they will bestow on you a free medal. On the medal is a picture of the bomb itself. This way you can be honored for the part you had in such destruction and killing. I couldn't believe it.

What is needed has been lost. Science is taught in separate departments from any humanity in the modern university. But, no worry, it will all be over in five billion years when our little sun is done.

And are we nearing the end of Christendom? In this country, some churches are dying and some seem to be flourishing. It seems the general societal approval and support of the church I enjoyed early in my life may be coming to an end. This might be a good thing! First, we would quickly recover an eschatological view of the gospel. We would see that we live between the times as opposed to being immersed in time. We live in two aeons simultaneously. The old age was characterized by sin. The coming age, made possible by Christ through the Holy Spirit, is redemptive. We can rationally believe, as the New Testament believes, that Christ has triumphed and is reigning, but yet the powers are still rampant. *The preaching of the gospel is why time does not stop!* The church does not have a political mission, her very existence is a political mission. The church gives an alternative to the politics of the world. We only know there was a beginning because we have seen the end in Christ! *The end is the beginning*. The story told in the Gospels states the meaning of creation. It is impossible to separate knowledge of God as Creator from God's work of redemption. By the word, the world exists. Again, we *know* there was a *beginning* because we have *seen* the *end*. So, all things flow from our knowledge of Christ!

Jesus, to be seen as sitting at the right hand of the Father, not only indicates Jesus' role in the cosmic victory; that He is at the right hand of God is also a declaration of his rule of the world. This is the one God who uses the world as his stage of divinely purposeful action. History has an end, and could we be it? The politics of eschatology simply is the existence of a people who refuse to acknowledge the claims of worldly rulers to be kings. And from the way Jesus became Lord, it is also clear that nonviolence is a central commitment in defining this kind of politics. Christians can even claim the church knows better than the state what the state is to be and to do. Thus, the meaning of history is to be found in the existence of the church. This is apocalyptic politics! Christ carries out the purposes of the Kingdom. He is the one who is sovereign by ruling over the rebellious structures of the universe. This rule is hidden, but is made visible through the servant church. The place of the church in the history of the universe is the place where Christ's Lordship is operative. This is where it is certain He rules, as well as the kind of rule he exercises. Christ is the suffering servant whose rule is decisively revealed in the cross. The church makes history, not through domination, but through being the servant of the crucified and risen Lord. The relationship between the obedience of God's people and the final triumph of God's cause is not a matter of cause and effect, but of cross and resurrection.

The simple fact is the universe did not have to be. We are created, contingent beings who did not have to be. Only God exists by necessity.[2]

But Christians further believe the God who exists by necessity is known only through contingent creatures. "Witness" names the truth that the only way we can know the character of the world, the only way we know ourselves, the only way we know God, is by one person telling another.

The only way we can reason about God is from the existence of a world which did not have to be. Aquinas sought to faithfully describe the world in all its contingency. The theologian is to read the world as God's creation. Modern philosophers have become entangled in the Enlightenment's mechanistic conception of causation. Cause, according to Aquinas, was rooted in Aristotle's sensible pre-modern view that "cause" was carried in its meaning by what is for us human beings to cause something.

Witness, then, is required by the Christian faith. To witness is to speak the truth about the world as God's, the God of Israel, the God who raised Christ from the dead. This is our witness. It requires a language. Witness requires the faithful display of Christian speech sufficient to test what is said in the light of how it is said. Christian speech presumes those who use the language have a character commensurate with it. So, theology and ethics cannot be separated.

As Christians, we are called to come out of the world and to die in Christ. We are followers of the way, and the way leads to the cross. Jesus calls the disciples (us) to worship him and follow him into the Kingdom. The work we have to do is the same work Jesus did. If the Gospels say anything, they say that!

---

2 This is an ontological argument.

We are called to witness not only to what has happened but also to what will happen. There is a new age to which we witness. Eschatology is the name given to describe this new beginning. The story of Jesus is the story of a new creation. "Martyr" is the New Testament Greek term for witness. The book of the Acts of the Apostles uses the term "witness" 23 times. The task of witness in Acts is no mystery (Acts 1:8). The message is to be carried to the ends of the earth.

The truth to which Paul and others witness in Acts is counter-cultural and comprehensive. It re-narrates the whole of human life in such a way that change in the entire pattern of life is required. When the gospel took root in Acts, it was witnessed to by people who both spoke it and practiced it. The Kingdom grows from person to person. We cannot know Jesus without those called by Jesus. The politics of witness is a politics of speech. The language must be taught and learned. Church words are necessary, but these words should include rather than exclude.

The eschatological character of the Christian faith will challenge the politics of the world in which it finds itself. We believe in history. It is an extraordinary thing for Christians to believe we come from a past which will find its fulfillment in the future.

Back to my own denomination. Methodism is a movement which, by chance, found itself as a church in America. All my life in the church, we have failed to teach a theology or to shape a witness which could stand as a clear alternative to the culture. We have emphasized sanctification; yet this was mostly a pietistic construal of the faith shaped by revivals, and that was only at certain times of the year.[3] Holiness was thought to be about individuals, not the church. Methodists have confused salvation with having their own personal relationship with Jesus Christ, which meant the church simply became the place which confirmed what your personal decision already was. There has certainly been a rampant anti-intellectualism which has been evident in the church of my experience. There was no encouragement for me to keep working hard on theology. I was to simply get up something to say on a Sunday morning. If I went to Cokesbury bookstore, I would run into other pastors, but it wasn't "have

---

3 Seasonal, like football!

you read this?" it was "have you heard about?"—not learning, gossip! Success in my work was the same thing as the world's success. How many people have you signed up? What have you built? Have you paid all our apportionments (taxes)? Now I am retired.

Now let me be clear. I am very fortunate to have had the life I was given. If there were justice, it would not have been so. But it was not a matter of grace against justice. It was that I didn't get caught! There were unforgivables in my behavior, and I'm not sure I have repented to sufficient degree even yet. I hurt people and certainly let down a whole lot more. Hauerwas wrote a sentence to the effect of, *we are not so much punished* for *our sins as punished* by *our sins.* The total effects of alcoholism on my life have been punishing enough, but here at the end times, after more than a quarter century of sobriety, I look back on a very fortunate life. It can be said that, were it not for the people I hurt, if all this was to be my destiny,[4] it was worth all that went before to have arrived where I am now. It is neurotic to keep digging up past sins for their entertainment value if I have been forgiven for them. And, *if* I have asked for the pardon in the light of the Twelve Steps, why would I not accept the relief which stems from the forgiveness? We have no secrets anyway. God knows our innermost selves, good and bad. We can run, but we cannot really hide. God can always find us, and if I run away somewhere, I am then there also. May as well stay the course. If humility is revealed in being accurate in my self-assessment, and I think that so, then I bring who I really am to God as offering. God keeps the offering, good and bad, and gives us what we need as a good and perfect gift. It all winds up as God's good, gracious gift.

4 Do I believe in destiny?

Addiction

Addiction represents the ultimate effort to control, the definitive demand for magic, and the final failure of spirituality. It is turning to the "magic" of chemicals in an attempt to fill a spiritual void with a material reality. It is an attempt to make magic a substitute for miracle. Addiction has been described as the belief that whenever there is something wrong with me, it can be fixed by something outside of me. We want to be "fixed," right now[5], and a false beginning inevitably generates ever more drastic illusions. The cycle begins and will become ever more demonic. Looking for transcendence in chemicals becomes a sort of spiritual death. Alcohol is the ideal magic in the beginning. The result produced by it seems to be that which we had been looking for, so long as we speak of our drinking careers. Alcohol seems to work for many for a long time, but there are inevitable difficulties. What to do when it quits working? Well, then the AA program works. It is a mystery that it works, but magic is no longer a part of it. It is process, and it takes a long time. It is hard work. It is to be earned.

We had sought to will what cannot be willed; we were trying to bring control from the uncontrollable; we demanded to coerce that which could not be coerced; and we entered into a vicious cycle. Seeking to control what cannot be controlled destroys precisely what we are trying to control.

What came of all this is *story*. Story details the gap between intentions and results. We alcoholics become at home in this gap. It is no longer destination but journey; we had sought a fixed state, a place where the drugs and alcohol were mixed just so. Now, we have been set free from being determined by things from outside ourselves. As we have learned to tell our stories, we also learned that the story conveys the reality of human freedom. Although "real," our freedom is limited, and although "limited," our freedom is real. Our hope is that we are right where God wants us.

---

5 Instant gratification takes too long.

The most helpful thing Bill Wilson ever did for AA was what took place between 1961 and 1971 (when he died). In April of '61, he planned to write one last book. It was to be *the* book of AA Spirituality. He ran some installments of the Grapevine pertaining to the subject, even a series on various aspects of spirituality, but he also kept going to meetings. In meetings he would seek out the members who were thought to be "really" spiritual. He gradually realized a great spiritual paradox. He said those who have spirituality don't know they have it. He never finished the book on spirituality, because spirituality is one of those things you have as long as you seek it. As soon as you think you have it, you've lost it. It's like the guy wondering what he will wear to the banquet when he accepts the humility reward.

More important, if Bill W. had tried to describe what each member of AA was to seek in some definitive sense, it would not have been a book worth reading. We do not capture it; it captures us. Humans like to surround a thing with their eager cogitations and wrap things up. Spirituality will not yield to being fenced in. The word 'pilgrimage' originally referred to the distance one could travel in a day. What a clue there for us to stay in the day. Day by day we make our way.

Our peregrination (the old name for pilgrimage) is not a straight-line progress. There are twists and turns and backtracks, even detours, but we are *on the way*. In AA we are on the way as a group process. It is not a religion wherein we follow a Lord. This would not be acceptable in AA. We each have an 'inner light'. We share hints, suggestions, even advice (though we deny giving advice), and we make our way as a group *and* as individuals (all this within a group). The group principle is love. Acceptance is the key. The steps and the traditions are read every time. We tell our stories. We don't drink, and we *do* go to meetings. That is AA.

Church, on the other hand, is first of all *on the other hand*. Don't try to combine the two things. If a person gets sober in church, it is a good thing. I'm one who simply requires both communities. Now, as I grow (progress, not perfection), I am, of course, developing my spiritual muscles both at church and in AA. This growth is a good thing, and I need not concern myself with just where I am in the journey. It really doesn't matter. Even picking up a chip in AA is not a thing for me, but a witness that one can keep it going for years without drinking. In church we have the Eucharist to help us re-orient ourselves. Our destination is never a place, but a new way of looking at things.

In both church and AA, the reality of spirituality is that it must touch all of life. If it's not pervasive, it is not spirituality. As one reads the 12 Steps of AA, the little word *all* keeps showing up again and again, reminding us this is an all-or-nothing reality.

The earliest version of Step 7 read: "Humbly, *on our knees* asked him to remove our shortcomings—*holding nothing back*."[6] Can you imagine the meeting when this wording was discussed? It should be short, clear, and simple because it speaks of our preparation and God's faithfulness. God will set us free! God will do for us what we cannot do for ourselves.

In AA, a person gradually changes. They begin to experience life in a new way. It does take a while, so new people are urged to keep coming back. As people tell their stories and listen to the stories of others, this change takes place. Clearly, drink and drugs have been put away, for no one can grow spiritually while drunk and stoned, but as the story of change is exchanged, the newcomer starts to live in a new way. This involves, as any seasoned AA-er can tell you, learning the language of recovery. Language thus fashions experience and becomes practice. It is not a theory: we must live it!

When we let the truth about ourselves be revealed, we experience a kind of release. Where there had been fear of being found out there comes relief. It is not yet 'true' freedom, for that comes with the Steps, but it comes as a welcome change for the newcomer. It is giving up the illusion of control. It is not taking ourselves as seriously as before. We do not cling to self-interest but abandon ourselves to a higher power. We begin to develop a spirituality. A day at a time. We surrender. "Letting go." If we are in control of all in our lives, and if we are in a continual mess, then we will want to entertain notions of release, of finding a new way. AA brings this.

---

6 W. B.

Spirituality is itself a gift; no one can acquire it or possess it, for it is a reality freely given and gratitude is the only possible response to this gift. In this response of gratitude, we begin to gain a vision of how truly gifted we really are. That vision, which comes only to those who in some way have given up trying to control, makes it possible to help in giving up other areas of control. We give up control because we realize we were never *in* control. It was an illusion based on our efforts to play God.

Murdoch

I keep alternating between the novels of Iris Murdoch and Anthony Trollope. What a wondrous thing it is. The way each understands seeing—the virtues, morality, and the character development is endlessly fascinating. Certainly, I have to distinguish the differences in matters of faith. Murdoch is an atheist, and we then ask, how can she contribute much to Christian ethics? Hauerwas helps me see how this question can be answered. Trollope is quite situated in the faith and ethics of 19th century Anglican and British morals and ethos. Again, I keep asking, how does he help advance the faith and ethics and practices which undergird my existence? I agree with Hauerwas: "The redemption that Christians believe God has offered, is not a 'mystical' possibility, but one that is made possible only because of and through the Jews."[7]

Murdoch concluded we need a theology which can continue without God. Christians believe our lives are at once captured by sin and yet sustained by hope. You need God for that belief. Murdoch did not believe that the Jews are God's chosen people or that Christ's resurrection inaugurates the end time. Murdoch would say what she understood as orthodox Christianity is waning rapidly and that religion must come to terms with autonomy. What Charles Taylor in *Sources of the Self* helps us to see is that people do not decide to stop believing in God as Trinity. Rather, they gradually or suddenly realize that the "sources" which once made such beliefs intelligible are no longer in place. Or that a person can still "believe" such things, but they simply don't matter anymore.

Murdoch would point out that even among churchgoers, they already think in a non-literal way without bothering about metaphysics and theology. She has written much about philosophy and she posits: "The Cartesian era is coming to an end. Wittgenstein said he was ending it. In

---

7 Hauerwas, S. (2018). *Wilderness Wanderings: Probing Twentieth-century Theology and Philosophy.* Routledge. 156.

moral philosophy it may appear that the Kantian era is coming to an end. Theology not only reflects these problems but is forced to struggle with them in ways which bring it closer to philosophy now than it has been for some time."[8] She then goes on to say all of this might be expected in a materialistic, technological society which would marginalize theology. She has described herself as a neo-Christian Buddhist Christian.[9] She dismisses revelation, yet keeps a framework of how a person might 'get saved' as they discover a living force within each human soul which can console and save. She then calls this a Christian tradition which can be 'generally believed.' She would keep a sort of *imitatio Christi*, but would have redemption possible without God. But as I read her, the characters in her novels are certainly in search of redemption of the sort that I profess can be provided only by the God of Abraham and the rest. The deal is that her characters are so very well known to her readers. She has them praying often enough and implies the loss of God is a great loss, but they are always in a "muddle." They love the wrong person or get so caught up in illusion that no good can come of it. Those muddles are the results of self-absorption. She presents the psyche as:

> ...an egocentric system of quasi-mechanical energy, largely determined by its own individual history, whose natural attachments are sexual, ambiguous, and hard for the subject to understand or control. Introspection reveals only the deep tissue of ambivalent motive, and fantasy is a stronger force than reason. Objectivity and unselfishness are not natural to human beings.[10]

In her novels the characters are caught up until some near tragedy happens or an angelic avatar appears. Murdoch's morality is a metaphysics and, in the end, everything must be given up so the good can be depicted. I will continue with Dame Iris, but carefully.

---

8 Ibid, 159.
9 An oxymoron
10 Ibid, 160.

History, and Beginning in the Middle

None of us begins at the beginning. We start from where we are in our journey. Why isn't that more obvious? Because we must first take our bearings to find out where, in fact, we are. It is not possible to always answer "where shall we begin?" First, we must find out where we are standing.

I stand firm within my two communities and can only tell my story from both perspectives. I can only live forward because my firm foundation lies ahead, not behind. Both science and theology are *not* able to say: this is the absolute beginning. Why should we humans keep trying? As Christians, we need no place to begin. Our task, then, is not to find the perfect place to begin, but to lose nothing which can help us to live faithful to "the way." Luther said, "Here I stand."[11]

What must the church teach if it is to be the church? We very much need to move from the modern question of, "How little must I believe to still be a Christian?" to "How really wonderful it is that the church has always believed in all this."[12]

We begin with God's rule and God rules from the cross. *Thus, we stand in "eternal now."* The function of the past is to move the story along. The place we stand in *now* has us always facing Jerusalem. The end is the thing. Eschatology is our perspective. The shape of our history is our narrative. History is not what I once thought it was. It certainly is not what I was taught it was. I can remember having to take Mississippi history in Junior High. Just imagine what a sterling experience that was. The legislature of that great and sovereign state had to approve the textbook and insure it was taught. I wish I had a copy. The legislature of

---

11 Not in those exact words
12 Like Catholics do

that state is the best example of the appeal of the least common denominator, as also can be seen in our current national congress.

History is written by the winners and its subject is warfare (or how you get to be a winner). But Christian history is different. You begin from where you are. You ask, who really rules? The answer is God, and the seat of his throne is the cross and resurrection. Since through Christ we have been made a part of the end, the story is never done. It is an ongoing narrative. We are to be patient. We wait upon the Lord. We have "great expectations" to be sure, but they are within the framework of the biblical imperative: "no one knows when he shall appear!" We know so little. Just try to come up with an acceptable "theory" of the Atonement. Thank God the church has never done this!

Barth says we can know history only when it is something that has happened to us, and sometimes happened against us, as we participate in it. I was given a half century in the church and the clock is still running. That is the history I know. The rest is just what someone wrote, either about their own times or what they thought happened in other times, and people *will* lie. It's been demonstrated! So, if understanding any history is difficult, and even the original source can mislead, how do we get the sense of the scripture? I have preached for a while now. I'm my own history with an ancient text; I have come to the realization that none of it really matters, except my faithfulness to the task, and the Holy Spirit using the effort in the incredible time called worship.

The Word came into this world and dwelt here. I like to think of it in cosmic terms. It's not because this tiny blue planet was 'hardly significant' that the Word came. It's that, of all the universe, this particular place became chosen! It is a concept so amazing we hardly consider it. If life is as unlikely to appear anywhere else as the experts say it is, then the sudden appearance of the key to the whole thing is so incomprehensible we can miss the whole deal. Now, certainly this whole notion can be dismissed as being, even, ridiculous. But I believe it is not only true, but that this signifies that Jesus is the center of the universe! God did all this so you and I might have life! It is such an abundant life we can never fully grasp the gift. In fact, if all this is not true, then we are dead in our sins. This to me is not only true, but radical, and the most radical thing Christians say is "Thy Kingdom come". It is most of all a political statement, and I actually believe that not only do we speak of the politics of this planet, but in a real sense of cosmic powers and principalities. The way the world is now is certainly without hope or help unless 'Thy Kingdom Come' is true. No one knows how this history will play out; we only know that a radical, sweeping, eschatological transformation that only God can bring is what can bring the change necessary. And yet, because it is God's time we are talking about, this kingdom of God is also a *present reality* Jesus brought, a Kingdom which precedes and judges all our concepts and experiences of the kingdoms of this world. Christianity is essentially eschatological. Our faith demands we must think differently than we have been taught and tempted to think by the world. The history of the world is a "tale told by an idiot, signifying nothing."[13] Christianity brought an end to history. History as in our faith is not of this world, but a great contradiction to the world. *And* Jesus *will* come again, and he *will* be pissed off. As long as I can line up with the sheep it will be alright.

I have never wanted to live in any other time than this time. Not because this is the best of times, but because this is the time I was given. The homiletical challenge of these years is great, but this is true of any other period of what we call history as well. It has been a radically transitional time. As we went from the modern world into whatever this current reality is, my thinking shifted gears. I had to keep reading and studying and going to as many conferences as possible, because seminary in the 60s hardly prepared me for what would come. The longer I have lived, the harder I have worked. This is the best mental, intellectual, emotional, and spiritual time of my life, and yet I am only starting to begin. God, please let me linger for a while.

---

13 Shakespeare, W. *Macbeth*. 5.5.26-28.

Preaching the Unspeakable Word

The book which really got Karl Barth going was Romans. When one reads Barth's famous commentary on Paul's Romans, his rhetoric seems to burn with zeal. It can be tedious, repetitious, exaggerated, but it's as if he knew this one bible commentary was to be a huge turning point in 20th century theology. When I was in seminary, I was *not* introduced to Barth in such a way that he became a dominant force in my life. Through the years, the things I came to believe were also those things which Barth lifted up. It was only as I was able to study and read deeply that I realized this theologian was the strongest influence in my life and work.

Barth understood how the Bible is to be read. He presents scripture as a vast, loosely structured historical novel and the subject of the book is Christ. It is, of course, not fiction. Barth understood the narrative quality of scripture in a way that differentiates him from the scripturalists and the scriptural expressivists. Barth rejects both topical and expository preaching! His preaching was Christological! He saw the events of scripture to be unique and unrepeatable events which demand a particular sort of attention and narration. One must have a certain type of imagination, which is used by the Holy Spirit to allow our little lives to be lifted up into His life. Our lives thereby become a figuration of the story of Jesus.

The text itself carries the message. The message (flow, narrative, even meaning) is to carry itself to the ear of God. Then, with the help of the Spirit, to the ear of a thirteen-year-old girl who has been told that this is one of the few times in her life she is absolutely not to fiddle with her cell phone. She is pissed and besides, her little brother has some stuff from

Sunday School to play with. To get through to her, to excite her in the faith, to convince her that the youth choir tour or the mission trip just might be a thing to remember for the rest of her life. To bring a tear to her eye because she finds out Jesus loves her even though she has trouble fitting in at school. This would be carrying the message. That is what a sermon *does*. The girl is just one of those sitting out there. One doesn't address her needs. One preaches gospel. The Holy Spirit is the active one looking around the room for one who is ready to get it. The preacher cannot use a rifle. We may know of a definite need. (We always know of a definite need.) Alas, we cannot address this need from the pulpit. One can story-form the need after (one has, as a pastor, prayed). One can bring up one's personal experience. One can illustrate (most any source will do) an event or a story from the culture in such a way that especially touches that need. It can even be a real tearjerker, but be careful if you make them cry. It's better to leave the intense stuff to the Holy Spirit.

If a preacher is absolutely in need of a direct approach on a Sunday morning, prayer would be the best preparation. You can count on something going wrong. Any time the preacher must unload a personal passion and she simply lays it out there, watch out! I used to do it. I did it more than anyone I know about, but it was not wise (well, maybe a time or two). Getting people pissed off with you simply is not an effective pastoral move. If you can no longer communicate with them afterwards, what have you gained? If I still did it, it must be the something that Jesus also gets pissed about. I must be able to absolutely show that as I make my defense (the opportunity will be given).

When I did throw down the gauntlet and then stood my ground, there was given protection, because I had shown them I had first loved them. Maybe I had just warned them of hellfire, but I seemed sad about it. Maybe it was even something political. I spent all those years believing in some things which were so different from what the congregation thought. I'm sure I voted differently. That would have been most always true. The irony has not changed for many years, expressed wonderfully by G.K. Chesterton, who said something to the effect of 'the job of the progressive is to keep making mistakes; the job of the conservatives is to make sure those mistakes never get corrected.' I am certainly not drawn to partisan politics, except that all my voting life has been spent in the Democratic voting booth. That is not what I preach of on a Sunday morning; yet I hardly hide the fact. I try to preach gospel. The scripture does not hide material which directly applies to each person in the pew. It is clear enough, and it is always dangerous (fatal) if a person uses the Bible only to find backup for what they believe. The book itself won't let you do that if you read carefully.

As I look back, except for the damage caused by my alcoholism, I can say it was fun. I was largely at play. I sought to do artistry among my clan, to re-arrange the furniture, to change focal points, to pick new music and make it attractive, to be silly even. It mostly worked, but if one is seeking a career in the pulpit of the UMC, I would hardly suggest emulation.

Nietzsche[14] rediscovered the essentially metaphorical quality of most of our language, even language which claims to be non-metaphorical and reasonable. He wrote:

> What is truth? A noble army of metaphors, metonyms, anthropomorphisms—in short, a sum of human relations that were poetically and rhetorically heightened, transferred, and adorned, and after long use seem solid, canonical, and binding to a nation. Truths are illusions about which it has been forgotten that they are illusions.[15]

Nietzsche's acknowledgment of languages as metaphorical helped undermine the Enlightenment's confidence in its transparent, rational speech and helped give birth to a postmodern evaluation of language as figurative act, a way of thinking which was not less than the rational *but considerably more*. Barth sees the paradox—our ability to talk about God, despite our inability to talk about God, as evidence of God's redemptive condescension to sinful humanity in the Christ. As we speak about God, we should begin with confession about our basic sin—conditioned inability to speak about God. Our broken, metaphorical speech about God

14 And Wittgenstein
15 Willimon, W.H. (2006). *Conversations with Barth on Preaching*. Abingdon. 91.

is appropriate in the sense that we are kept from saying more about God than God says! We are time-bound creatures speaking about God. It is when we confess our inability to speak about God that God speaks to us. The sermon speaks of the interplay between speech and silence, of now-and-not-yet, of having-and-not-having, of the end of language. Barth thus invited his readers into the strange, new world of the Bible. Always strange, always new.

William James said at the beginning of the last century that every time we say, "I know," the claim to knowledge is based on the prior affirmation of "I believe." James challenged Kant's notion that somehow we can escape to a world of pure 'facts' untainted by belief. James said, "Our faith is faith in someone else's faith, and in the greatest matters this is most the case." He said life always exceeds logic: "It is the practical reason for which the theoretic reason finds arguments after the conclusion is once there." [16] The cosmos is never complete, but is always becoming or coming into existence. And this was 1908, before Einstein made known and before science would demonstrate how dynamic the universe truly is.

Words make the world. Observe a young child learning a language. This happens in a matter of months. *It is the process of words making the world for the child.* This is the beginning of language. When language reaches the heights of expression it tends to poetical, metaphorical, and evocative as means of expression. This is where we meet the rhetoric of Karl Barth, and he gets there by bypassing traditional rhetoric. One can sense, even in his early Roman's commentary, that what he was about was the creation of a world through words.[17] This is, after all, the way God created the universe. He spoke it into existence. Words have power.

When Lincoln gave the Gettysburg Address, he was not giving out information; he was reconstructing the whole rationale for the Civil War, reconceiving the war, and changing his hearers. And on my birthday in 1963, the greatest sermon in American history was given. We don't think of it as a sermon, for it was delivered on the steps of the Lincoln memorial facing the capitol building. Not given in a church but 'field preaching' like Wesley did. Dr. Martin Luther King spoke words which changed the

---

16 James, W. (2019). *The Pluralistic Universe*. Andos Books. 87.
17 Genesis chapter 1

nation and ushered in great progress in civil rights. [18]

Words are powerful. Many have thus characterized Barth's work as a bomb thrown into the playground of the theologians. Barth's work, over all, reminds me of his favorite music. He loved Mozart and regarded him as an angel. It came to me long ago that the way to build a sermon is like the sonata—allegro form of a symphony. Think of any first movement of a Mozart symphony... Introduction, Exposition, development, Recapitulation, Coda. Or, warm them up, tell them something, play a while, and then remind them you have told them something. The whole thing can then end big or not.

The really radical thing about the whole process of doing theology or preaching the gospel is the incredible irony that in speaking about God, we preachers speak for God! We are thus caught up in the impossible situation of having to speak a word which cannot be spoken. One of Barth's most famous assertions about preaching: "As ministers we ought to speak about God. We are human, however, and so we cannot speak about God. We ought therefore to recognize both our obligation and our inability and by that very recognition give God the glory."[19]

Barth never tired of the dialectical, rhetorical form... it's always either-or and both-and, on the one hand this, but on the other hand that; but in his later works he moves from the expressionistic forms of his commentary on Romans to the more realistic forms found in the Dogmatics. He was also moving from the pulpit to the classroom. He had been run out of Germany by Nazis and back to Switzerland. Barth thought preachers must be told something (through prayer) before we can speak. Knowledge, as Barth's epistemology goes, is an active, engaging event which embraces both personal and cognitive, subjective, and objective elements. The modern world tended to have a fixed, inert view of knowledge. Barth points to the Bible's considerably involved notion of what it means to "know God." Theology must be passionate. Plato had taught that there was even an erotic quality to true knowledge. Barth speaks of knowledge as if it were a sort of coitus; Barth's dynamic, gifted view of knowledge is

---

18 "I have a dream."

19 Barth, K. (1957). *The Word of God and the Word of Man.* (D. Horton, trans.). New York. Harper & Brothers. (Original work published 1924).

behind his statements linking theology to prayer. "Theological work is surely inconceivable and impossible at any time without prayer."[20] Prayer is the way Christians think. See Paul, in 1 Thessalonians 5:17: "Pray without ceasing."

20 Willimon, W.H. (2006). *Conversations with Barth on Preaching*. Abingdon. 124.

Sanctification

In John 17, Jesus prays to the Father that those who follow him be sanctified in the truth. As a Wesleyan, I still hear about Sanctification from time to time but mostly when I bring it up myself. The movements of grace just don't get far in the churches of my experience. And 'Sanctification' and 'truth' are seldom found together in the current culture. People say they believe in Jesus, have met him as their own personal Lord, and even pray to him without ever thinking there should be obvious disciplines in their daily lives because of what they believe. The thing I like best about Stanley Hauerwas is his insistence that theology and worship cannot be separated. The Wesleyans with whom I have lived think otherwise. So, recovering the power of Christian speech is the place to begin, and it is what I have been about for the last 20 years or so. It was not possible for me to do anything but go through the motions for the first half of my ministry. Drunks add very little to the faith. Yet, even then, some of the passion was just below the surface. I have always been one who believes. I just was not capable of doing anything about it. I certainly had no notion of going on to perfection, even though I had promised so to do when I was ordained. *Perfection is simply the claim that we have been made more than we could have been otherwise because of God's work in our lives.* In other words, as the scripture says, God has done for us what we have not been able to do for ourselves. How then to speak of such things as holiness without using categories of individualistic and pietistic displays? There are so many things we Protestants have lost in the split from the Catholics. Chief among these things lost is to have our sins named by the church. That plus the loss of holy communion being normative in worship!

Back to Jesus' prayer in John 17: The sanctification which characterizes those who are made disciples of Jesus through the work of the spirit is that which makes it possible for us to see the world, which includes ourselves, in the truth that is Christ. For Wesleyans to be made holy, to be made capable of attempting forgiveness of our sins, to be put right with God, is not just personal holiness. We then can worship God justly. This is of crucial importance. Our worship must produce our ethics. Theology and ethics must be joined.

For there to be no dis-connect between head and heart is one thing but between talk and walk is quite another. No one I know in our current culture aspires to be a saint. We claim 'chief of sinners' status eagerly, however. Perhaps bragging on badness is as much a problem as disclaiming an affinity for growing up into the status which the church has bestowed on some with navels such as I am. It's not as if we should think less highly of ourselves as is accurate and call it humility. It is, in fact, learning to think of ourselves accurately which is key. The way I aspire to that lofty goal is participation in my two communities, AA and Church: both help in different ways. In AA I'm given the gift and the opportunity to find honest reflection about who I am. Since I become so well known in open sharing again and again, I dare not become morose or grandiose. There is no place to hide in AA. Sponsors and sponsees, both are allowed to call your hand if you posture and prevaricate. In Church, the love and acceptance grows and then the miracle happens: we worship together. In worship, all the gifts get given because we come before God. The ability to learn to worship together is that which constitutes church after all. The Sacraments are the times when God is acting in the worshiping community in the most obvious way. In singing and prayer, in confession and scripture, in preaching and offering, all the good gifts get exchanged. God is the unseen prompter as well as the audience for all of this, and we become God's people more than we could have ever imagined. If sainthood and perfection seem too far beyond our capabilities, we might ask, what direction do we then choose?

Thoughts on Sermons

John Calvin had an image of the preacher as someone the church sends to the Bible week by week to dig up parts of its treasure and bring it to us in the Sunday Sermon.

From the well-known poet, *Anon.*, we get:

> The written word
> Should be clean as bone,
> Clear as light,
> Firm as stone,.
> Two words are not
> As good as one.

One of the remarkable texts in the gospels is Mark 5. Jesus heals the demoniac. The town sees him then clothed and in his right mind. The preacher prepares the sermon so when Sunday morning comes, the sermon may appear 'clothed and in its right mind'.

God is such a master of irony, that God hits straight shots with crooked sticks.

Sermons should be clear enough to discern the main thread of thought, lest it be all 'beads and no thread'.

Our words can, after all, be 'wiser than we are', and never more so than when the Holy Spirit is in the room.

Ernest Campbell said this about writing sermons: that one should write a sermon half again as big as you need it to be, and then trim it down. He said what you want is to "prune luxuriance instead of fanning scarcity."[21]

Good preachers don't say too much. Good writers don't explain everything. Show, don't tell.

---

21 Plantinga, C. (2013). Reading for Preaching: The Preacher in Conversation with Storytellers. Eerdmans. 56.

Poetry

W.H. Auden said, "poetry makes nothing happen."[22] Well, in a sense, the poet does not write to encourage revolution or incite rebellion, perhaps, but I have a different report. It was not at sobriety that I changed the aspects of life which now keep me alive. It was after the long stay in Emory hospital. The first heart "trouble" stay. When they tampered with the heart the first time, they instilled a thirst and love for poetry which had formerly lain in wait. I had always thought I would get around to celebrating my love for words in my daily life. Of course, the heart is just a pump, say the moderns; well then, what to do with all the ancient literature which declares it to be the seat of emotions? With all their trying, the moderns have not destroyed metaphors and other figures of speech. The post-moderns have hence said there is no 'scientific' way to speak of truth; it's all metaphor! Well, what it is to me is a coming-alive. Poetry made something happen in my life indeed! From the time they first messed with my heart 'til now could be said to be my 'born again' moment. I have been *writing* as opposed to *taking notes* ever since. I even thought I would myself write poetry. I still would if I could; I should—but there I go 'shoulding' on myself again, and I said I would quit that. The words, *could*, *would*, and *should* ***should*** be deleted from the language and replaced with the shoe commercial ("just do it"). So here I am, alive at last and just in time.

"What will be will be;" not fatalism, but awareness that God will do what God will do. My part is to be faithful in my two communities. Here we are in the twenty-first century. It is a time in history when we don't know what to call history. Are there clear indicators anywhere? (Ones which are not economic, at least?) Does one look to scripture and poetry for answers? I think *yes*.

---

22 Auden, W.H. (2020). *In Memory of W.B. Yeats*. Retrieved from https://poets.org/poem/memory-w-b-yeats.

It's all about Jesus. Like Mary Gordon I am drawn to the "figure in a mist, a shape on the horizon. That shape, that figure, embodies itself in a person, Jesus."[23] She goes on to say the elusiveness of the figure leads her to be a person of hopeful faith. Jesus is ungraspable; he said so himself as he cautioned Mary in the resurrection garden. We do not grasp his form, but we certainly recognize him as Lord of Life. She says, "the incomprehensible, is nevertheless rooted in profound attachments."[24] It is the attachment she 'feels.' She is Catholic, female, and married to a Jew, so my understanding of Jesus would be spoken differently perhaps, but she does write rather well. Jesus was not a writer, nor did he tell others to write it all down. We find this a bit strange, don't we? What creative expression Jesus left us was stories. There are many other words he gave us, of course, but don't we resonate most with those stories which appear made up on the spot? They say there is no unstoried form of the gospels. *They*, being some leading lights, so let's go with that. If one actually took the gospels as books to be read as a whole, rather than picking at fragments, one could then see the authors' intent. One would also sense how it is that the gospels have no unstoried form. We then read how these four authors saw things, how they wrote from what they had seen and heard. Remember, we are looking for Jesus as we read. What do we find of him that we can relate to, a relationship which builds itself into the one all other relationships can be understood from, the prime one we have in Jesus.

We must start at the end. The future is assured by the victory of the crucifixion and resurrection. The Lamb is on the throne and rules the universe from that place and He will come again to establish God's Kingdom once and for all.

John Wesley wrote:

> The full assurance of faith relates to present pardon; the full assurance of hope, to future glory. The former is the highest degree of divine evidence that God is reconciled to me in the Son of his love; the latter is the same degree of divine evidence ("wrought in the soul by the same immediate

---

23 Gordon, M. (2009). *Reading Jesus: A Writer's Encounter with the Gospels*. New York. Anchor. 3.
24 Ibid.

> inspiration of the Holy Ghost") of persevering grace, and eternal glory. [25]

This assurance perseveres unto the end. Wesley's idea of complete renewal carries a doctrine of sanctification to its logical conclusion. The misunderstanding of the intent Wesley had can be found in the words used in the West compared with the way those in the East understood this advanced state of sanctification. The Western Latin translation of *perfectio* (perfected perfection) and the Eastern *teleiotes* (perfect*ing* perfection), for example. The West had the sense of an achieved state of perfection. The East spoke of a never-ending aspiration for all of love's fullness. Wesley thus spoke of going on to perfection, *teleiotes*, a never-ending journey which is not an individual achievement, but one characterized by the practices Wesley had employed in small groups from his earliest days at Oxford.

---

25 Kirby, J.E. and Abraham, W.J. (2009). *The Oxford Handbook of Methodist Studies*. Oxford University Press. 611.

Medicine

I'm reading some theological ethics by Hauerwas as he refers to Aristotle and Aquinas, his favorites. He speaks of the unity of body and soul. Habits and virtues are formed of necessity. It is a question of what kind of habits and virtues we develop. Aristotle thought that how one becomes proficient in craft is quite similar to how one acquires the habits necessary to become a person of virtue. *Repetition.* We become virtuous by performing virtuous actions.

For Aristotle and Aquinas, we are purposive beings capable of acquiring a history through the acquisition of habits. So far, well and good. We certainly do not want to separate any of these things. (We will bypass the modern era—we are post-modern.)

It is crucial that the young acquire early in their lives the right habits. The goal is to become a person of such character that what we do is not different from what we are. "Mastery" is Aquinas' description of what it means for us to be able to act in such a manner that *what we do* and *who we are* are inseparable.

For Aquinas, the will and reason are interdependent because every act of the will is preceded by an act of the intellect, but it is also the case that an act of the intellect is preceded by an act of the will. Reason's grasp of the good depends on the will being disposed to the good through habit. (Is attention to liturgy through habit important? Well, only if one wants a Christian!)

For Aquinas, the soul names that we are bodies destined by our desires to be befriended by God. Accordingly, he understands reason to be rational desire and will to be desiring reason. This is close to Wittgenstein's remark that the human body is the best picture of the human soul. For Aquinas, the soul is the principle of life in the body, and the organizing principle or form of the whole person. We can say that to be human for

Aquinas is to be a body destined by love. Aquinas argues that the presence of the passions is a sign of the intensity of the will, indicating a greater moral goodness than would be the case if the passions were absent. Aquinas, drawing on Aristotle, describes habit as a disposition—that which is disposed well or ill, and thus, either in regard to itself or in regard to another. Thus, health is a habit. The enduring quality of habits is the result of their relation to acts which are done in such a manner they make the agent good as well as the act good.

So now we are ready to explore why I deplore going to the Doctor. Any attempt to care for the body which fails to so recognize the storied character of our bodies cannot help but distort the practice called medicine.

Medicine refers to the pills I take. The pills I take are expensive, and they are passed out by people who pass by the bed in a hospital. But then, they are obtained by another sub-set of people who have a whole library of pills and "medicine," who hire other people who work counters, and you give them a note and they count your pills. The large drug companies have prepared these pills and have a process called R&D. This means they can secure a patent and charge hundreds for what it takes pennies to prepare. The government has agencies to make sure this is done properly without getting in the way of the whole point, *profits*! Thus, the pharmacies and prescriptions are then dispensed.

The physicians are other people. One must have a primary care physician who has an office. She hires other people who work behind glass walls. One must phone the physician to get an appointment three months later. Then the patient proceeds to the primary doctor. She has a "waiting room." You then sit with the sick for a few hours. Then a person calls your name and you proceed to have various procedures done after you have produced your insurance information. All these people must be paid. Then another person comes to get you and you sit in another room for at least an hour, until at last your primary physician shows up. What happens then is you get a note, so you have to go back to the pharmacy and get some more pills. This is medicine, or pills, in my experience. Now excuse me, the sun is up; I must count out my pills for the day.

Medicine is dominated by economic and political ideologies which claim to be, first and foremost, about securing the freedom of the individual. Medicine becomes yet another impersonal institution which delivers services to consumers. A medicine so determined cannot acknowledge that the body, which is after all the whole point of the medical arts, is a storied body. A storied body is not the body of *anyone*, but a body determined by a particular history of a particular community. Wendell Berry says health is just that, namely, membership in a community. Berry argues that if this is recognized, no hard and fast distinction can be drawn between the physical and the spiritual. The body as a machine has come to dominate our lives and, in particular, medical care. So, we are a collection of body parts which can suffer a systems failure; it is clear if I cannot piss, I must seek out a piss doctor, but if I cannot shit, a whole different specialty is called for. This explains how, since I have lived in Augusta, I have sought appointments with sixteen different physicians. [26]

It reminds me of the woman Jesus healed in the gospels, as it describes "she had suffered much under many physicians."[27] Now, please understand. Some of the doctors I have known are some of the finest people I have ever known. I have received what we all say we want: "the finest medical care available." I'm not trying to return to the old mythology of the small-town country doctor. The medicine we have is the medicine we have. Modern medicine can be quite brutal, but the medicine of the past was even more so. Nor do I deplore the incredible advances of modern medicine. I am deeply grateful for the medical care I have received and without it would have been long dead. I must also address my impatience and arrogance as I relate the current state of medicine, *but*—and it's a big butt—let me continue. Berry reminds us that who we are is indicated by our bodies in relation to other bodies. When we as bodies are abstracted from the communities which constitute the trust and love that give life, we get an abstract notion of the body which can

---

26 That's more than one a year.
27 Mark 5:26

only be destructive. The whole experience of submitting to gain entrance to a hospital bed explains what I am talking about. (This is not really the fault of individual doctors.) What the body really is, is a body which has been formed by the body of Christ. It is a body which is *not* going to get out of life alive. My point is, medicine not only names what physicians do but also is a determinative relationship between doctor and patient. It is often forgotten that physicians are human beings. They would like to be liked. Physicians would like to help those who are sick and come to them for help. The problem is enlarged when the patient is focused upon an unreasonable expectation of a cure. The patient wants to be fixed! We bring expectations as patients which are unfair to the doctor. The fear we bring to the physician makes it hard for the doctor to tell the truth. Think of all the different patients a doctor sees. They care for people in a manner they have been taught and according to their skills, but the patient may not understand the limits of what a physician can do.

Medicine is the name for a tradition of wisdom concerning good care for the body. As such it is not a 'means' to health, but it is part of the activity we call health. This is ideally an activity which involves participation by the patient and the physician. In terms of creation, as well as the classical understanding, the body is the artist of its own healing. We are to learn to live through our bodies, not beyond our bodies. We are to learn to live through a body that is destined to die. We are a body that is not simply a physical body but a lived body. If being a Christian is the fullest expression of what it means to be a human being, then how do we train ourselves with the physician's role, as well in what it truly means to dwell in this transitional vehicle? Think of this... what body does the medical student first experience in medical training? A corpse. Thus, they learn the body, like the world itself, is essentially of no purpose other than our ability to impose our will upon it—our arbitrary desires. This is a mechanistic understanding which right away teaches the learner that true knowledge of the body is knowledge of a dead body. A lived body is an unpredictable body. A dead body makes possible predictable knowledge. If you remove the patient's story in providing medical care, you are no longer truly a doctor. To be able to see the patient, one must listen to the patient. We all want medicine to be an orderly field of knowledge and procedure. But it is not; it's an imperfect science, an enterprise of constantly changing knowledge, uncertain information, and fallible individuals. There is science, yes, but there is also habit, intuition, and guessing. Thus, doctors must talk to patients about life and death. We need help in understanding what is happening and why, and what is possible and what is not.

The body the church presents to be cared for has been formed within the body of Christ. It is a baptized body of the people of God. This body cannot die apart from the church which is responsible for it. This body has been formed and shaped by practice, carried by the story of God in which illness, suffering, and even death are not regarded as the final enemy. The grace of God insures this to be so. Even human finitude can be seen as a gift.

If we can learn to die, there must be training, and the initial training is also ongoing; it is provided by the church as we gather together (weekly is not enough). In my case I also have another community, AA. In those two areas I am provided with what I need. These groups are made up of individuals. They are ones formed by the groups and trained by those groups. To cut off the individual from the community is like picking a flower from its plant. It can be pretty, but not for long.

As I move in my two communities, I am learning my story. Like all stories, it is made up of 'what it was like, what happened, and what it is like now.' The story will also have an end. I will try to tell my story for as long as it is possible. If the end is an intensive care unit, I can only hope for consciousness. What a wonderful thing to tell your story still, even as they pull the plug, so to speak. There are those who get to attend such events who can testify that the one in transition will allow the ones who are gathered to go with the traveler as far as possible, or as far as a person dares to go, in attending the dying person.

All of this is part of what keeps me alive today. I learn from many sources. I see courage and nobility and selflessness demonstrated as well as despair and fear. The final enemy is not death, but fear of death that detracts from the grand adventure the body makes as it goes elsewhere. How can the person of faith consider it otherwise? How do we learn all this? 'Now I lay me down to sleep', from speaking to sponsors, mentors, from scripture and preaching, from reading, from watching others in the acts of living and dying. It is all a gift.

The problem with church is that it is only weekly, thus weakly. One lives from day to day. This is why I crave the monastery. The ideal life would be a monastic one, with daily AA meetings and some good work to do, and encounters with sponsors and spiritual advisers and worship. We do not live ideal lives.

So many live unexamined lives. They move from event to event with no cognizance of connection. Their body awareness is turned off as they seek happy and feel-good. This is what the culture teaches. How can we change things? Only by changing ourselves and telling the story of what it's now like. It reminds me of Wesley's characterization of the movements of grace. If the Holy Spirit is made manifest in the community, the news will spread. It must be witnessed to.

Health is a reflection of the love of God. In the church some are well, and some are sick and not going to get well. We accept this as a part of the body of Christ and see human finitude as gift. Our health is not an absence of suffering, but a reliance on Christ, even when facing illness and death. It is faithfulness to Christ which makes the difference. We learn to suffer, but since our hope is in Christ, we can never lose hope. We pray for our doctors, not only for their craft among us, but also for their courage to tell us when they cannot help us.

It should be obvious when we Christians are gathered in the ICU waiting room. There should be a spiritual power which radiates from such a group. This should be the case when it is clear the 'patient' is dying; this should also be the case when we want them to 'pull through.' We are those taught to pray "Thy will be done." And if we are to overcome, we pray to believe the Holy Spirit will pray on our behalf. Also, we have our story formed by the one who came to dwell among us, "God with us." We have been baptized into Christ, which means we have already died. Therefore, we are not those who expect to get out of life alive, but we are those who have been taught to remain faithful to the end. Our hope is a resurrection hope.

We would rather live our lives uninterrupted by illness and death. When we are confronted by those realities, we must once again learn the lesson of control. We must learn to live as those who are out of control. This is not only a lesson we must learn (yet again); this can also be the hardest of lessons. When we as Christians gather around the 'death bed,' we have been taught God is in control and we are comforted by Romans 8: *nothing* can separate us from the love of God in Jesus Christ. This can obviously be the hardest thing a Christian can ever do; it can also be the most glorious.

These last words may seem so far from the current state of the church and the practice of medicine as to be unrealistic. It is simply true that from time to time I have been a part of the story of such bodies which can tell the story told above. It is the most holy of times when it happens. I'm there as a pastor and get to witness a faith which sustains my faith. It brings all we have been taught together. We stand by death, not as final enemy, but as those who don't have to live in fear and the illusion of control. This can be taught in the church. It is rare, but worth the effort.

Stan Hauerwas quotes from the Book of Common Prayer the following, entitled "Prayer for Use by a Sick Person:" [28]

> This is another day, O Lord. I know not what it will bring forth, but make me ready, Lord, for whatever it may be. If I am to stand up, help me to stand bravely. If I am to sit still, help me to sit quietly. If I am to lie low, help me do it patiently. And if I am to do nothing, let me do it gallantly. Make these words more than words, and give me the Spirit of Jesus. *Amen.*

Well, with the Spirit of Jesus, what else do we need? Yet the part I want to lift up is "doing nothing gallantly." As Hauerwas points out, if we

---

28 Hauerwas, S. (2013). *Approaching the End: Eschatological Reflection on Church, Politics, and Life.* Eerdmans. 200.

have been properly trained for death and illness, this training will get us into the body formed by Christ, and we will be able to do well in sickness and in death. Note that the prayer is for the person who is sick. I so wish I could have learned earlier some of these things. As a pastor, I would enter the hospital room and defer to the doctors, "O Lord, help the nurses and doctors do their deal." I see the whole thing in a different way now. Our job is to prepare *ourselves* in a way that the physician *can* do his or her job. As it is now, the doctor and the patient are desperately trying to defeat death. The Christian will help heal the physician in a realistic understanding of what is going on, if the gift of God called a good death is about to be given. The physician can learn to be honest and clear with the patient. The patient can learn to be and to do those things which can enable a good death to occur. As it is now, the PA system sounds the alarm, "code blue," and some patient is turning blue while everyone runs to overturn that which will come to each inevitably.

It's a matter of language, after all. If communication is at the heart of medical care, then it is crucial to teach the language to all concerned. The doctor is trained to believe what shows up on the x-ray is true in every way. When I am shown an x-ray, I have no idea what I'm looking at. Nuanced communication is called for. Technology explains little to the untrained person. Again, it is really about control. Modern moral discourse provides no vocabulary to deliberate about the meaning of this limited shelf life which we share. We need to learn to speak to the meaning of suffering and death. The church is where this should take place. Then this training should be taken wherever necessary.

Again, we turn to Barth. And, again, Barth is radical. Life is to be the object of an explicit command of God. We are responsible to God for it. That is simply because life, even our own life, is not that which we possess. "Life as such means to live for the One to whom it belongs and from whom it has been received as a loan... We must accept the fact that in respect of this natural direction of his life towards God, man is not its owner and lord."[29] So our respect for life is because, in Christ, the living God has unmistakenly chosen human life as different from any other form of life. Life is a mystery made possible because God has accepted us and

29 Ibid. 212.

identified with us. And, because of our existence as God's covenant partner, we respect our neighbor's life also. When sickness threatens us, we tend to isolate from ourselves and from one another. But we must learn that in the church, when one is ill, all are ill! The body of Christ is not meant for isolation, but for fellowship.

Our lives have God-set limits. Our lives are loaned by God for the service of God. This temporal life is bounded. It is not eternal. Thus, and this is hard, respect for life cannot consist in an absolute will to live, "but in a will to live which by God's decree and command, and by *meditatio futurae vitae*, may perhaps in many ways be weakened, broken, relativised, and finally destroyed."[30] Barth does not allow us to live as if we were God. The point is, we are to see in this limit to life the goodness of God. This life is a gift, not cruel fate.

Health is not absence of pathology. "Health is the strength to be as man."[31] We are to be the wholeness of our created potential. In all cases the question to be answered is, "Do you want to be healed?" (Jn 5:6). If the Christian has been formed to be in partnership with the Creator and to give glory to God for the gift of life, as it is given us, then the physician can do his or her job in support of this gift.

---

30 Ibid. 213.
31 Ibid.

A Temporal God

That I sit here is miracle enough. To merely exist is an extravagant gift of God. What *all* does it mean to consider the impulse of God to create *ex nihilo*? God had certainly no *need* to create. But whenever we talk about God's needs, purposes, and motivation, we are on shaky ground. The thing that's clear about God's viewpoint is that only God can have it. But let's just say (as those who would please the Creator) we are exploring the grounds of our gratitude. That we exist at all is a miracle. When we find ourselves in this *"alive state"*, what then is our purpose? Well, to praise God and enjoy his benefits. God, after all, left us a record. As he created, he established and entered into what we call time. Timeless as God was, He gave us time. He is apart from this dimension which binds and defines us (he always has the option to enter history again, he just does it rarely). So, as God began to create, after each day he would say, "Damn, I'm good!" And when one explores the things we can figure out, science and such, He was spot on. In fact, this may be the best work in the universe! It's hard to say because God made it hard to say. That he stepped back from time is clear. Someone should count the times he has made a personal appearance. My personal favorite was when he spoke from Baalam's ass (Numbers 22:22-35). A sense of humor was something the deity shared (in fact, created).

This whole time business is important to explore. Could it be God is more 'temporal' than we are? I think so. God is ahead, behind, before, above, all of the above. What of the quantum world? If God is moving quarks around like chess pieces, then the basic building blocks (how he did it) is as much a mystery as ever, but we are given a world teeming with God's glory, just the same. How do we witness to all of this? How do we tell this story? This, I believe, is the whole point. Christians have a special opportunity. We know there was a beginning. Is it because we have read Genesis? No, it's because we have seen the end! When we speak of creation, it is not on the grounds of "well, *something* had to start all this." We are those who have been intervened on, and have a story to report, because of the doctrine of eschatology. The end is our beginning! The kingdom has been established as well as our place in it. We cannot conceive of an atemporal God. The church fathers knew this. The Logos was with God in eternity. If Jesus Christ and his cross and resurrection are *real* events, then God's purpose must be historic. What is history? Our silly efforts to record and tell this story. And the story can be told only by those who have been formed to tell the story. In other words, were it not for the ways God enters temporality and forms and guides the church, the world could have no story.

Certainly, it is telling that the earliest "history" we have ever found is an inventory of how many sheep and goats or whatever this ancient guy had in Iraq. Then if one reads the rest of history, it is a record of war after war. Hauerwas says the church is to make the world the world. This is an eschatological claim which says we have been shown the end. It means creation is not "back there;" creation is about God's continuing created efforts. It's about how God continues to reach out to us with the love Jesus spoke of and demonstrated through the cross and resurrection. Thus, the eternal is not atemporal. John Yoder said, "...in the Bible the eternal is not less like time, but more like time. It is like time to a higher degree. The Kingdom is not immaterial but is no more like reality than reality is."[32] This is extravagant stuff!

How do we support such claims? By living true to them! Being a Christian is what I get to do in this writing. What I am trying to do is to make sense of my life in the light of the gospel. If this is the case, then I do not even get to say what is true in these words I have written! It is a story I tell. The only way to judge the truthfulness of these words is if they are judged true by others whose lives are formed by the gospel. We do not live and write to ourselves. Each of these words are given to those fellow pilgrims I meet within AA and church. And again, it must be acknowledged,

---

32 Hauerwas, S. (2010). *Hannah's Child: A Theologian's Memoir*. Eerdmans. 158.

these words have no utilitarian purpose. Therefore, these words must be more like prayer than anything else!

Prayer is a form of communication. Does prayer change God? Who's to say? It is clear enough that God wants to fellowship with us.

As I wrote above, God did not have to create. I suppose things were just fine before the big bang. Or could God have been lonely? I guess we should not think of God as being needy, yet look at the plethora of created objects, to say nothing of the great distances involved. It must be that God loves creating and travel. We also can infer that diversity is dear to God. It is so far beyond our ability to imagine the infinity of possibilities represented in what we know of the universe.

I'm reading an interesting book about how we may be alone in the whole of creation. The author strains himself considerably, but does a pretty comprehensive job; then he confesses he can only speak for this little neighborhood we call the milky way. What a cop out. Why not the whole damn thing? But if he is right, it could be that God does crave a word now and then. If we are so special, it is because we were made so. Then our prayers should be mainly ones of gratitude. So we turn to the poets, who alone have the language to express these wonders.

I have loved poetry for many years now. This craving for words was awakened for me when I first encountered the reality of my mortality. It again was as if the ancients were right when they spoke of the heart being the seat of emotions. We realize during great distress that words are what we have. Words give us the ability to tell our stories and God made this so from the very beginning, when he began to create and spoke the universe into existence. Words are what we have, and here toward the end of this time for me, words are all I have. So I rise early and write these words.

More on Worship

On a Sunday we get to worship. I have written more about this subject than any other and will continue so to do. We take our place each Sunday. Yes, I have a place and woe to anyone who sits in my pew. We are all like that and if something is always true it must be OK (just kidding). So, we meet and greet and then settle down. I scan the menu to see what specials are offered. The scope of the service is given. Jamie has planned the flow-and-go so that word and music are joined in a powerful way; yet the design is often a very subtle artistry. Gary is the co-leader of the process. He announces, prays, preaches, and presides over the presentation of our offerings at the altar. Jamie praises the whole thing, and the design elements cause the whole hour to flow seamlessly. It takes great skill to do what they do. I love it and remember my delight in doing a similar thing for half a century. That's a chunk of time, and yet I only scratched the surface of the possible expressions. We are the people of a book and my old study bible has been in many ways *the* book in my life.

God's Word—that's what we call it. It's what we preach. What a conceit! What a calling. We don't really consider the immensity of the act. If we did it would crush us. We pass out bulletins to the pew-sitters. It would be better to provide protective gear. We unleash a power which changes everything as we worship, and we finally realize that's the whole point. We must be changed. We shall all be changed at the last trumpet. A trumpet clarion call at the end of worship from the balcony would be a good way of expressing this given fact. I will think on this. I wish I could start over with what I know now, but with the original equipment I was blessed with. I wasted this gift and yet can remember the times I almost got it right. Praise and Prose have been my life in the church, and I can think of no better life. But we get only the one chance. Sad.

Hauerwas wrote:

> Being Christian requires the recognition of the difficulty of reality. We are suffering creatures whose suffering tempts us to be more than we are, which ensures that we will be less than we are created to be. We create hells for ourselves and others fueled by false hopes anchored in the presumption of our significance. We are wounded by sin, we are wounded by our illusions of control, we are wounded by our inability to acknowledge the wounds our desperate loves inflict on ourselves and on others.[33]

Bearing reality is the difficulty of being a Christian. I believe only church can prepare us for the reality of living in this broken existence. We hold on to extravagant claims in the church. The continuing reality of existence is not only hard to bear, but harder to reconcile in terms of our claims that God is somehow guiding the whole enterprise. We see injustice, violence, suffering, and death everywhere we look. In the century just past, more killing took place through technology than in any time in history. Now that we are beginning a new century there is little change. Christians do not have a handle on history. We simply have the promise of a new type of Kingdom. This is past, present, and future gift brought by the risen Lamb. We are sinful creatures trapped in time. The Lamb of God reminds us of what only he can do. We can learn from him what only we can do. We are Christians and believe history can be seen doxologically. We have been redeemed, and we do not have to bear the burden of our self-inflicted wounds alone. We share the burden by participation in the body of Christ. The Church does not make any of this any easier. To be a Christian does not mean we ever cease to be human beings. We are called to be a witness to a world which does not believe anymore that anyone can speak the truth.

---

33 Hauerwas, S. (2013). Bearing Reality: A Christian Meditation. *Journal of the Society of Christian Ethics 33*(1), 3-20.

On Knowledge and Rationale

A New York Times op-ed guy has a column and recently did a thing on keeping a journal. It made me think of what these words mean. I have already decided there is no value or moral purpose. It is hardly therapy either. The readership is non-existent, so the question remains. I freely admit to narcissism and self-absorption.

This writing helps me to name the claims. Repetition is a necessary discipline for one as scattered as I am. I will forget valuable lessons without reminders. I guess this is introspection and my assumption is that it is basically healthy. It is certainly possible this whole enterprise is neurotic. I can only try to be honest, and I'm never sure I reach that level of honesty. My mind has rarely had my best interests at heart. It is a dangerous neighborhood at best. Our brains are complex, and self-awareness is tricky. But, if I have failed at this, then all is a lost delusion.

How do we know something? If I seek to justify my belief, I can only do it by relating it to other beliefs. If my belief is called into question, the other beliefs are also called into question. This chain of justifications must stop somewhere. It cannot infinitely regress, so we use the image of a building. In this metaphor we say the building must have a *foundation*. This thinking goes back to Descartes (1566-1650). He lived during the Thirty Years' War (1618-1648). In this war over differences of belief, there was urgency for a "foundation" which could lead to universal agreement. Descartes said science and religion stood for two paths to knowledge: pure reason verses tradition. From his time into the modern age, the ideal of human knowledge focused on the universal, general, theoretical—in contrast to the local, particular, the timely, the practical. The problem is that the modern quest has failed us. This foundationalist picture of linear (bottom to top) thinking is an over-simplification leading to circular reasoning. One cannot begin at the foundation. If we use language, we run into trouble immediately. There is really no "bottom" even in science. It is not built on bedrock. The piles go only so deep.

Quine has a better metaphor. His "holist" theory has no un-revisable beliefs. Also, we reason not only in one direction (up from the foundation) but in many directions. So from a post-modern perspective, when we look at knowledge on a large enough scale, it all turns out to be an interplay of texts and experiences. Language in our times has been referential and representative. That is, language has been thought to get its *meaning* by referring to objects or states of affairs in the world; its primary *function* has been taken to represent its reality. We must come to realize language has many functions. We look to the relation of language to its context and to the community which uses it. For example, the fundamentalist, desiring a firm foundation, turned to an inerrantist doctrine of Scripture. When the historical critical treatment seemed to fail to carry the freight, some theologians turned to religious experience for a foundation and the liberal tradition was born. To me it is clear what is needed lies beyond these two approaches. What we need is a practical problem of choosing a way of life. That leaves us at the door of the church.

Here is our problem. There is no conviction-free place to stand from which to evaluate religious convictions. There is no foundation from which to work toward consensus. Wittgenstein said we really do not know what language means unless we can see how it is enfleshed in human life. *And* doctrinal claims fail the test if they cannot be lived out. Both meaning and justification require exemplification in life. Arguments for the existence of God are secondary to discovery of a community's actual concept of God. The question is whether there is or can be a suitable coherence between the Christian concept of God and the one true God, as we have come to know that one in trust, worship, and obedience. The Enlightenment distinction between fact and value (theology and ethics) does not hold up. We must find ways of living and thinking which are faithful to the biblical story. Life and thought are to be expressed in a communal nature. Faithfulness is found in how this particular people in this situation perform the biblical stories. By extension we also find *there can be no formal method for theology in a world without foundations.* There is instead only the church and its practices. Take the Christian Scripture: while the Scriptures are of a particular community, they intend to give a true account of the origin, character, and final end of all people and of all creation as well.

Martin Buber has written "we understand others by reiterating our self-understanding."[34] We are formed in the church to learn to tell our story. There is a recovery of the significance of narrative for understanding both the Scriptures and our own lives. This is in contrast to the modern attempts to reduce Scripture's content to propositions or history or religious meanings, and to the Enlightenment project of attempting to know all things 'objectively' or 'from the standpoint of eternity.' *We have the recovery of the importance of the community epistemologically, ethically, and linguistically.* In contrast to the Enlightenment ideal of certitude and universality, the Renaissance practice of reason was tolerant of diversity and ambiguity, modest about its own powers, and concerned with the practical. We are to proceed stripped of Constantinian pretensions and clothed with the wisdom of the Gospel.

---

34 Walzer, M. (2002). *The Company of Critics: Social Criticism and Political Commitment in the Twentieth Century*. Basic Books. 67.

Hauerwas on McClendon

This is how McClendon has helped us move into the narrative of how knowledge has lost the absolutes and how we can tie what we know with what we do. This is the practical and particular emergence from the old modern worked into what we are thinking *and* doing in these transitional days. Hauerwas writes we must "give up our need to control the world. We must instead believe that truthfulness, not war and violence, is the way the world acquires a history befitting its ordering to God's Kingdom."[35] Then McClendon would have us escape the way education has specialized theology in order to meet the demands of being a science in the modern "research" university. If theology is a subject matter for professional clergy, it risks being of no significance to the faith. We are to train leaders for the churches. Theologians today are to be found talking to other theologians. McClendon challenges the presumption that theology can be true to the teaching of the church and at the same time be of service to the state. This results in distortion. Academic Theology is an oxymoron, on a level with military intelligence. *The resurrection has determined that one cannot domesticate theology*. It means you cannot begin at the beginning but at the end. Our lives are based on miracle. McClendon says, "Every Christian doctrine seems to require every other for its clear presentation."[36] Thus, we get story and narrative. It is a complex story to be sure, but the deeper I get in all this theology, the more it seems God holds everything together. The tale is ongoing, but by beginning at the end, we are given the assurance that through Christ we have been made a part of the end. The teaching of the church is eschatological.

---

35 Hauerwas, S. (2018). *Wilderness Wanderings: Probing Twentieth-century Theology and Philosophy*. Routledge. 173.

36 Ibid. 179.

McClendon resists the "theories" of the atonement which de-eschatologize the cross. If we read the accounts with care, we come to see that *we are also characters* in the story. It is the story of creation, after all, and we will find ourselves popping up eventually, but we will recognize ourselves truly as those of the community we call the church, *itself* an *interim institution*! In our day, the stress on individual salvation and so-called doctrines of atonement often betray an attenuated Christology. The church thus becomes just a collection of individuals who are only concerned with their "personal" relationship to Jesus Christ. Religion in America is like shopping in a market, finding what suits your personal lifestyle. Thus, the church gets lost and the politics of Jesus have no power. If we are, in fact, losing the form of Christendom in North America, it may be a good thing. God is fully capable of bringing another interim institution into existence. It will always be those gathered around the great banner Stan the Man has proposed: "Jesus Christ is Lord, everything else is bullshit."

I finished another Murdoch last night. It was quite a "muddled affair." Not her writing, but the constant state of the affairs which involve her characters. She is becoming an addiction. I must be careful in not being drawn into the net. That Hauerwas can claim her as one of his great teachers is enough for me. I also can take a break every once in a while with a good Trollope.

When I write, something first flits from tree to tree in my mind; then I have to find a way to express it. The expression gives life to the idea. I doubt I have anything much to say. I am still a learner. Mostly I borrow stuff from my books and arrange my own words around the notions of others. As Hauerwas has taught me, if I have something to say it is because I am a Christian. What does it mean to be a Christian in such a world as we have? There is a huge difference between the glory and particularity of this created world we have and the mess we have made on this planet. This cosmos is too much. The conclusion that we are alone here and on our own is based on the fact that we will die before we can make or receive contact with anyone else who may be 'out there'. The distances are just too great. And as we find ourselves on this little blue planet today, we are in a time of great transition. The planet itself doesn't realize we are moving from the modern world to whatever lies next. If it did, it would breathe a great sigh of relief that we haven't destroyed the earth yet. We still may, of course, because the only clear thing we have learned about history is we don't learn from it. So, my own task in these words is the task of imagination. To image with the mind in the realm of poetic expression would just about sum up what I am about.

We Christians have extravagant things to say. That Jesus rules the cosmos from the cross is an incredible notion. Our task is to find the words to express this radical fact. We have learned from Barth to avoid the apologetic mode. Yet how do we reach folks for the sake of the gospel today? Again, from Barth, the message of the gospel is a joyful exclamation. We are to be found working with words in the light of faith. Faith is nothing more than the words we use to speak of God, and yet the God to whom and about whom we speak defies the very words we use. Why would God do this? After all, God sent Jesus. We believe he is the very word of God. W*hy is it the nearer we get to God, we discover that we know not what we say when we say "God?"* (Barth). How do we address God and begin our prayers? When we try to pray, we start with "Father," "Son," and "Holy Spirit." God is the name we use to speak of this relationship revealed in the Trinity. We can know this only because Jesus has taught us to pray to the Father. Thus, we begin to learn how to pray, and we learn of whom we pray only by praying and worshiping and learning a story which takes a lifetime to learn. Only God can make God known. Aquinas refused to separate God's essence and existence. Thus, we may account for God's simplicity.

The familiarization of Christianity since the Reformation has had disastrous results for everyone. The presumption that the normative way of life among Christians is marriage and family is clearly wrong and contrary to what Jesus said! The church grows not through necessity or biology, but by witness to the stranger. If you become a Christian, you learn your true family is now the church. A Christian's first loyalty is always to church, not a family or a nation. The idolatry of today's family is one of the worst faults of the church. The church does remain, however, a nifty place to bring the family on the day after the Sabbath. And not only that, but "family values" are best learned in church. It's just that the church is not the place where we learn about how to preserve the American Way of Life. I think the best way to go about teaching the above today is to demand the church be the church. We could begin by not allowing people to come to church to have their "needs" met. They must learn to come for Christian reasons.

In my active days I would always say, "Yes, we are a family church and if you are a carbon-based life form, you *are* family and *are* welcome." Maybe this stretches the matter a bit, but Jesus reached out to every conceivable type and style and level and form of person when he gathered followers the first time. Why would he want us arranged in neat split-level suburban groups with an SUV outside?

Now, as to once you join up, then what? Well, Christ simply bids you come and die. Not good market strategy, but true to the "good news."

Ethics

The Peaceable Kingdom is Hauerwas' 'text' book on ethics. Written early in his Notre Dame years, he has already come to his "themes" which are repeated through the years. He has already found Murdoch and Wittgenstein. He is more in favor of R. Niebuhr than he would become. He quotes Reinhold thusly:

> Christianity stands beyond tragedy. If there are tears for this man on the cross they cannot be tears of 'pity and terror'. The cross does not reveal life at cross purposes with itself. On the contrary, it declares that what seems to be inherent defect in life itself is really a contingent defect in the soul of each man, the defect of the sin which he commits in his freedom. If he can realize that fact, if he can weep for himself, if he can repent, he can also be saved. He can be saved by hope and faith. His hope and faith will separate the character of life in its essential reality from life as it is revealed in sinful history. This man on the cross who can say 'Weep not for me' is also able to save us from our tears of self-pity. What he reveals about life transmutes tears of self-pity into tears of remorse and repentance. Repentance does not accuse life or God but accuses self. In that self-accusation lies the beginning of hope and salvation. If the defect lies in us and not in the character of life, life is not hopeless.[37]

So, this brings us joy. We learn we were not meant to be tragic but joyful. This is an Atonement we can preach. Life is not tragic. The cross mirrors our condition. We are not lost. Christ will do for us that which we

---

37 Hauerwas, S. (1983). *The Peaceable Kingdom: A Primer on Christian Ethics.* University of Notre Dame Press. 146.

have been unable to do for ourselves. We are not overcome by grief, but we are freed to move into the joy of salvation. Our nature is God-created and thus we were meant to be those who know the truth. We can thus live with one another in peace with the assurance of God's redemption.

We usually think of joy as a sudden release when we are drawn out of the darkness into light. 'Surprised by joy,' if you will. We think of joy that it is spontaneous but has little staying power. Hauerwas writes, "the joy we receive as Christians is not that of a passing occasion. Rather it is a joy that derives from finding our true home among a people who carry the words and skills of God's kingdom of peace."[38] We are not 'happy,' although we can try to be. We are instead joyful *but* not through our own efforts, but as the gift that comes through that which is given through the cross and the resurrection. We didn't expect joy, but when it was given, we were freed from ourselves and all our attempts to control our lives. And the irony is, the more we give up, the greater the possibility for living life joyfully.

We live our lives by making choices. All of life, day by day, hour by hour. We choose. Is it to be life or death? Following our risen Lord or making out our calendars, health or sickness, selfless love or failure to care for others. Is it to be a genuine spiritual quest or living in the world as if we were meant to live to ourselves in the world? God gave us the horrific gift of freedom. How shall we use it?

38 Ibid. 147.

Wesley

What of the Church according to Wesley?

We, in these times, as we lament the stress upon the individual and thus the resulting loss of Christian community, need to remember how this individualism came about. *It is the result of pietism.* The dominating view in Western culture is that the individual is the measure of things and religion is a private matter. If, among secular people, religion is brought up, it is an embarrassment. This is in sharp contrast to history and most of the non-Western cultures today. Religion has been in history a very public matter. It has been normally a celebration of a common story and common values regarded as bestowing identity upon a people. We turn to etymology; the very term *religio,* "that which binds together." It seems among us today that religion has become unraveled. If religious institutions are places that are artificial creations for the benefit of individuals, what happens when an individual feels as if her needs are not met? Well, she shops somewhere else, right? Where then is the church? The community is not first, but secondary and subsidiary; in our culture, the individual is primary. One of the things which makes Wesley such an interesting figure is he combines *both* an early stage of this pietistic individualism *and* a strong protest against it. On the one hand, he insists the church is not a human product—not even of pious individuals. He wrote it is "not the appointment of men, but of God."[39] Moreover, it is the God of the Trinity. Wesley borrows a line from the poet Virgil to express this divine power "that fills, pervades and actuates the whole."[40]

At the same time, Wesley insists whoever does not participate in this power of God on a *continuing* basis is not a genuine member of the Church. He said *the rite of baptism does not grant permanent*

---

39 Wesley, J. (1872). Sermon 92 "On Zeal" in *The Works of John Wesley* (T. Jackson, Ed.). Via wordsofwesley.com.

40 Wesley, J. (1872). Sermon 111 "On the Omnipresence of God" in *The Works of John Wesley* (T. Jackson, Ed.). Via wordsofwesley.com.

membership in the church. His point was, we must live answerable to our baptism. There is no *status indelibus* granted to the baptized without regard to their response. Again and again, we encounter Wesley's consistent claim that Christianity is all about changed lives. The holiness of the church is made manifest when its true members participate in the holiness of their Lord, and we are transformed by it in a continuing process.

Wesley was not a sectarian in the usual sense. He simply wanted the church to be church. Also, we must remember he was no separatist, and he strongly *resisted* any separatist sentiments within the ranks of his own movement. He much preferred the example of those who "lived and died" in the churches to which they belonged. He sought not to found a church but to bring renewal to the life of the church to which he was committed. Wesley thought the Church of England, in her worship and government, to be closer to the model of the early church than any other national church.[41]

He believed that zeal for the church only makes sense if it is zeal for those tasks the church was to accomplish. It is of interest that Wesley gives priority to *works of mercy* (feeding the hungry, clothing the naked, visiting those who are sick and in prison). Yet, at the same time, he insists that *works of piety* (public and private prayer, the Lord's Supper, reading, hearing, and meditating on the Word, and fasting) are also essential. And he makes it clear that *the two kinds of works* are not to be considered apart from each other. Both serve God's ends. Neither is possible without constantly receiving from God.

We need to remember not only Wesley's Anglicanism but his philosophical heritage as well. There was a clear dominance of Aristotelian thought at Oxford. Cambridge was the stronghold of Platonic thought. The Cambridge Platonists were the dominant philosophical school in the seventeenth and early eighteenth century. But at Oxford, the Aristotelian orientation was the prominent school of thought. Wesley, as a tutor at Lincoln College, had taught Aristotle's logic using the textbook written by the former dean at Christ Church, Wesley's own college. Platonic thought

41 Of course, being a "national" church is a huge problem in itself.

assumed direct access through reason to the universals, those archetypal ideas which lie behind, inform, and guarantee the reality of everything which exists. Aristotle questioned this immediate—and thus mystical—approach to the universal through innate ideas in the mind, and insisted instead that it is by our experience of existing we arrive at universal principles, which are rational abstractions derived from experience. John Locke had followed this Aristotelian pattern in his rejection of Descartes' innate ideas and in his derivation of knowledge from experience. With Locke and Aristotle, therefore, Wesley denied innate ideas and the corollary of immediate and mystical knowledge of God, arguing instead that the ordinary way in which God is disclosed is through *means of grace*. The initiative lies with God rather than with the capacities of our reason or the human spirit; yet, Wesley had no difficulty with "immediacy" when it referred to the action of the Holy Spirit in the life of the believer, the *action initiated by* God. Wesley's approach could be termed "sacramental." When the spiritual senses are quickened, we are enabled to grasp through the means of grace the God who approaches us. Thus, the pattern of Aristotle: we go through existing things to arrive at spiritual reality. In the Christian community we live for one another, and "fellowship" is the mark of the church from Pentecost onward. Christ calls us to build up one another. Yet Wesley does not intend to downplay the importance of time apart for prayer and meditation.

The influence of the American frontier had a watering down effect on the original movement Wesley started. The revivalistic and camp-meeting tradition have given us a picture of the American revivalist and pietist traditions of individual salvation and people going down front to get "saved" and "born again." The communal structures he established with the Societies, Classes, and Bands operated in a different manner. Statistical research on the spiritual lives of early British Methodists, whose spiritual biographies were published in the Armenian Magazine and the Methodist Magazine, shows, according to their own testimony, only 1/4th of them experienced new birth in the context of the preaching they heard prior to joining a Methodist society. By far the majority needed the nurture of the society, classes, and bands, and spent an average of 2.3

years in this nurturing process before experiencing what they themselves identified as new birth. Methodist preaching at the time ended not with an "altar call" but with announcements of where the local Methodist's societies met and an invitation to attend.

The "Holy Club" at Oxford is often seen as an example of an Anglican society. It had rules drawn up by the members. Regular attendance at the sacrament and use of the stated prayers of the Anglican tradition were read. They collected money for the poor and also ministered personally to the poor and to prisoners and their families. They held each other accountable and encouraged each other. Sometimes they used the disciplines and worship of the early church as models. Wesley often used the rhetoric of the recovery of the faith and practice of "primitive Christianity."

Early Methodists flocked to the celebration of Holy Communion. From Wesley's journals we get a picture of how from church to Cathedrals he would administer the sacrament to hundreds at a time. Sometimes the buildings would not hold the numbers of communicants. It is important to recall the Eucharistic theology informed by the Anglican efforts to provide an alternative to the Roman Catholic doctrine of transubstantiation. Yet they wished to retain a strong sense of Christ's presence and activity through the Spirit (Article 28 of the 39 Articles). The Anglicanism of the seventeenth and eighteenth centuries followed Calvin in insisting Christ was in heaven. Wesley agreed and stated that he will remain there till the time of the restitution of all things. Thus, the Roman Catholic adoration of the consecrated host is rejected. Nor is Christ's presence to be understood in terms of a miraculous change in the elements. Yet, Wesley does not intend to downplay the divine presence but, if anything, to heighten it and make it more comprehensive by bringing out its Trinitarian nature and communicative purpose.

Thus, Christ is no less present than in the Roman Mass, but his presence is by virtue of the Spirit, who makes Christ present to the soul of the believer. The change in the bread and wine is "not in substance, but in use."[42] They remain bread and wine still, such as before in nature: but

---

42 Nicholson, W. (1842). *An Exposition of the Catechism of the Church of England.* Oxford. John Henry Parker. 177.

consecrated and set apart to represent our Savior's passion, an exhibit and seal to a worthy receiver the benefits of that possession. Christ is "truly and effectually there present"[43] through the power of the Spirit who applies to the human heart what God accomplishes for us in Christ.

Charles Wesley in his hymns, for example:

> O the depth of love divine,
> the unfathomable grace!
> Who shall say how bread and wine
> God into us conveys!
> How the bread his flesh imparts,
> how the wine transmits his blood,
> fills his faithful people's heart
> with all the life of God. [44]

---

43 Ibid. 179.

44 Wesley, C. (1745). *"O the depth of love divine."* Retrieved from https://hymnary.org/text/o_the_depth_of_love_divine_the_unfathoma

Yahweh's People

Walter Brueggemann brings out a strong resolve of Yahweh—that Yahweh *will have a people*. Yahweh's own people in the world. This is clear in the canonical texts of Jews and Christians; there will be a new Israel. Israel again, healed, blessed, brought home rejoicing—by no claim of its own but by Yahweh's resolve—there will be a time. So, when is that time?

"The Book of Comfort" collects together all the hopes and possibilities of the Jeremiah tradition (Jeremiah 30-31). The ones scattered will be gathered up, like a shepherd with lost sheep (see, the New Covenant). This new place is a home beyond exile.

Ezekiel expresses hope and new possibility in chapters 33-48 with the vision of a new temple and its new divine presence. The "breath" comes to "dry bones". The carcass of Israel lies in wait before new life. This new life is restoration and homecoming. Yahweh has been shamed by Israel, yet remains faithful, and the holiness of a new temple will be functions of Yahweh's own holiness.

Isaiah 40-55. The poetry uses the term "gospel" (*basar*) in an intentional way to declare Yahweh's transformative presence. Israel is alone in the world without Yahweh, yet Yahweh will not be "Israel-less."

The point is, the apocalyptic imagery here is as decisive and massive as any current scientific scenarios about the undoing of the world. The creator of heaven and earth can and will form a new creation. It will be a place imagined in these scriptures, a hoping against hope. God who calls into existence things that do not exist (Rom. 4:17) will accomplish this.

In the Old Testament only two texts are regarded as entertaining any notion of life after death: *Isaiah 26:19 and Dan. 12:2.* These statements are quite late, cast in apocalyptic language and influenced by the entry of

Judaism into a world of Hellenistic thought. There exists Old Testament scholarship that posits the Psalms refer to life after death (eternal life, the future life, beatific vision, etc.) but the Psalmists voice their urgent petitions as acts of hope. Yahweh brings new life out of a variety of forms of death. We have not yet arrived at resurrection.

Atonement

People are often surprised to discover that in the whole passion narrative, there is scarcely a single image which belongs to the traditional language of "atonement!" All my life I have pondered over this and have noted earlier in these pages that it is good that the church has never come up with a standard doctrine. Therefore, I'm going to quit worrying over it and will encourage others as well. We don't have to have a standard model doctrine! We will continue with various interpretations which have provided the means by which many generations of Christians have dealt with the reality of the cross. There are no clear signs of a "theory" by which the reading of Jesus' death becomes a reconciled experience. One can accept the gospel accounts as primary source material and without bringing theological presuppositions to the passion material, simply read the story as ironic. Christ crucified is a scandal and a folly. If God's will and Jesus' mission have been accomplished, then we read that Jesus is crowned and proclaimed King, then there is violence and death. The *story* has two ideas which don't fit: Jesus' kingship and humiliating death. How to *explain* this theoretically? Each reader must simply come before this ironic story. What if the story simply portrays life as it is? Examples abound. Life is mysterious, impenetrable, eluding the grasp of all. Now, everything depends on what God does in response to Jesus' execution. The necessary doctrine here is the doctrine of the Trinity. This doctrine is also not spelled out in the scripture. The Trinity is the way we look at *all* of scripture. *God sent Jesus.* The doctrine of the *Incarnation* is clear. Jesus was with God before creation. Jesus came as one of us. The Spirit is ever present. Now, how will God respond after God has raised up a people to keep a covenant which they have never kept, and now this man, Jesus (the King of the Kingdom) has been crucified? What do we do with Jesus' promises? How do we read the accounts in the light of the end of the story?

But wait: it's not the end; God will surely respond. We note that, by itself, irony can be very upsetting. But there is one who is still to speak, one who knows the end of time. We listen to the "my God" to whom Jesus' last cry is directed. Now we understand Jesus has not been forsaken. Now we who will follow him will never be forsaken. "It's Friday but Sunday's coming." Look at the end of the story as Mark tells it! A "young man" tells the women, "You seek Jesus of Nazareth, who was crucified. He has risen; he is not here... Go, tell his disciples and Peter that he is going before you to Galilee. There you will see him, just as he told you" (Mark 16: 6-7). These women were terrified and amazed. They said nothing, for they were afraid. The end. Talking about irony! This is the original ending of Mark! What's up with that? The ball is always in God's court.

If the ending is so disappointing, we will want to look at the rest of the story; after all, Mark has given us a whole gospel, so where's the good news? What *is* the end of the story? We think back through the pages, Jesus (3 times) has predicted his death and resurrection. Yes, we can trust his promises! But we look back to the end of the story and then suddenly realize deliverance will require being acted upon. We then do not require redactors who assure us things do not come out to our satisfaction after all. Maybe we were meant by Mark to be dis-satisfied. All the versions of Atonement I have ever heard have been less than satisfactory. Perhaps I am to wait for deliverance. I now know such waiting is required. When I charged off on my own, the outcome was always not from God. Those were my plans, not God's plan. But deliverance did come. New life, abundant life, was given. Resurrection did occur.

The conclusion I clearly see now is that this encounter with Marks' gospel is an eschatological experience. Here we experience the end which is expected from God. There will be deliverance only if God raises the dead. I see no other way of reading the gospels. In our world, most people regard God as absent or silent. They may say otherwise, but if people must undergo the necessary lengths that it takes to reach these conclusions, we have a lot of work to do. Yes, there can be no denial of death. The gospel as read is the "word of the cross." It is a word which takes death seriously. The cross of Christ is eschatological not only because it does not evade death; it is an experience of the last things, most especially because God does not allow the cross to be the last word. Mark knows this. The testimony of the canon of the New Testament is that God raised Jesus Christ from the dead and, behold, all things have become new!

Begründungszusammenhang

Begründungszusammenhang is what the Germans refer to as the theological context of justification. Hope is not the same as optimism. The Old Testament has Yahweh making covenants with Job and Noah and Abraham, and as they kept the covenant of God's faithfulness, they received hope. The Apostle Paul received the story of Abraham in Gen. 15:6, *"that from Abraham acting in faith, the Lord credited it to him as righteousness."* Paul calls this "hope against hope." Hope is based on God's promise. So, how do we reconcile the science of the day with the biblical promise of the end which can be expected from God? Our hope in God's promise is inseparable from God's power to create the future and give hope. And once again we must turn to our risen Lord. Our hope is focused on the resurrection. The Lord of history gives us hope. Martin Luther, in his study of Romans, tells us "this hope leads across 'into the unknown, the hidden, and the dark shadows, so that he does not even know what he hopes for, and yet he knows what he does not hope for.'"[45]

Now, we can only think of finitude in contrast to infinitude. We think of never-ending processes. Can we even have any knowledge of the end? Do we know what it means for something to come to an end? Think of those we have loved and lost. Do we really understand the end of their lives? Is this quest for understanding demonstrated by those who attend funerals? Would we even go to funerals if we had all this worked out in our heads and hearts? The story of Jesus Christ is a paradigm for something which comes to an end and comes to a new beginning. The life of the risen Christ depends upon God's judgment of existence. The natural sciences tell us the world is finite. To that we reply, as long as there is life there is hope. We have a strong sense that life goes on. We think, well, it always has, and God will carry us on to that which God alone can really determine. We have a strong belief that changes do not constitute an

45 Sauter, G. (2000).Our reasons for hope. In Polkinghorne, J.C (Ed.), *The End of the World and the Ends of God.* Trinity Press International. 215.

ending. But just saying 'life goes on' is at least ambiguous. It's like saying 'the show must go on.' Must it, really? The scientists say there simply is no scientific justification for hope. Arnold Benz, in advertising his book, writes: "Every prognosis we have, be it for living things, planets, stars, galaxies, or the universe, finally amounts to disintegration: the sun will cool off, the earth will be lost in space, and even the matter of the universe will radioactively decay. Therefore, there is no hope which can be backed up by natural sciences."[46]

No hope. The poet wrote of the end, "not with a bang but a whimper."[47] It will either get cold (really cold) or hot (really hot). Or as regards this little blue planet: we could just blow it up in the meanwhile. What confidence do we have in those 'in power'? Well, don't get me started.

Some still shrug and say, 'well, life goes on.' Really? When I consider the powers that be, I am terrified. Gerhard Sauter reminds us of Blaise Pascal's words: "The silence of the infinite space makes me shudder."[48] Well, Christians do what Christians do. It's not what is to come. It's rather who is coming. It is said Martin Luther said the following, but it was really someone else, probably that anon. guy: "If I knew that tomorrow the world would end, I would still plant an apple tree." Wendell Berry suggests a sequoia.

But still I'm left more than nervous, and how do we preach eschatology (which almost no one does, at least authentically) if there is no end to be expected from God? How can there be eschatology without a future? My faith is as strong as the next guy's, *but* and again it's a big but—God will have to provide a grace-motored continuity. The world moves to its consummation, but God brings the end according to God's will. If there was creation, there can be a continuing, and it from the gracious Trinity. After all, we are aware of the interplay of scientists and theology in terms of creation. Just think of all that. The doctrine of creation stands nicely up to the scientific (and philosophical) theories of the big bang. Could a

---

46 Ibid. 218.

47 Eliot, T.S. (1925). *"The hollow men."* Retrieved from https://msu.edu/~jungahre/transmedia/the-hollow-men.html

48 Sauter, G. 221.

Christian eschatology be articulated reminiscent of the classic example of Thomas Aquinas' efforts to interpret creation in the face of the best of the Aristotelian science of his day? It would have to be a comprehensive cosmic eschatology. Its preoccupations would not center on the world of the future, but on the world as a whole, and on an ongoing redemptive relation to God who gathers up the past, present, and future. But we still have yet to come up with an eschatology (I think) which explains what the world is like on its own, the Christian response of what the world is like independently of the salvific relation the world enjoys with God. Is this even possible? (I think no.)

Science, likewise, cannot show us a quark. They say, well, the evidence shows it must be so. How scientific! I believe, in the quantum sense, Science takes more on faith than does theology. Now, the brain scientists tell us one half the human brain is "wired" for religious experience. (Note the word 'experience.') Some have even called this 'neurotheology'. It may tell us some new information about the circuits of the brain, but about God it tells us nothing. Barth taught us theology is first and foremost about God. Feeling ecstatic is an emotion. Certain brain areas may 'light up' when emotional stimulus is occurring, but scientists have not discovered the seeds of religion thereby. Religion involves a whole range of acts and insights which acknowledge a transcendent order. This does not at all require a transcendent experience. In fact, few believers experience what Christian theology would call a mystical union with God. Neurotheologians confuse spirituality with religion.

What religion is about is doing the will of God. I suppose if we gain what could be termed as peak experiences, it is an occasion for thanksgiving, but it is not necessarily a religious moment. It could be sex (again thanksgiving is called for). A mutual meltdown of ecstatic sex is certainly a peak experience. These neurotheologians say evolution has programmed the brain to find pleasure in escaping the confines of the self. Meditation does certainly help us to escape the stresses and selfishness of our self-interests. To "be still and know that I am God"[49] is an important part of spiritual disciplines from many religious traditions whether the brain lights up or not. We rewire our brain to transcend just

49 Psalm 46:10

pleasure centers and to then focus on ethical imperatives. If we are successful, we can be certain a gift of grace was given from outside the brain, which enabled us to escape the realm of self long enough to get to that place! To assume that the brain alone is the source of all our experiences would be reductionist. We have the will, the external environment, the very beauty of holiness to consider. If we are to love our neighbor as ourselves, then quite a bit of self-transcendence is going to happen. Maybe we won't be happy about it, but after a while we will experience joy.

Stanley Hauerwas believes the mystery of God is found in the trivialities of everyday life. (Yes, I add, and also in the cosmos.) He addresses almost no words to science that I have found. His emphasis on language is partly responsible. Part of the Wittgensteinian legacy would posit that the language of science and the language of religion are totally incommensurable. We must somehow subject theological claims to correction and revision in terms of what we have learned from the social and physical sciences. The problem here is, if theology represents a very different way of knowing, it can only result in making Christianity unintelligible in a world in which fewer and fewer people are formed by the Christian language. How can we reach out to each other if we don't understand each other at the level of language? Recently, I was surprised to read about the number of top scientists who were devoutly faithful in their churches. Scientific language is mathematical to a large degree. Therefore, this language must be learned. Those who don't learn it must remain on the outside. Likewise, if we are formed in the language of faith, the narratives of the community give shape to the way in which we interpret life in the world, and the way we understand the world itself. The church must escape tribalism somehow. We cannot be isolated from the rest of the world.

Think of religion on the modern university campus. If the Duke campus were being put together today, would an enormous neo-Gothic Chapel dominate the landscape of the school? Usually the religious stuff is off to the side or even off-campus. But Christians are never just members of a church but very much live in the world. Hauerwas writes,

"What Wittgenstein has taught me, however, is that if we attend to the diversity of our language we learn to appreciate what a marvelously diverse world we inhabit and how complex claims about the way the world is will inevitably be."[50]

Hauerwas believes if we are to adequately see the truth of Christian convictions we must be transformed. Thus, sanctification is central for assessing the epistemological status of Christian convictions. Judging the truthfulness of religious convictions cannot be separated from the truthfulness of the persons who make those claims. Christianity is not one world view among others. Our faith must truth itself. We turn a noun into a verb to establish what the great moral philosopher Steven Colbert calls 'truth-i-ness.' The problem here is that one might think we are left with 'try it, you might like it!' Can the content of the convictions of our faith stand the challenge scientifically, metaphysically, or morally? We must answer from the standpoint of what it means to live eschatologically. The subject of transformation for Christians is not the isolated individual, but a community in a historical setting. We know what can be known only through witness. Our worship requires us to be open to continual reality checks. Christians are not required to face the stance or choice of complete involvement with the world or complete withdrawal from the world. We can be *in* but not *of* the world.

Hauerwas makes a great point: "Unless the church and Christians are trained first to understand their community's language they will lack resources to notice times when the language of the state is not their own!"[51] We may hear a view of the state as a general well-being and yet the reality may be a narrow range of economic and political ideologies. There are so many examples of this in our times that the ability to know who we are is crucial. I think of the many Christians quite willing to attend the various political tea-parties of today. I cannot believe they have developed the habits of 'truthiness' from being formed in the language of Christian community or for that matter why anyone who is not really rich would ever vote Republican.

---

50 Hauerwas, S. (1988). *Christian Existence Today: Essays on Church, World, and Living in Between.* Eugene, OR. Wipf and Stock. 10.

51 Ibid. 12.

Probably, the view Stanley H. proposes would be alien to all forms of secular political institutions. Just his opposition to violence would separate him from the state; yet he maintains strongly that pacifism demands strenuous political engagement. Christians must stand ready to be citizens. We must prioritize our participation certainly. Selective service is called for from our experience of having been formed in the church. Which brings us to Jesus.

Christian ethics has tended to make "Christology" rather than Jesus its starting point. Many would also claim there is no way to know the 'historical Jesus'. Yet I think it is clear enough to be able to find Jesus as he is portrayed in the documents of the New Testament. His emphasis was on the establishment of the Kingdom of God. Jesus through his teachings, healings, and miracles tried to indicate the nature and immediacy of God's kingdom. The synoptic gospels present a Jesus who does not draw attention to himself but to the Kingdom the early Christians felt had been made present and yet was still to come. (The fourth gospel has a different slant.)

So, following the way of God's kingdom means following the teachings of Jesus and thus learning to be his disciples. We are called to be like God: perfect as God is perfect (Matt. 5:48)! Christian ethics means we attend to the life of a particular individual who was also a member of the Trinity. We can only learn perfection from him. We are called on to be *like* Jesus, not to *be* Jesus. To be like Jesus requires that I become a part of a community which practices virtues, not that I try to copy his life point by point. Jesus was not one who taught a whole new thing. Israel already knew what it meant to walk in the way of the Lord. Israel is Israel. She remembers the way of the Lord, for by that remembering, she in fact imitates God. In Jesus' life, we see God's way with Israel.

Now, the above is the realm of Sanctification. There is no way to speak of it other than as a God-granted movement of grace (after Prevenient and Justifying). It is where I am now in my journey (I hope). Or, at least, if I'm ever to get there it must be now. (I'm glad to be Wesleyan here.) There are certain times and actions which give hope. It is also what I mean by sainthood. If I'm going on to perfection, can I claim it at this late stage of life? Well, yes! Let's say the call goes all the way back to childhood. I remember a missionary from the Belgian Congo. I was hooked. I would do that too when I was older and learned whatever language they speak. Well, I didn't go there, yet even in high school there were signs. There were prayers. Even though I was marginalized there were clear signs. It was to be in college that I answered the call. I said yes, even though I had no clue. Let's call this God's *prevenient* work. Then came seminary (God still going on before—I was still clueless). I made muddles (Murdoch), wrong choices, and yet I've always maintained I was still following the call. Addiction blocks all the movements of grace! I had a half career in church music. If God gave some good during all that, it was because *good* is what God does. I cannot declare it a waste: marriages, fatherhood, musical achievements, ministries, relationships, misadventure, sin and, what else? Well, I kept the sense of the call in mind. What happened, at last, was God's final big prevenient push. I was done with running my life by frantic willpower. Then came the door of *justification*. I was able to get off the porch and to go into the rooms of AA to undergo the process of early sobriety. It's all process! It is God doing what I had never been able to do under my own power. Glory Halleluiah. Holiness, well, yes Mr. Wesley. A whole second career that lasts and lasts. Movements of grace which are part and parcel of what we call *sanctification*. It goes on and on. It is a journey. I make this journey with my partner and the love of my life. We make journeys within the journey.

How much fun can you have? Does it get any better than this? Well, we don't know. We have not yet arrived. Thank you, Jesus!

The last few pages show my life in depth. I'm not bipolar, but I can go from high to low in an instant. *Steadiness* is what I long for. Perfection and Sanctification are categories most folks I know would flee from. I have written of them carefully in these Journals as they reflect not only 12 Step work but my Wesleyan heritage and the huge range of influences from my study and readings, my relationships, and the various gifts of grace God has given in the journey. I read back through these journals from time to time with great satisfaction. God has always blessed me and at this stage of my life I feel like the end of the James Wright poem, "A Blessing" (page 143 in Complete Poems *Above the River*). Life is good and God is Good.

Christian Life

If the world is under the lordship of Jesus Christ, and I believe it is, then the fundamental character of our life is that of a gift. As we learn to accept the gift, we realize we are not alone. We are being formed into a community. The Christian life is made up of those attempts to live into a narrative. This narrative is determinative. As we "live into" this story, our characters are formed in such a way that this history becomes our own. The fellowship formed by AA operates in the same way. It is as if we are chosen by a higher power to be 'in' AA (irony). We once were lost, but now are found. We are then placed in 'these rooms' where we learn a history and practice a heritage. The stories are again determinative. We share the way it once was, what happened, and the way it is now. We continue with spiritual mentors called sponsors. We have a big book like the *really* Big Book (the Bible), which is again filled with stories. We proceed a day at a time.

Back to Hauerwas, who wrote:

> I remain convinced that nothing is quite as uncontrolled or radically unpredictable as Christian orthodoxy. To learn to see our lives (as well as the cosmos) as created; to learn that out of all the nations God chose the Jews; to learn that our destiny lies in the crucified and resurrected Jesus; all of that is to learn to see the world charged with God's grandeur. Surely a theology that has at its center a God of such wildness cannot be enclosed.[52]

He goes on to say, 'be not afraid.' The only fear then comes from our unfaithfulness to God.

---

52 Hauerwas, S. (2018). *Wilderness Wanderings: Probing Twentieth-century Theology and Philosophy*. Routledge. 5.

Then he posits one of his most characteristic themes; he does not think there is, in principle, any way to ensure the Gospel can be made intelligible to someone who is not a Christian. Well then, what to do in our outreach mission? It's easy for him to say such a contrary thing, but we in the church have to keep signing up new members so as to subscribe the budget and pay the bills. Well, he does allow that Christians can have still a lot to say to each other as well as to the culture. *And* if the church would act as if it were the church, God always provides what is needed.

Hauerwas says the tradition of Protestant liberalism has given the church (the one I know) a misguided sense that we actually know where we are. The church I know has sought to represent the faith in a manner which will appear both intellectually respectable and politically responsible. The result is an accommodated church that "fits in" with the culture. If the church is then reduced to "beliefs," then God is removed from a continuing role in history. If history names a world which is not God's creation, there are inevitable difficulties. Hauerwas asks, "How can hope be sustained in a world that is not created?"[53] (He uses Niebuhr as a case in point.) The doctrine of creation only makes Christian sense as part of the doctrine of the Trinity. Stanley H. says the doctrine of the Trinity is necessary, if we are to render the world intelligible both as we find it and as we hope it will be. This claim is orthodox Christianity, but only if it is worked out in the Christian community, only if the church is seeking to be the church.

The problem with liberals is they do not recognize the New Testament "powers," but in their engagement with the culture fall under the influence of the very powers they would rid the culture of. In becoming accommodated with the liberal culture, the liberal Protestant church too easily forgets liberal culture is unintelligible without the God we Christians worship. (And, once again, I'm not using 'liberal' in the left/right sense we have in the popular culture.) In this reduced sense we see how the culture handles thought, especially in the early 21st century. Perhaps from the bicameral form of government we practice, we have only two sides to pick from. Left or Right (both are wrong!). Perhaps we could go back to the early twentieth century and remember the battle between the

53 Ibid. 7.

fundamentalists and the liberals of that day, but we are still left with only two ways to think. Surely, we realize the tremendous diversity of our day. There simply are more than two choices. My voting decisions are always on one side of our current choices, but this doesn't mean I'm happy about the situation. Nor does it mean, *by extension*, that my theology be also liberal! I have learned from Hauerwas and others, the way forward is to be found in restating the whole enterprise.

If I had church to do over again, it would surely be different knowing what I know now. But the main thing would still be the main thing. *Jesus Christ is Lord.* The good news is that there is no salvation without the church. (This assumes the church is the church.) This claim sounds arrogant and imperialistic, especially as we consider the Constantian history of the church. But if we are quite beyond this legacy, we can consider the church as it is today, a struggling minority, so unsure of its current position. We follow Jesus as we worship the Trinity. We are no longer in control, and this is the very essence of the good news. Gerhard Sauter has written, "the freedom of the church is not where it has possibilities, but only where the Gospel really and in its power makes room for itself on earth, even and precisely when such possibilities are offered to it."[54]

Wittgenstein wrote in *Tractatus*: "Death is not an event in life. We do not live to experience death. If we take eternity to mean not infinite temporal duration but timelessness, then eternal life belongs to those who live in the present. Our life has no end in the way in which our visual field has no limits."[55]

Well, whatever that means, I like it.

---

54 Hauerwas, S. (2018). *Wilderness Wanderings: Probing Twentieth-century Theology and Philosophy.* Routledge. 32.

55 Wittgenstein, L. (2010). *Tractatus Logico-Philosophicus.* Retrieved from Project Gutenberg. https://www.gutenberg.org/files/5740/5740-pdf.pdf . (Original work published 1924).

Christians must embrace the doctrine of creation *ex nihilo,* because it then impacts what we mean by our ontological and moral commitments. We call on Aquinas. Aquinas says an important thing. Not all who hear the word *God* understand it to the point to that which nothing greater can be thought. The word exists in the intellect, and some have thought themselves capable of something greater or some have thought God does not exist. Aquinas goes on to say that, although it is clear *truth* in general exists, the existence of a First Truth is not self-evident to us. Aquinas objects to the ontological argument, not because existence cannot be a predicate (Kant), but rather because the intellect cannot have *a priori* knowledge of God's nature. Any Being whose essence is existence cannot be known through the idea of such a being, but rather through arguments from its effects. Therefore, if God's existence is to be "proved," it must be through an examination of God's effects (Phil. 101). So, Aquinas' "proofs" (5 ways) are rightly understood against the background of the doctrine of creation ex nihilo. This Creation is the Christian and Jewish view that the existence of all that is, is the result of the free decision of God. This creation is fulfilling no natural need. God did not "need" to create and gains nothing from the act of creating. The will of God can only be investigated through those things God must will of necessity, but what God wills about creatures is not among these. That the world began to exist is therefore an object of faith and not a demonstration of science.

Ex nihilo is a strictly theological predication of God. It secures God's transcendence over against the world. It is God's graceful gift, a contingent and finite gift of God who was not in need of the world. Creation then is an overflow of God's abundant love as reflected in the inner life of the triune God. The contingent is created. Some see the purposelessness in the sheer existence of the contingent (Murdoch). The task is to see the contingent as gift whose purpose is to praise the creator.

Christian History, and a Way Forward

History needs to be done over again. What if I were given the task to teach "Basic Christian History" in today's Theological Seminary. What would one do? First, write a textbook. Then what? Well, begin at the very beginning, of course. Then after establishing the history of the Jews and Jesus' Lordship, I would begin with the Big Bang. What was God thinking as "He" flicked his finger and started from scratch? Those who begin with scripture start in the middle and think it's the beginning. From Hauerwas:

> Everything we have to say about ourselves, our history, the universe, is distorted if what we profess does not reflect the truth that God has created ex nihilo. The great heresy of modernity is the assumption that human presence in the world is sufficient to summon out of chaos and emptiness order and beauty.[56]

God created and called it good. It was a quite decisive act. God also redeemed, and this was also quite the definitive act. The church points to the resurrection as the restoration of God's good order in creation. We who would follow are indeed set free to have joy. The Gospel is good news, which gives us the ability to look back to creation and forward to consummation. As we seek to escape the confines of modern theories of history, and especially the Constantinian history of the church, neither do we seek to return to some golden age of the good old days. We seek a new orientation, which is called for by the church as it finds itself in the current situation. The church in any age has a mission. The church *is* a mission and the same is true of politics (the church is a politic). The church will also be enculturated (the church has always been so enculturated). There

56 Hauerwas, S. (2018). *Wilderness Wanderings: Probing Twentieth-century Theology and Philosophy*. Routledge. 201.

is a theme for citing the history of the Christian church right there. Now the church and state coexist. The church must address and instruct the state if the state is to be humble. *When the church failed to preach salvation history, but had some liberal open-ended concept of historical development, the Christians no longer had any idea what the state should look like; but even more, they undermined the intelligibility of the doctrine of the Trinity.* As an enculturated institution, the church may have to make the best of whatever political context it finds itself in, but making the best certainly with boldness and clarity.

We then read Scripture forward. If we have lost Christendom, perhaps we will have to learn, with God's never-failing grace, to preach in Babylon. What we preach is the Reign of God. This *kingdom* among the people of Israel and in the person of Jesus is quite unlike the secular rule of the nations. The difference is not only the manner or mode of this rule but also, and especially, in the particularity and uniqueness of its subject and relations. Jesus, the anointed one is, after all, both servant and messiah, victim and priest, sufferer and liberator, afflicted and physician. Theology is a manifold witness. The Gospel is the unified object upon which it consecrates its witness. Theology needs more than political images; it needs a full political conceptuality. And politics needs a theological conceptuality. Both need focus on the one history which finds its goal in Christ, "the desire of the nations." Christians need to be assured God's rule will prevail. The chief difficulty for Christians in America is that many of the religious right have no concept of such a politics of the Gospel. They don't see themselves as "resident aliens," but have embedded themselves in the secular culture in such a way that idolatry can be the only possible outcome. What must be shown to them is that they too, even in America, continue to live in exile. American Christians also need to hear that Yahweh's final restoration of his covenant people is assured! But until America quits assuming the rule of God is not always through them, or even predominantly through them, they will flounder in an idolatrous system of civil religion which parades under the guise of the Christian faith.

We need missionaries. Christians today, like the Jews of the Exile and the Diaspora, are in a situation where the temptation to cave in to the reigning forces of the day (bombing the hell out of brown people, money, civil religion, the myth of the Right, football, etc.), to fit in and be accepted by the power of those with the big bucks, is for many virtually overwhelming. We do not take seriously the witness of the Hebrew prophets. We do not take seriously the words of this young and fearless prophet of ancient Galilee. We do not take at all seriously the legacy we have inherited from the rampant genocides of the twentieth century. We do not take seriously the mentality we have inherited as post-Holocaust citizens, the magnitude and character of the evil unleashed in the eruption of primordial chaos, which continues to threaten the very structures of creation.[57] And we do not take seriously the role we play as Christian citizens of the world's only remaining super-power, the role of witness, of a genuine stewardship, of how to live on this tiny speck of dust called planet Earth. And so, in retrospect, considering what science says about the end of the universe, and what one can clearly see in the current political climate and the absence of a vigorous and faithful witness from the church, from where can hope be found?

Well, from where it always springs forth. I would suggest a good start with the great hymnbook of the Bible, the Psalms. If one desires great lament or if one is greatly pissed at one's enemies, this is a good place to vent and lament, but if one sticks with the task, the whole soggy mess will become lifted to the sunlight of the spirit. A real hope will emerge as the glory of creation is celebrated. Singing the Psalms would be the best. The music helps the word sink in; our whole body can be an instrument through which the gifts of the Spirit can be given. The prophets can be next. They are timeless, as well as being those who were chosen to carry the word of God to the nations. By speaking to a chosen and particular people at a certain time, through their faithfulness, they manage to translate God's truth to all times and to all people. The power of this prophesy has not only never been surpassed; it has rarely been tried. Then, as people come together because they have been called apart, the Epistles speak to the challenge of what and how to do. Complete operating

57 The rabbis say that God needs to be forgiven.

instructions are not included. The church is enculturated in every age, but there are words of how to keep the main thing the main thing on every page. As the church struggles to be the church in every age, the Gospels are then given as the message of what God would say through Jesus. We lack not for hope. We are given faith through the practice of God's word as we work it out in the church. God's spirit is promised and given in our experience. The problem is not, once more, that all this is not given attention in the 'modern' world. The problem is that all this has not really been tried. We have looked for answers in all the wrong places. We have followed other gods without even knowing what we were doing. We have tried to fix ourselves instead of the deep reliance upon God, which is called forth in the pages of the Scripture. We have failed to follow. We are to be in, 'but not of the world'. We are in it up to our necks. We are floundering in our own foolishness. 'O God, come to us and deliver us.'

And God will come to us if we truly turn to him. We have everything we need. We have only to begin.

What will be next?

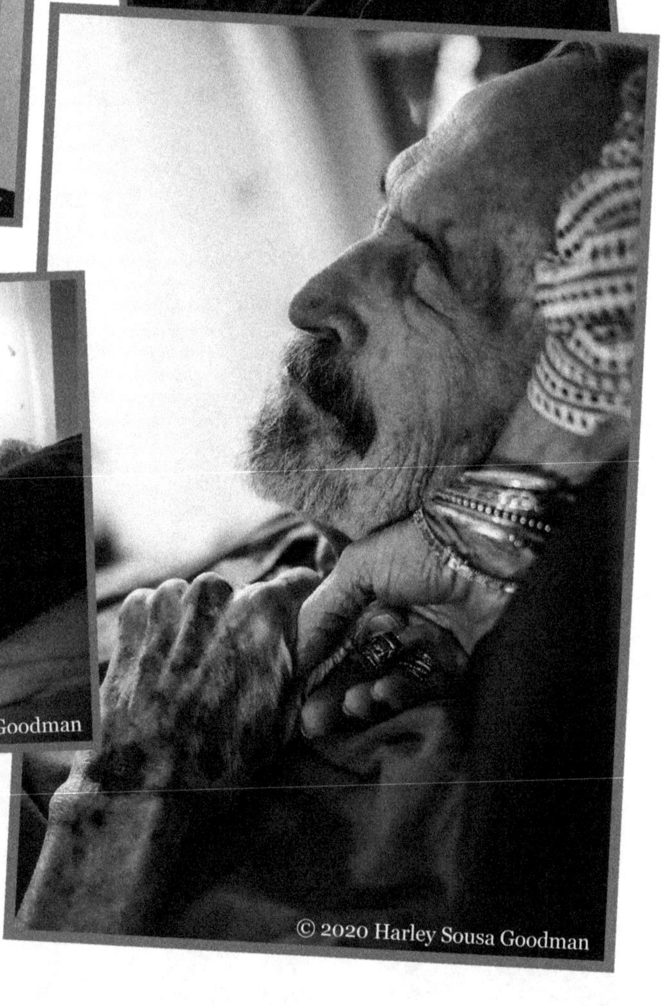

Journals Volume Four

Mouse Turds

So much of life is just stumbling over mouse turds. We go from one moment to the next with small 'good orderly directions' (god). Why proceed that way anyway? Boring! To set our agendas and fill up our calendars willfully each day "seems" more satisfying, as if we know where we are going. Yet we *can* decide where to go... Wendell Berry says it well: "to keep oneself fully alive in the Creation, to keep the Creation fully alive in oneself, to see the Creation anew, to welcome one's part in it anew."[1]

This way we participate in the particulars. We get to partner up with the Creator. Now, God has not required this by rule. But if one seeks a life with God, this is the way to proceed.

If one is too caught up in cursing mouse turds or blaming them for one's lack of forward progress, or if one simply expects the stumbling to be a part of the Design, then the point can be missed. God the Creator doesn't care, but if you want to know God, you must take certain steps. Always keep in mind, however, these steps work on you, not on Him.

God puts in a personal appearance only rarely. Read the Scriptures from beginning to end and count the times. In fact, read the start and finish of the Bible and see it's all the same story, from when it says, 'when God began to create,' until finally the New Jerusalem is let down from the creative hand of the same God. It's all the same. I want to be a part of that creation, that story. I am a part of it, after all.

Jesus called his disciples not from their ordinary lives; he called them out from their belief that life was ordinary. He was the very son of the very God; yet all he had to work with was the ordinary. It could be that the ordinary is sufficient. It could be the more ordinary particulars are the places wherein poetry may be found. Certainly poetry trumps prose.

---

1 Berry, W. (2010) "Healing.". *What are People For?: Essays*. Berkeley. Counterpoint. 9.

Anyway, this stuff I don't understand: *science* has a language I don't understand (mathematics). But why not look at what I still don't understand—metaphysics, philosophy, theology, ethics—yet do have some language for?

Poetry is the language.

Panties

Panties are a relatively recent invention. Drawers of any kind are believed to have been unknown before the sixteenth century. If one lacked drawers, one would have no need of a drawer into which to place them.

Naturally, the first mention of panties in history came from a sermon. The Cardinal-Archbishop of Milan preached that God Almighty intended the bottom area of women should be kept bare in remembrance of Mother Eve's weakness. This insight was first preached to Italians. During my marriages, my practice was that whenever I encountered a stray pair of used panties, I would wear them on my head like a hairnet. I liked the effect. I persisted in the practice even after the day—not remembering I was thus adorned—I answered the parsonage door to find the chair of the finance committee standing there. Of a certainty, most pastors would not have done a thing such as that, nor would there have been three separate styles of panties possible for presentation. I like to think of such things.

I have been blessed.

Soul

Something beyond life lives within life and calls the soul. Well, first, what is the soul? But wait: everyone has one, and most everyone has enough of an idea of what an ensouled life is, so we may continue. As for the beyond and within, I'm still not picky. I have no trouble with "the indwelling of the Holy Spirit". She comes riding upon the wind, from outside us, and lights the pilot light within. If she doesn't come, we remain dark and cold. If we are not open and listening, we can remain "lost in myself' and miss the voice. One cannot speak of all this without using metaphors and various images. That's how we know we are in the realm of the metaphysical language, which must extend itself into poetry. No matter what, we damage ourselves. We always do, and so some repair of the soul is before us. The premise of this: we can do no good daily work if our spirits are not aiming at the invisible, unless we reach deep and far. We need anchor for our souls.

All of this is especially true as we get older. We long for otherworldly things as we approach the 'other worlds'. In "Sailing to Byzantium" Yeats expresses it: "An aged man is but a paltry thing / A tattered coat upon a stick,"[2] unless he transcends the earthly mortal realm by transforming eternal yearnings. The beyond seems to remain beyond. We give in to the journey itself. We remain unsatisfied; yet on the way, in growing orbits.

"The world is too much with us."

Wordsworth[3]

dry-cleaned deacons and anusless angels, and even Jesus farted.

---

2 Yeats, W.B. (1994). "Sailing to Byzantium." *The Collected Poems of W.B. Yeats*. Hertfordshire. Wordsworth Editions Ltd. 163.

3 Wordsworth, W. (1807). "The World is Too Much With Us." Via poets.org

Obscurity of Writing

As hard as I work at this writing, I might as well in all seriousness dedicate these pages to obscurity. Oblivion is the writer's greatest fear, and there is a lot of evidence to support this fear. It is like death. It comes rather relentlessly. One would like to be remembered for something. I had half a century of work which gave me a sense of being a part of something big and ongoing. If one serves the church and the kingdom, time gets all its dimensions lifted up. We are a part of past, present, and future, if we are a child of the purposes of the kingdom of God. Even ego eases a bit. What if one can publish a book? It will mostly sit on a shelf somewhere, won't it? That's where most of my books live. Well, a few are lifted more than others, but we who are writers (and I really don't think of that as my primary diagnosis), we who write, write because, being who we are, we can do no other.

Think of Emily Dickinson. She was a recluse who eavesdropped on visitors from the top of the stairs. Now whose grave is visited daily? Venerated as few other virgins have ever been. Why? Because her words live, they breathe.

Think of Dylan Thomas, who could turn words into blood.

Politics

I live in a place where the sitting president[4] is excoriated and demonized as is, as I can recall, without precedence. Although no one admits the chief reason for this (because he is black), indications abound. Midway through his second term in office, he faces a nation wherein 25% of the populace thinks his presidency is illegal because they maintain he was not born here. 17% think he is a practicing Muslim. And 10% believe he is the Antichrist! We are rather deeply divided.

American politics has taken an extreme turn; the result is that the function of government has ground to a halt. Bipartisanship and compromise have ceased. Previously, such a thing as a government shutdown would have been unthinkable, but now it describes that which sporadically occurs.

Think of FDR's four terms. His last election victory, he had 98% of the electoral vote. Think of the lasting legislation legacy. Or, how about LBJ's legacy—not only the 1964 Civil Rights Act, but Medicaid and Medicare, protecting the environment, supporting the arts, rural development, *and* urban renewal. Unthinkable in today's world.

And—here's the real deal. In 1964, the top income tax rate for the wealthiest Americans was almost 90%! The income disparity between the wealthy and poor Americans was among the smallest on record, and most folks trusted the government most of the time. Today the highest income tax rate is just under 40% (those thus taxed never cease their bitching and moaning) and barely 20% of Americans say they trust the government.

4 Obama

Marilynne Robinson

Finished the third of the trilogy by Marilynne Robinson last night. The books of Gilead (*Gilead, Home,* and *Lila*) are strong, and make me cry alone in my bed as I read them. Her Calvinism shines through and reminds me of that part of Calvin which still infects some of my deep impulses, having been exposed to it from birth to high school. Then I went to the Wesleyans, who didn't know that's what they even were, but their music was better.

I'm told Marilynne can rip you to pieces if you try disparaging old Calvin in front of her, but that's her story and burden to bear. The point is, she is among the best of writers today. Gilead is a living place; those two old men ministers who sit on porches and argue theology and enjoy friendship will forever be a part of my life. Robinson writes of Iowa, of a town, Gilead, where there is a home for all of us. Her characters are those we care deeply about. But mostly, they are just getting by. Maybe that's what all of us are about. She writes of daily bread, her people eat when they are hungry, or when (Lila) they can find food. Home is her basic theme, and family and love.

I'm not bipolar, but I can go from being Master of the Universe to the scum that grows on the bottom of whale shit at the speed of light. This was more characteristic of my earlier life when I was trying to get the "mix" just right, when I *was* perhaps crazy or at least did crazy. I have watched enough Dr. Phil to know one *can* get better. I have gotten better. Nowadays, if I were interviewed by a Court-mandated shrink, I would not be found crazy at all. Thank you, Jesus.

Sex

Now, about sex! (Thank you, Jesus.) There are those who have a hard time with the notion that God could have created the cunt. Count me not of that fold. We spend much pleasure rooting around between the piss and the shit. You may ask, why must you be so scatological? I reply, I'm not the one who formed the man to explore; I did not think up the placement of parts either. I simply accept all of this as a gift of God's grace. You say, well, this is no way for a retired UMC minister to talk. I reply with my curious evangelistic self and say, "fuck you very much," itself bestowing a blessing, right?

Do you remember the old "you are what you eat"? I'm not an asparagus; yet I ate them last night. In these days we try to say, not 'tell me what you eat, and I will tell you who you are'... we say, 'tell me who you fuck and I will tell you who you are'. Bullshit. Male or female, hormones are shared and are found in both sexes. If you know how you "love," do you then know who you are?

I like sex in the English classics (18th and 19th century). Sex was as strong as always. One simply did not dwell on it in the drawing room. We could conjecture, did Jane Eyre ever get an orgasm? How has the concept of "I" changed in the last two centuries? Well, as usual there is the bad and the good. I don't know how much sex goes on in Charles Taylor's "The Sources of the Self" because I just can't get into the damn thing. I keep trying. If you want to get scared, read Dr. Tissot on masturbation and know he was one of *the* doctors of his day! Oh well. It is said that after Augustine, we experience sex in the head. Did he mean that in an 'after the fall' sense? Or was it those who interpret things thataway? The answer is yes. We come to the modern age of anxiety; we love to heap drama on sex till it is mostly covered over. Actually, sex is just not that important, or is it? Again, the answer is yes. It is one of those on the one hand, but on the other hand things. Most guys just use one hand. They may say they need both hands, but few do. It is also true that boys are much prouder of their little things than are girls. That's why boys name their dicks. They don't want a stranger making most of their decisions.

Sex is supposed to be just among those legally married, man and wife, mostly for the stellar purpose of continuing the race. That's sort of what I was taught. Then think of this: the female is capable of making an occasional egg. A lunar, monthly target of opportunity. The male is capable of firing at that target at least several times a day, each outburst containing millions of little swimmers, only one reaching the golden egg. It's like an oak tree and its acorns: only one is needed to produce a giant tree; the rest is squirrel food and for children to throw at each other. So from the Creator's point of view, there is a ridiculous extravagance built into nature. This is not just among mammals and trees. Think of fishes and the plethora of eggs sprayed about. They don't all turn into other fish.

The Genesis story is always the place to start. Our first parents and their fruitful garden. Naked they came, and it was all good. Goodness was built into things from the get-go. They had everything needful. We cannot know everything that was in the Creator's mind. The committee who wrote Genesis gave us perhaps all we need to know. I don't really know.

Genesis is a great favorite for me, always has been. It was not just Adam and Eve; think of Abraham and Sarah, the promises, the millions of little swimmers released in search of the egg of promise. Diversity came quickly. There were all kinds of people, thinking all sorts of stuff about sex. God kept trying to get things as He wanted them to be. He would erase some of it and start over again. Some got drowned, some burnt up. The rabbis speak of God needing forgiveness for some of his blundering. But somehow through it all, some sense of 'your mama and them' came to us. We belonged together. It was a place where the women were strong and the men were good looking. *There became a home in Gilead.* All was well, and then came marriage.

Then there was the rest of the story up through the New Testament. But it's too early for Jesus yet. Let's look at the children preparing for him. Boy meets Girl. They are drawn to each other. Why? Is it a matter of God's will, or do they simply like the way the other smells? There is always the marital bed. Now they lay them down to sleep, but first they must diddle one another. Let me count the ways.

God intended all this for good, we say. Then why is there such eternal confusion, longing, unfilled desire, violence, and 'using' going on? Well, there is also the loving coming together, the deep satisfaction which stems from the duly concreated marriage relationship.

In each age, according to my cogitations, the number of really good relationships is rare. Quite rare. Do we not say, if you are able to have one true friend, you are blessed? (I am thus blessed.) Then, how many really great marriages can you count? Your own count of all those you know.

We were at church last night. Old Buddy taught. Big crowd, the children were there as well. Since All Hallows Eve is Friday, the children had their costumes on, and they paraded around for our edification. It was wonderful. The meal was great: pork chops and macaroni and cheese. The question is, how many people went home (or elsewhere) and had sex? Why do you even ask?

Sex is a part of our created self. Most of us have some experience with it. I think of John Updike. He wrote much about it. I love the ways he lifts it up and dwells in it. He can even masterfully speak of the act itself. Why do we emphasize that which takes three minutes to complete with such fascination and fixation? The average male goes through the day and considers sex. How much of the day do we thus dwell? Well, I have often said it's good to have achieved the biblical promise of three-score and ten, and my libido has cut me some slack. I can think of something besides sex for, oh, I don't know, maybe thirty minutes or so. I have virtually no idea what women think about. They remain a mystery. It's hard to get a girl to talk with you about it, and if you are able to converse thusly, after a minute or two you want into her britches. What's up with this? Well, it is enough for me to admit I am a horny old goat. I have no idea if I am normal in that state. Probably so, but I am where I have been placed in life. It's just fun to write about all this.

Which brings us to love and marriage in New Testament times. ("It's better to marry than to burn in hell."[5]) Thank you, Paul; that helps a lot. The Corinthians must have been a randy lot. The great apostle must have known the race would somehow advance itself in the way it always had: man on top, get it over with quick. In fact, in later years the missionaries gave a name to that position.

But Paul expected the end to be near. The end which is expected from God, that end. The end had no need for marriage, so we had to make do when the end did not come. We have been making do ever since. Making babies too, making love, eros in search of agape. Is agape sex a possibility? I should like to think so.

What would Jesus do? What did he do? We have no record. Conjecture about Mary Magdalene is not helpful. That was a matter for celibate Popes to cogitate over. It's not in the Bible. This brings me to homosexuality. It *is* in the Bible, in just a few verses, but I believe what my personal Lord and Savior Jesus Christ thought and said about it. Look it up... Nothing, nada, enough said for now. I'm tired of sex. I'll move on.

A funny cartoon teacher sitting on a desk in Psych 101. He says: "If your family tree falls in a forest and no one hears it, are you still dysfunctional?"

What does an agnostic, dyslexic insomniac do... lie awake at night wondering, "Is there a dog?"

5 1 Cor. 7:9

Spirituality

I was reminded of my brief sojourn at the View. How do you begin to do 'spiritual' if you are the Spiritual Director at Ridge View Institute?

Well, I started with them. I asked them what, to you, is spiritual? They were all crazoids... Drunks and druggies, bi-polar, depressed, sex addicts, etc. I was there because the industry has long known, if you want to get them better, there *must* be a strong spiritual component involved in their recovery. So, we started slow.

What does the dictionary say? They answered as one would expect, that vague, woo-woo, crystal seeking, new age bullshit one picks up from living in America. It's like dragging a piece of spiritual Velcro across the culture to see what sticks.

So I tried to narrow it down a bit and remember the spiritual traditions of AA. The 'view' hosted many 12 Step gatherings, so I assumed we could proceed on the basis of the approach the leaders of the program strongly enforce. One is perfectly free to pick the God of your understanding. We say, if that doorknob over there is your god, you are welcome; if the local group is the god of your understanding, you are also welcome. You see what I mean? There must not be any 'religious stuff' allowed. Outside issues, etc. nothing must violate the traditions of the program of AA, and I agree completely!

So, I asked them: what is spirit? What is soul? Then the big one: is it inside us? Like a pilot light that will fire the thing up if we can gather about the campfire and sing the right song? But the song cannot be "Kumbaya" because it means, "come by here, Lord." It means there is something outside us which must come to us, which has the POWER to pull our heads out of our butts. There is always that big popping sound when this occurs, and we can sit around in meetings and call it spiritual.

That's just fine by me, but when you hear the 'pop,' it's not spiritual; it's religious! You are unable to do for yourself that which is needful. There must be something like what theology calls *revelation*. The only effective power comes to us from outside ourselves and delivers us from the captivity we had enforced upon ourselves.

Now gentle reader, you must remember, I was not working for AA. I was getting paid! I was a professional (don't try this at home folks, just do what *I* say). The problem was, I was in the realm of the medical, therapeutic, psychological structure of the dominant culture, and I was the lone religious guy. Feces were going to occur.

But, as long as I could refrain from being who I am, all was well. Well, what were the odds of that? Now, don't get me wrong: if your ass needs to be detoxed, get us to the View to check you in. People die from that! Good doctors are essential. Good therapists are key. You always hear from one who has managed to stay sober that one of the counselors has strongly said, "you only gotta change one thing: you gotta change everything!" What that really means is when you graduate from the Ridge, you need to find a home group and a sponsor. Group process is key here. If you are seated in a circle, look to your right and your left, of the three of you, only one will make it. Two of you will crash and burn. Jail, institutionalization, death, whatever. You get scared straight; is that it? No, the fact is, if you want to recover, you leave your enormous ego in the parking lot and sit in AA, day after day. Look for the winners (someone of your same sex who has what you want), ask them to sponsor you, work the steps, and do what they do. *If* all that takes place—and the chances it will are quite small—then you might be the "saved" one of the three. Now, it's important to note that the crowd who came to my lecture days and our 'Spiritual' Sunday afternoon time was composed of all sorts of folks. Some had already sort of 'got it.' Some were on their second or third or another attempt to get it. Some were really messed up junkies who had already lost more brain cells than they could afford. Some were rich neurotics who were on a sort of therapeutic vacation because their families simply wanted them out of the house for a while; some were young people, spoiled brats whose parents could afford to send them to the Ridge for a while because they didn't know what else to do with them.

I was hired to *do* spiritual, whatever that could mean. I was reminded of what it must be like to lead church if you are a Unitarian Universalist. It means all are allowed, no matter what. There is a clear tradition going back to some good New England intellectual roots. You can do artsy-fartsy, good music, fire and water kinds of things, but *do not* mention God; some might be offended. And whatever else you do, never mention that Jesus guy! (It must be hard at Christmas and Easter.)

But we gathered on Sunday afternoon when people should have been taking a nap or watching football and we *did* spiritual. Music and some poetry helped. Some carefully guided meditation, and then I would launch into a talk, flirted with some rhetorical elements which could be thought sermonic, then offered it up to the 'spirit of the universe' and went home exhausted. You must also remember I hadn't read Hauerwas yet, at least not deeply.

It was all in all a good experience for me. I, of course, got fired. They said, you're too religious; there have been complaints. Oh well.

Now I know better. I have written so much about where I am coming from in these volumes, we won't go into all that again. Do as I do and skim back through all of this. That is only surface-scratching. We've only just begun.

I don't make much witness. Too tired. I am now what I fussed about from my various pulpits. All know I'm a worn-out old preacher, but none (few) come to me for advice. I go downtown to St. John UMC to engage in Christian community. We have mission, worship, and music there. It is in a certain building. The facility is beautiful, historical, and on the national register of such things which go back a couple of centuries. Significant things have taken place from our church since it began. They worry about the future. They should!

Timor mortis conturbat me. (the fear of death scares me shitless)

I sit here at 8:48am at my desk, looking out on a cold, rainy day. U-tube has Berlioz Symphonie Fantastique (1830).

He sounds later.

Poetry

The 'Roaring Twenties'. America has been a cultural wasteland for poets. Yet there was that one decade...

1923 – Denise Levertov, James Dickey, Louis Simpson

1925 – Donald Justice

1926 – Robert Bly, Robert Creeley, Allen Ginsberg, James Merrill, Frank O'Hara

1927 – James Wright, John Ashberry, Galway Kinnell, W.S. Merwin

1928 – Anne Sexton, Donald Hall

1930 – Gary Snyder

1931 – Etheridge Knight

1932 – Sylvia Plath

Why them? Why then?

Well, we came out from under the thumb of Europe, and made some stuff regarded as American—jazz, etc.

There are so many other poets, afore and aft. I relish in words and their combinations. The meaning and the sounds.

I collect poems. They are everywhere.

Christology

Some more provoked by Hauerwas. (I did take a little time off from theology.)

Stan thinks the only reason one would be a Christian is because Christian claims are true. Moreover, the only reason to be churched is that *it* is the community which pledges to form its life by the truth. (*How we act because the word is true.*)

Any community and any polity is known and should be judged by the kind of people it develops. Okay, fair enough. Hauerwas contends that the truest politics, therefore, is concerned with the development of virtue. This is the familiar theme in these journals, as this line of reason has been traced from Aristotle and Aquinas up to today. Now, to look at church and state as we have them in today's culture. We are really caught up in freedom in our American experience. Freedom, however, can only come by being a part of a truthful polity capable of forming virtuous people. Also, this must not be an oppressive uniformity, but a truthful community, one wherein a variety of gifts and virtues can flourish. Hence, the church should not only be a community of character. The true church is always a community of characters. Does not God demonstrate a propensity for diversity everywhere one looks at creation? Why not also in the rich diversity of those who come to His church?

The way the church can become a useful agent for social change and justice in the world today is not by finding a new program to chart the way, but by simply being the church. 'We have a story to tell to the nations.' It is a narrative of the greatest value. It is a claim which is extravagantly presented in this story (Bible). It is a story that witnesses to the kind of social life made possible for those whose lives have been formed by the gospel.

To be a Christian implies substantive and profound convictions about the person and work of Jesus of Nazareth. Christians have always argued about how to understand the significance of Jesus, but the centrality of Jesus for Christian identity has never been questioned. Jesus Christ is lord indeed! The Gospel is the story of a man who had the authority to preach that the Kingdom of God *is* present. It was, it is, it is to be. It's not that Jesus had a social ethic; his story *is* a social ethic. The social and political validity of a community results from its being formed by a truthful story, a story which gives us the means to live without fear of one another. There can be no separation of Christology from ecclesiology, of Jesus from the church. The truthfulness of Jesus creates and is known by the kind of community his story should form.

Yoder has written:

> The Jesus of history *is* the Christ of faith. It is in hearing the revolutionary rabbi that we understand the existential freedom which is asked of the church. As we look closer at the Jesus whom Albert Schweitzer rediscovered, in all his eschatological realism, we find an utterly precise and practicable ethical instruction, practicable because in him the kingdom has actually come within reach. In him the sovereignty of YHWH has become human history.[6]

Wow! It's all there. Jesus' story already *is* a social ethic, and the church must exemplify that ethic. We also lift up that this man of Nazareth is also the savior of all people, but this proclamation can be claimed only by learning the particular form of discipleship required by this particular man. The *real* Jesus is only known through the kind of life he demanded in his disciples.

---

6 Yoder, J.H. (1994). The Politics of Jesus. Grand Rapids. Eerdmans. 103-4.

Grace

I desire *mirabile dictu*, to dream of the possibility and the dream coming true. It is always a miracle if that happens. It is also part of the story. The story, of necessity, is of a whole, from Creation to Apocalypse. The Bible tells that story. It is shaped by canon; they arranged it so it knows its end in the beginning and its beginning in the end. All of reality is embraced. As Dante says of what he sees at the end of *Paradiso*, all is "bound up with love together in one volume."[7] The good news is, while the Bible is a closed canon, it also reaches out whenever it is opened to the contemporary reality of the seeker or the believer. Scripture has the power to 'evangelize' human experience in any age by making each isolated moment or event meaningful in terms of its whole.

Flannery O'Connor has expressed the reality well in her non-fiction. She writes:

> For the last few centuries we have lived in a world which has been increasingly convinced that the reaches of reality end very close to the surface, that there is no ultimate divine source, that the things of the world do not pour forth from God... For nearly two centuries the popular spirit of each succeeding generation has tended more and more to the view that the mysteries of life will eventually fall before modern man... In twentieth-century fiction it increasingly happens that a meaningless, absurd world impinges upon the sacred consciousness of author or character; author and character seldom now go out to explore and penetrate a world in which the sacred is reflected.[8]

---

7 Alighieri, D. *Paradiso*. Canto 33.86. (H.W. Longfellow, Trans.). Via Project Gutenberg.

8 O'Connor, F. (1969). *Mystery and Manners: Occasional Prose.* (S. Fitzgerald and R. Fitzgerald, Ed.). New York. Farrar, Straus & Giroux. 157-58.

That which is needed is grace. If it is so clear that the prevailing notions of existence are so shallow and impoverished, then, "where shall the word be found, where will the word resound?"[9] The answer is clear to me; God's grace is as active as it has ever been. God's messengers are still called and they faithfully respond. It's just that some of the old institutions and churches of my experience seem so bereft of power and witness. And the whole modern construct has failed to serve the time. The situation is bleak for us, but this does not mean God is not active in other places than the dominant nations and cultures of my experience. This current crisis is most evident in the Western civilizations where Christianity had experienced a Constantinian hegemony for century after century.

How can you speak about the experience of grace without assuming a knowledge of any religious tradition? How can you speak engagingly about such an experience, in such a way, so as to open the listener to the sense of mystery and transcendence, which the spirit of the present age has seemingly inoculated us against? Well, many are trying. The best do it indirectly and without coercion.

Think of the parables of Jesus. They serve as a paradigm within our common legacy of scripture. We first must remember that before they became scripture, they were first spoken by Jesus to people who did not share his assumptions. The background of many of his stories presupposes sharp antagonism. Joachim Jeremias calls them weapons of warfare! But we are talking about a language of grace. And the invitation is to enter a narrative world where we must discover our own responses and make our own decisions. But it is clear that if not open warfare, many of these devices Jesus used cloaked as story, offered objectively as an event, were, in fact, traps. Those caught knew they were ensnared in the story's net. There they must examine themselves. Jesus was not the only one who did this in scripture; the classic Old Testament example is in 2nd Samuel. Nathan tells the story of the ewe lamb—an obvious example of the rich exploiting the poor. David clearly sees the injustice and says so, only to have the tables turned on him. Nathan says to David, "You are the man!"[10] How do we then trap the listener into self-awareness? We must present

---

9 Eliot, T.S. (1930). Ash Wednesday. Faber & Faber.
10 2 Samuel 12:7

the action of grace to an audience whose faith cannot be assumed. That's even when preaching to a church full of members.

The stories also must take place not far from home, school, work, and play. Yet the examples from Jesus take us, as well, from the familiar to the ultimate. There is an eschatological element to be found in the good story. Often the grace shows up in the undeserved turn of events and an overflowing sense of extravagance. God's grace is always that way; the gift gets given in sheer gratuity. We expect justice, but we get mercy. This is often disturbing. (Just try to 'preach' some of these parables from year to year.) We expect the 'real world'. We get the Kingdom of God. God's grace is shown again and again, but all of this is difficult. With much of the Bible, the preacher can no longer assume the listener knows what he or she is talking about if a biblical reference is made. Though the Bible still has some credibility (even the president can quote it about once a year or so), people simply don't know what's in it. One must tell the biblical reference before trying to interpret it nowadays. The teller always runs the risk of being misunderstood.

Again, Flannery O'Connor described this whole state of affairs well when she expected her novel, *The Violent Bear it Anyway*, to get trounced by reviewers... "Besides the fact that nobody knows about the devil now, I have to reckon on the fact that baptism is just another idiocy to the gentle reader."[11] Or as she writes of the difficulty to explain the basics of the faith, "the writer has to succeed in making the divinity of Christ seem consistent with the structure of all reality."[12] In other words, the task facing the preacher or the novelist is so daunting that God's grace is necessary or else we are doomed, and we may very well be doomed anyway.

O'Connor seems to begin by writing of a recognizable real world. Yet in her fiction, the action of the supernatural would locate the mystery of grace in the solid flesh of our experience. Therefore (and it helps to have been brought up in the south), when she can take a detail of the farmyard or a town with the eye of a satirist who misses no tricks, or put words into

---

11 Hawkins, P. S. (2004). *The Language of Grace: Flannery O'Connor, Walker Percy, and Iris Murdoch.* New York. Seabury Books. 20.

12 Ibid. 21.

the mouths of her characters in such a way, you "see" in your mind what she is talking about. Mostly though, she is funny as hell, real humor which renders hell real as well. Her humor seduces the reader into her world; we let our guard down, and we can look forward to what will follow. Her Catholic orthodoxy underlies all, as she shows the world of the rural south as a gateway to the spiritual realm that at once inhabits and transcends it. She intends the literal level of her work to suggest the allegorical and wants the reader to be lifted up from the country to the True Country, let down from the heavens by a merciful God. For O'Connor the ordinary is sacramental. God is present in the tattoo parlor or the pig pen.

O'Connor's world is profane only when it is cut off from its true identity as a creation. She wants everything that breathes to be holy. O'Connor brings her characters to a point where they can no longer avoid their relationship with God; although they may not understand what is going on, the reader certainly gets a sense of it. We remember that her literary oeuvre is not large, only 32 short stories and two novels, all about the south.[13] Her south is hardly Christ-centered, but it is most certainly "Christ-haunted." Thus, the Christian writer has a unique opportunity: Religious enthusiasm is accepted as one of the South's more grotesque features, and it is possible to build upon that acceptance, however little real understanding such acceptance may carry with it.

13 O'Connor's two novels are *Wise Blood* and *The Violent Bear it Anyway*.

Soul and Body

We keep trying to keep soul and body apart, even if we know better. We have the biblical model of wholeness; yet since we cannot approach soul empirically, we tend to get pissed at these muscles and bones which carry us on to love. We live and move and have our being. We are gifted with the miracle of reflection and consciousness as we lurk about the planet, thinking, trying, feeling, planning, praying, and several other 'ings' as well. Our spirits are embedded in our bodies, which are found in our bleak universe. We exist because our dogs recognize us.

Why not divide our experience into spirit or soul, mind and body? Spirit is thought, and thought is transported by language. Language is an "electro-chemical" activity of the brain. Future times will have different names for all of this, but a reality will remain: mind and flesh are both made of matter. Why must they engage in conflict? Matters of the heart call for both the cardiologist as well as the poet. The brain's game is to think. Where do we get the impetus to live on beyond this life we think we have here? Why the urge to live? Does this all spring from the all-too mortal brain so capable of thinking way beyond itself? How much better it would be for our brains if thought were a distinct, lasting substance (what would you call it?) which only occasionally agreed to rent space in our house of flesh. The brain keeps firing. Thought brings much thought about thoughts, which only brings another thought.

Can the poem carry the freight of a one-substance view of the universe? Then there are feelings. Our most human emotions unite us with the most primitive organisms in the whole of existence. Yet the whole of the universe is not even theoretically apprehensible by means of the senses we possess and the equipment we manufacturer to stretch our senses. Our notions of time and space lead us to a ridiculous dead end at the edge of the universe. Scientists walk away. They have completed their task.

Whose business is it to pursue beyond the limits?

Or this, is thought other than consciousness? Thought is the electro-chemical activity of a certain organ. It is limited by the confines of our realities. Is consciousness simply another word for yet another activity of matter or another function of energy? What is this internal illumination? We only know that our human constitution leaves us helpless to answer questions which that very constitution poses. Our eager cogitations take us to a certain point, and then a black hole swallows it. We do not impose the categories of time, space, and causation on the universe. The universe imposes them on us. Consciousness, like time and space, seems to have one foot in our world of matter and energy, and the other in unutterable strangeness. We never can get in back of this consciousness; it is always itself in back. Can we not see that the world is full of tired scientists looking for spiritual refreshment?

"Even if God did not exist, religion would still be holy and divine. God is the only being who, to govern, need not even exist. That which is created by the mind lives more truly than matter."

- Charles Baudelaire (1821-1876)[14]

14 From *Baudelaire: His Prose and Poetry*. (T.R. Smith, Ed.). New York. Boni and Liveright. Via Project Gutenberg.

Christology Again

It is revealing to tack an 'ology' onto Christ. We don't say Jesusology, but maybe we should, because we must see him as he is in terms of all the incarnation intended. It ended in atonement, but in-between is his story. There is really no moral point or message which is separable from the story of Jesus as we find it in the gospels. Jesus' identity is prior to the 'meaning' of the story. *We learn who he is by learning to follow him.* In the history of Christianity, we should remember the big split of east from west. If one party [Eastern] has sought to find the essence of the gospel at Bethlehem, and another [Western] at Calvary, and each of them thereby presented a distorted picture of the gospel, it is because neither of them took sufficient account of what lay between, in Galilee and Judea. So we, as we have been taught, emphasize the particularity of Jesus' story! Yet, history also has a universal meaning. Jesus is not confined by history. His universal relevance is found in scripture and demonstrated by the fulfillment of the hopes and deep longings of humanity. This is revealed only by a particular community, trained by a particular man (Jesus), to articulate a particular set of responses as the necessary condition for living truthfully in this life. This then is how we come to understand how Jesus provided a story to determine the polity of the church. This is, of course, the Kingdom. The Kingdom is totally and exclusively God's doing. It cannot be earned by religious or moral effort, imposed by political struggle, or projected in calculations. Look to scripture: it is given, appointed, and inherited. Jesus is himself the established Kingdom of God. Or in Origen's classical phrase, Jesus is the *autobasileia*, the Kingdom in person. In the New Testament, as Jesus is depicted, his authority and identity are absolutely inseparable from each other. The Church must not separate what the Spirit has joined. He did not take on a role when they sought to proclaim him Messiah. His whole self is an act of participation in God's purpose for man. His story defines the nature of how God rules and how such a rule creates a world.

Salvation

"God intends to kill us all in the end."[15]
God must break you to save you.
God's gonna cut you down.

"Batter my heart, three person'd God."[16]
- John Donne

We come to salvation not on our own. We come out of our felt, lamented, and oppressive *sin*. We come not wanting to give up our vices. We want to keep all, so a radical conversion is necessary.

To me, the scriptures clearly speak of what we might call a universal restoration. (Wesley taught it as well.) Look at Peter's sermon on Solomon's porch, recorded in the third chapter of Acts; Peter alludes clearly to the times from God, the *chronon apocataseos*, or the times of restoration. The early writers—Origen, Evagrios, St. Gregory of Nyssa, St. Clement of Alexandria, and St. Isaak of Syria (there were others)—they all engaged the notion; as St. Paul puts it, it is God's will that *all* be saved.[17] Does not even Dante (why is it called the Divine 'Comedy'?) suggest the flames of hell may really still be the glory of God as experienced by those who have neglected him? Paul says *all* things are meant for good (Romans 8).

All this in the midst of looking again at Flannery O'Connor. I remember me and my seminary buddies cogitating over her works; she was recently

15 Hauerwas, S. (2018). *Wilderness Wanderings: Probing Twentieth-century Theology and Philosophy.* Routledge. 27.
16 Donne, J. (1571-1631). "Holy Sonnet 14." Via poets.org
17 1 Timothy 2:4

dead: we planned a pilgrimage to the former state capital to mourn her passing and praise her artistry, yet we never made it. Those were good times. I didn't take it seriously, seminary, because it was not really a serious place. I've only recently been really serious about the deep issues, the way of salvation, the wayward journey of sheer grace I am on, and about the creation that recalls Blake ("everything that lives is holy,"[18]), and about the extravagance of creation with its funny time and space stuff. The end that is expected from God.

But it was Christian Gottlieb Barth in the nineteenth century who observed: "anyone who does not believe in the universal restoration is an ox, but anyone who teaches it is an ass."[19]

The poet Scott Cairns helps me as he describes his growing understanding of these matters... his understanding of salvation is one which has us "moving toward and into a continuously thickening reality."[20] Since it is of God, the "thickening" does not weigh us down, but we can travel lighter, as I have always liked to do. What it is, is we are in 'recovery' from our separation from God (past, present, and future), but we are set free from 'earthy stuff' and can enter that part of the Kingdom which is provided as we stay alive. This is for all. You don't really have to take a membership vow or sign a pledge card. One accepts the One who is the way and the truth and the life, and one *does* then enter a community of those whose lives are being formed by the One who is the One—was, is, and shall be evermore. Amen. One who has found the One is never alone again and may not travel alone. A famous bishop from the East has said: "We can say where the church is; we cannot say where she is not."[21] The Spirit blows where it/he/she wills. We travel on by participation in what we have always called *church*. Before we had been sleep-walking through life, every once in a while we would pole vault over a mouse turd and call it progress, or we would drink or drug to dull the nagging slog of existence, or we would settle for that which was not *the Way* and commit the idolatry of calling it the Way. But now! We have been delivered! Manna is given daily. Still stiff necked, but on the way. St. Isaak of Syria in his seventh

18 Blake, W. (1757-1827). "America: A Prophecy." Via bartleby.com
19 Karl Barth would say perhaps a similar thing later.
20 Cairns S. (2009). *The End of Suffering: Finding Purpose in Pain.* Brewster, Mass. Paraclete Press. 72.
21 Bishop Kallistos Ware

century *Ascetical Homilies* gives us this wonderful assurance: "The man who has found love eats and drinks Christ every day and hour, and hereby is made immortal... and while yet in this world, even now breathes the air of the resurrection."

I'm together daily with an assortment of 12 Steppers. They have been encouraged to come up with the God of their understanding. What a goofy notion that is. AA has strong liberal, protestant, Judeo-Christian roots but the wise early drunks said no, we'll let them pick and choose. You can tell a drunk, but you can't tell them much. So, folks with no notion of Christian spiritual formation, without the guidance of a wise mentor (such as myself) can enter the 'program'. They then proceed in whatever direction they desire.

But wait! These are dear souls who have just been saved from the pit of hell. They remember what it was like and they don't want to go back there. The ship of return passage sails every day, and normal people cannot believe anyone would get a ticket. They have heard by now the message of their disastrous first drinks, but they do it anyway. To hell, from hell, back to hell.

We who come each day watch them and say, 'well, better them than me.' What's up with *that* warm Christian compassion? But what would you rather us do, get on that boat with them? No, and look! There's another newcomer; welcome them. The daily sitters are there because they have discovered their daily bread. Even in the desert, manna is given. We keep coming back because our lives are being saved thereby. I never tire of it because of all the miracles I get to see. That is the basis of salvation then.

Willimon has written a book about who then is saved. Very helpful. He is that rare Methodist bishop who actually reads and thinks. The book is very helpful on virtually every page. As one enamored of Barth, he is careful about appointing folks to hell. He considers Origen, who has nobody in hell, and also Augustine, who has practically everybody there. He and I are proud Wesleyans. Methodists always have a position meant to please everybody. I have not learned much from my church since high school, but I have learned a boatload of stuff from my eclectic reading. Seminary was a nice diversion and kept me out of Vietnam, for which I am grateful. And a career in the church was good, and we seem to have enough money to spend plus government help thanks to LBJ and FDR and pension plans based on our beloved capitalistic system (stock market). Life is very good.

In AA, all the above are 'outside issues.' We stick to the traditional purposes. Drunks established those beloved principles, and yet they work anyway.

Back for a moment to the universal restoration theme. Does God mean for all to be saved? 1 Tim. 2:4, Eph. 1:7-10, Col. 1:15-20, John 10:16, 1 Cor. 15:28. Then look at Rom 5:12-21—the word *all* is repeated five times. How could Augustine and Calvin have missed all that?

Spiritual, But Not Religious

I hear it all the time and I'm tired of it, and need to make peace or understanding with those who say it: "Well, you know, I'm very spiritual, but I'm not very religious." It pisses me off just to write it. The reason I'm upset is because there is something wrong with me! I know what they mean when they say this, but it tells me there is something quite wrong; it speaks to an ongoing failure—theirs, ours, and mine. Those dear ones who say this are floundering and need to find their way home. They must find a way to reconnect their faith to their communities and their communities to their faith. They are suffering a separation of spirit and body and need wholeness. They are alone, fragmented, and spend time shopping in culture's vast supermarket of fake spiritual trinkets and are cut off from the church. They are also easy prey. Satan is always looking for any vessel sailing without a fleet, and an individualized, isolated spirituality can leave a hapless seeker eagerly climbing into Satan's boat. I see it all the time. We have folks shopping for a church where they can fit in, an experience of something like worship which suits their clothes, a place that 'meets their needs' but asks for little. They are heads without a body. And that's just the people who 'try out' a church. The vast majority of people never come to a church for any reason.

Truth is, you cannot do it alone. In AA we are clearly taught that we must have the group. You get a sponsor and get involved with others, you come to meetings, '90 in 90'. What would happen if we told a first timer in church that they must worship 90 Sundays in a row and to hook up with a spiritual mentor or they may be doomed?

Faith is not something which can be both solitary and healthy. We have a classic contemporary statement of this in Dietrich Bonhoeffer's *Life Together*:

> The Christian needs another Christian who speaks God's Word to him. He needs him again and again when he becomes uncertain and discouraged, for by himself he cannot help himself without belying the truth. He needs his brother man as a bearer and proclaimer of the divine word of salvation. He needs his brother solely because of Jesus Christ. The Christ in his own heart is weaker than the Christ in the word of his brother; his own heart is uncertain, his brother's is sure.[22]

We need each other.

If the church is vibrant and alive, she will find a way to speak this truth. If the church is the church, this will get done. It always takes "two or more... gathered in Christ's name" for the flame to come alive and light the path.

I find myself wanting this so much for so many of those I come into contact with, and I am fairly isolated myself, alone in my lovely home writing about these things. My old pastor's heart grieves over this.

This is true even among the monasteries of Mount Athos, the Fathers' lives in Christ are necessarily *lives together*. The old idiorhythmic (individualized) rule has been set aside for the even older, more traditional cenobitic (community) rule. Even the rare eremite, the desert dweller in his rugged cave, makes way to the monastic enclave for liturgical worship and communion. There is no such thing as solitary communion. Until we come together, we dry up and wither away. One of the desert priests has written: "Only in the unity of the church do we find these defects[23] overcome. Man finds his true self in the Church alone; not in the helplessness of spiritual isolation but in the strength of his communion with his brothers and his Savior."[24]

---

22 Bonhoeffer, D. (1954). *Life Together: The Classic Exploration of Christian Community*. New York. Harper & Row. 23.

23 Ignorance and sin

24 Elchaninov, A. (1967). *The Diary of a Russian Priest*. London. Faber & Faber. 87.

Scripture proclaims that *all*—there's that 'all' word again. All are made in the image of God. The question is, how do we continue to bear that image? This image is not born alone.

Even God exists in relationship. It was in the wisdom of the early church to develop the doctrine of the Trinity. One God in Three persons engaged in a single *perichoresis*. This single expression of the one God brings us into the continuing creation of which we are a part. The *personal* is emphasized. An individual is not the same thing as a person. Personhood implies communion.

When Jesus told us "the Kingdom of God is within you," was he not inviting us to come together as those to whom the gifts would be given? The gift of His presence is given as we do those things that constitute the Kingdom.

Our constant fallenness weighs heavy upon us. Many do not accept the theology of man's fall. For me, the primal story of the garden has always been satisfactory. I have read those first few chapters of the beginning many times. Fresh fruit is given on every visit. I usually don't think much about what tree I am picking from. When it comes to my wants and desires, I remain on the two-year-old level. I want what I want when I want it. Move back, here I come. Of course, we are given some pretty clear directions and instructions. Don't do this; *do* do that, and that sort of thing. But there's another problem. If you tell me to do this or that, try to guess what I will actually do, for it won't be this or that. Again, behavior we associate with a two-year-old who has heard the word 'no' much more than any other word as they learn *words*. This learning of words is the whole key to me. Words then become how we are to shape our lives. We are taught the *word*. What all does that mean?

Human life is so fragile and tenuous and ambiguous that scarcely anyone can be expected to figure out how to do it. It certainly helps if Momma and them are the 'right' sort of people. How likely is that to happen? There are no sure bets. I think that is why early on in my ministry marriages were the hardest thing I had to do. How could 'I' stand there and say, "now by the authority vested in me, I now 'pronounce' you?"

I would choke up. I could much more easily plant someone. After all, they were done causing mischief. That young couple were without a clue starting out, and God only knows what was going to come of it. I shudder to think! At the end of my ministry, marriages were still hard to do—not because of the above, but because they were a sure way to fuck up a weekend.

The most beautiful thing St. Augustine ever wrote:

> Adam is thus scattered throughout the globe. Set in one place, he fell and, as it were, broken small, he has filled the whole world. But the Divine Mercy gathered up the fragments from every side, forged them in the fire of love and welded into one what had been broken... An immense task it was indeed; but think who the Artist was.[25]

I feel forged in the fire of love; not only is the alliteration pleasing, but the fact of the forging, that God meant it as good and necessary. Yes, we fell, ontologically as well as jumping into the morass of sin with gusto and even enthusiasm. We fell, we are fallen, I shall remain in this Augustinian camp. I remain a stinking lousy sinner, and that's all right by me. I get to go to both AA and church. My life is good.

---

25 Lubac, H. (1988). *Catholicism: Christ and the Common Destiny of Man.* (E. Englund, Trans.). Ignatius Press. 376.

Death Penalty

In capital punishment cases, why, during lethal injection, do they swab the condemned's arm with alcohol before killing him or her?

The experts say a more humane death dealer is the firing squad. Humane because the killee dies pretty damn quick. Why is it that one of the rifles is loaded with a blank?

Karl Barth asked, "Now that Jesus Christ has been nailed to the cross for the sins of the world, how can we still use the thought of expiation to establish the death penalty?"[26]

So, if there are biblical, moral, practical, and theological reasons for not doing it, why do it?

Bruce Cockburn has written that prayer is "a way of breathing and seeing."[27]

---

26 Barth, K. (2010). *Church Dogmatics Volume 3.4, Sections 55-56.* London. T&T Clark. 114.
27 Cockburn, B. (2014). *Rumours of Glory: A Memoir. New York.* HarperCollins. 199.

Jesus

Who is Jesus? Who was Jesus? His identity, his present reality? He lived in the ever more distant past; therefore, this is a real question. The ancient Greeks used the 'perfect' tense of a verb to distinguish the ongoing import of a completed action. So, what is the "isness" of the Jesus who was? We don't want a Christ figure; we want the ongoing meaning—the *perfect tense* of Jesus. Think of Jaroslav Pelikan's *Jesus through the Centuries,* the diverse impact of Jesus wherever he is known. There is also Schweitzer's *Quest for the Historical Jesus.* How do you bring out the perfect tense in the sense of Jesus' ongoing significance? For example, the critical historian cannot affirm as an attestable historical datum 'that' God resurrected Jesus; what they can say is Jesus' followers 'believed' that God has done so, and they acted based on their belief. Thus, a strict historical account of Jesus ends with his death. Easter belongs then to the history of beliefs about Jesus, but not to the history of Jesus himself.

Although Matthew and Luke are expansions and modifications of Mark, they generally retain his overall story line. Most of what Jesus did concerns the villages around Galilee until he resolves to go to Jerusalem at the end, which in the gospels is the largest portion of the synoptic texts. Also, the gospels do not portray anyone really 'getting it' even though he stated his mission purpose. (Mt. 5:17, Mark 10:45) Only Luke reports his age (about 30, Lk 3:23), none report his upbringing (except the 12-year-old account in Luke). Matthew and Luke give genealogies, but they differ in places. He was a craftsman. A *tekton* means woodworker, not necessarily a carpenter. Four of his disciples were fisherman, one had been a tax collector, and of the rest we only know their names.

Certain customs are noted but rarely are they explained. The accounts are not very detailed. They are short stories. It seems details have been pared away; the point is to emphasize what he said as he went. They are always going somewhere. Real villages are named, real people are there, and they do the ordinary things which are done in villages. Often people writing about Jesus will give much information about his context. What is the role of Jerusalem and the significance of the Roman occupation, etc.?

To ask, *who is Jesus?*, is to inquire about his present identity, which is inseparable from his past identity and also inseparable from his significance. For we who believe, of course, Jesus' identity is solved in that in the gospels he himself declares what he is about, and the resurrection confirms it. There is also his relation to the Old Testament. *And* there is an incomplete description because he was expected to return again (soon) as the Son of Man.

There is an obvious transitoriness to *all* historical reconstruction, and we watch out for pretentious claims based on such 'history'. Also, in the case of the Jesus of history, "the past isn't what it used to be, and never was," because the people studying him are not what they used to be; they themselves live in 'history' and cannot settle any matter definitively. Who is Jesus? Well, he was a Jew, his mission was the Kingdom of God, he was executed without validation from the God he trusted, and he is the central figure in the moral life of those who follow him. Pretty bleak, all in all.

There is no reasonable doubt that he existed. In all historical study, there is a distinction between event and report, and even a very accurate report is bound to be an incomplete account. One can give only part of what occurred, and there is always a point of view expressed. Thus, there is a fundamental distinction between the exegesis of a text and the reconstruction of the event it reports. As early as the second century, one could regard the gospels either as portraits or as pieces. The Church opted for seeing the gospels as four portraits, each with its own integrity, and as an adequate rendering of the event. But the gospels differ often, so there is an ongoing debate: what *did* happen?

For us moderns, the 'quest' begins in the Enlightenment. The idea arose that the Jesus of history differed drastically from the Jesus Christ of the Christian faith and the four gospels on which it was based. Protestant theology has then wrestled with the relation of the gospel's 'Christ of

Faith' and the historians' 'Jesus of History'. There have been a veritable plethora of divergent notions which have arisen in 'our times.' I'll not go into all that in this Journal.

At the very beginning, the Jesus people (followers of the Way, called Christians only later) had a 'gospel' message about Jesus before they had a gospel *text* about him. Nothing was written down (that we still have) for more than a generation after his death. Jesus himself never wrote anything, except for doodling in the sand before the woman caught in adultery (what happened to the man?). The gospels rest on traditions reported orally by Christians and for Christians. Jesus was not a Christian. Strange that we must always remind ourselves of the Jewishness of Jesus. So, we get irony: the real Jesus of history is distanced from the Christianity which emerged in his name and embedded in the Judaism which largely refused the message about him. *And* it is not possible to know, in terms of the historical record, just what kind of Jew Jesus was!

To be sure, the Book of Acts does continue the Jesus story. We see the valuable story of the Church from Pentecost, but these were still Jews. They had only the basics of Jesus' story and the formative Resurrection witness, but we get little about the earliest community in Jerusalem, and really less about the disciples in Galilee. Paul's letters, written *before* the gospels, deal mainly with problems which arose in his mission to the Gentiles in the cities around the Aegean Sea. There are references to his relationship to the leaders in Jerusalem; he brought them offerings to appease conflict. The fourth gospel is so different from the first three, it must be considered separately. To get a clear picture of who Jesus was, we must do difficult work in the earliest Christian community (non-canonical works).

Jesus was a Jew, a particular Jew who can be placed in a particular time, place and map of Jewish religion and culture. So, we straightaway come to the Scandal of Particularity. How then did this Jew become the Christ of history, and particularly in the Gentile Mediterranean area where the Christian Church developed? We must be very careful here because of the historical record of stereotype and ignorance which led to antipathy of Judaism. Adolf von Harnack was a great historian of the faith. He said: "The Christian religion is something simple and sublime; it means one thing and one thing only: Eternal life in the midst of time, by the strength and under the eyes of God."[28] He distinguished between the kernel and the husk of the Jesus material. He opposed the conservatives in the Kaiser's Reich; saw them as Pharisees. He looked at the situation even in Jesus' time when the normative Jewish worship was synagogues and not temple, because of the Diaspora. The early liberal Protestant attitude said while Paul had a Jewish/Gentile attitude, Jesus had a truly universal outlook. Ernest Renan's *The Life of Jesus* said Jesus was surrounded by Judaism but was not really a part of it. Rudolf Bultmann's Jesus book does not separate him from Judaism but portrays Jesus as superior to it. He says Jesus expected God to bring in the Kingdom by force. This same pattern continues in our day. Crossan does not denigrate Judaism; he idealizes it in some ways. He has Jesus' words as "a religious and economic egalitarianism that negated alike and at once the hierarchical and patronal normalcies of Jewish religion and Roman power."[29] This results in an ideal vision and a social program.

What needs to happen is a scholarship that does provide Jewish readers with basic historical information about Jesus, that shows Jesus can be integrated into Jewish history and not as a renegade, and gives Gentile readers news that the Jewish religion of Jesus' day was no less worthy of respect than the early Christianity which was taking place in the area. Today the quest of the historical *Pharisee* is even more complex and controversial than the quest for the historical Jesus. We know only of two, Paul and Josephus! Actually, the New Testament is better evidence for the history of the first century Judaism than is rabbinic Judaism for the origins of Christianity. Also, the *Apocrypha* and *Pseudepigrapha* and the *Dead Sea Scrolls* do not add much more than further difficulty for the historian who wishes to reconstruct Jesus' world.

---

28 Von Harnack, A. (1851-1930). *What is Christianity?* (T.B. Saunders, Trans.). 9.
29 Arnal, W.E. (2005). *The Symbolic Jesus: Historical Scholarship, Judaism and the Construction of Contemporary Identity*. Oakville, CT. Equinox. 60.

NT Wright, who urges "the third quest" for the historical Jesus (he excludes 'the Jesus Seminar') says there is now a serious attempt to do history. He asks, how does Jesus fit into the history of his day, what were his aims, why did he die, and how did the early church take shape the way it did? Then what of the gospels? Wright's work is helpful.

The best book I have found about all of this is Keck's book, *Who Is Jesus.* That study reveals Jesus as teacher. What is the meaning in the "words in red" in the New Testament document?

This is our moment. We are part of a race called human. We exist in a garden. Very slowly we came here, and gradually declared ourselves the owners. What does it mean to own something?

Things are currently spinning wildly out of control. Who has control—who is at the controls? What came before? We have no idea. It could be that our garden is one of many, but for all intents and purposes, we are quite alone.

We declare ourselves definitive. What could be more than us? Yet, according to the sum of our wits, we wither away. Then where are we headed and what is the meaning of it all? And what *is* meaning? We exist because our dogs recognize us, and god is dog from the omega point.

It's all about power and who has it. Power is the release of energy. Someone cracks a whip high in the mountains. Energy, vibrations in the air. The snow is loose. Watch out below.

There were many gardens before and below the avalanche. They are gone now.

Who's to say our type was meant to last? There are seasons. Evolution is real. What dinosaur is to come?

I don't remember exactly when I became fonder of questions than answers. It is perchance from Jesus that the tendency comes. I like him a lot and the way he looked at things. He was the new son of man, the initial one had fallen away. Jesus didn't last long in this garden. He was the Omega (the true beast slouching towards Bethlehem [30].

---

30 Yeats

Church and World

The Church and World are companions. The world is sometimes enemy, sometimes partner, but they are never the same. The church is a community formed by the gospel. The world is the community to which Christ comes and to which he sends his disciples. Hauerwas says that through the church the world is given a history. The "world" derives its intelligibility from there being a people who can supply a history for the world. Many would disagree, but I do not. It's just that, as is always the case with Hauerwas, it's hard to sustain such a vision in a time in which the church is so accommodated to the things of the world.

Hauerwas goes on: the task of the church is to be faithful to the story of God which makes intelligible the divided nature of the world. The church, and the social ethic implied by its separate existence, is an essential aspect of why Christians think their convictions are true. For it is a central Christian conviction that even though the world is God's creation and remains subject to God's redemption, it continues eschatologically to be a realm which defies his rule. Church, though often unfaithful to its task, must lay claim to the promise and reality of God's Kingdom and then provide the 'institutional' place for the community of faith to understand the disobedient but still God-created character of the world. If Christian convictions are true, then the power of those convictions can shape a community able to face truthfully the nature of our world. This is the world to which God gave his gift of a chosen people and then Jesus. The character of the stories of God requires a people who are willing to understand that there will always be conflict in terms of other understandings of the traditions which are to be found based on the gift of God to the world.

The true church is able to exist and to grow only through tradition which is sustained by memory over time, by ritual and habit, and it sets the context and boundaries for the discussion required by the Christian stories. Again, the gospels have no unstoried form. It is true that the way to interpret a narrative is through another narrative. The power of a narrative lies precisely in its potential for producing a community of interpretation sufficient for the growth of further narratives.

But the church cannot be tribal; it is the world in which we live which has a divided and tribal existence. We in the church learn what the story entails as it is lived and lives through the lives of others. This is the particular story of the Kingdom of God and the history of Israel and Jesus. The criterion of truth for extended historical narratives is notoriously complex. Yet morally we cannot live indecisively. This becomes a dangerous action in such a world as we have it now. Yet the world itself is under Christ's lordship. We trust that the truth 'will out'! When that happens a community capable of truthful witness is made possible. The community then can tell its story to the world in such a way that the truth of the story of God's Kingdom can be given to a sinful and divided world. The church, itself a sinful community, is in but not of the world.

I Live My Life

I live my life in growing orbits,
which move out over the things of the world.
Perhaps I can never achieve the last,
but that will be my attempt.

I am circling around God, around the ancient tower,
and I have been circling for a thousand years.
And I still don't know if I am a falcon,
Or a storm, or a great song.[31]

31 Rilke, R.M. (1899). From *The Book for the Hours of Prayer*. (R. Bly, Trans.).

After Christendom

In his book *After Christendom*, Stanley Hauerawas says Christian adherence to foundationalist epistemologies (Kant and his school) was commensurate with social strategies of Christendom of the past. Such strategies were the attempt by Christians to create societies in which it would be possible to think Christians believed what anyone would believe upon reflection. Ironically, this strategy turned Christianity into a set of beliefs to legitimize the false universalism of liberalism. Hauerwas hopes to challenge that strategy by reasserting the significance of the church as the embodiment of the necessary practices to sustain Christian affirmation of God as Trinity. This leads him to the statement that outside the church there is no salvation, no saving knowledge of God. Now this is, to many, a quite fideistic position. It sounds sectarian to the extreme, but the issue is that questions of the truth or falsity of Christian convictions cannot be separated from how the church understands its social and political stance. Again, it is important that what he means by liberal has little to do with the right/left stance our secular politics has stuck itself with. We must remember what the church is. It is not a strategy. We turn from the Constantinian presumption. The church always exists over and against. The church clearly is in, but not *of*, the world. We are "resident aliens." The thing to note is how both the left and the right in contemporary Christian theology continue to assume the old Constantinian presumptions. The gospel is always a fresh social alternative. It is this refreshing turn to the being possessed by the Trinity and the purposes of the Trinity Hauerwas wishes to lift up in his books.

Why is it that, in countries where we have freedom of religion, it is difficult to make a serious reference to God in the public arena? The church has become so accommodated in our time that no clear Christian witness to God has been proclaimed. Theists are offering atheists less and less in which to disbelieve. The faith is stronger and growing in places where such freedom of religion has not been the practice normally accepted (namely "third world" countries). In liberal societies, Christians gradually divorced their convictions from their practices so that we lost our intelligibility as Christians. Where one has separation of church and state, it is often assumed Christianity has been disestablished. In America, we came to understand that legal disestablishment presumed the continued social and cultural hegemony of generalized Christian presuppositions. You do not need an established church if you assume everyone believes the same as you do. Our forbearers were at ease in their beliefs because they accepted sources which made unbelief incredible. Secularization has caused masses of people to come to a position which does not necessarily suppose a God.

What Hauerwas seeks to show is that the church must uncover its radical political stance. It is not belief which saves, but doing the right thing for the right reason. So, the church ideally provides the necessary formation for Christians to be able to act out of their convictions. We don't then cave into the prevailing winds of this or that secular alternative, but we have been taught what a clear witness means. What then are the politics of salvation? This is Hauerwas' question to us. As Charles Taylor (*Sources of the Self*) has pointed out, the Enlightenment taught us if we could just move into the "modern" experiment by giving up our superstitions and parochial attachments we would be in a position to benefit mankind (as if that is what we accomplished in the twentieth century). The separation of church and state has led to America's political arrangement of subordinating religion to the political order, this in the name of democracy. The founders wished to tame and domesticate religious passions of the sort which had convulsed Europe (Thirty Year's War). They did this by establishing capitalism. Religion was to be submerged, and peoples' energies were to have a *self*-interest in pursuit of the American dream—material goods. Thus religion is OK; just keep it private—it is mere belief—it must bend to the political will (law) as regards conduct. Jefferson, following Locke, said religion could be good or could be bad, but its truth could not be established by reason. Thus, we would not "establish" religion. It would rather be private and subordinate. Religious tolerance was good because pluralism meant civil peace—order.

We became a 'liberal' society, believing our task was to make the world *work*. Christian practice was relegated to the private realm, and that was fine if we had peace in society. Thus, I grew up in a church which preached love and justice, which meant freedom and equality would be balanced in the best interest of our society as determined by the findings of the Supreme Court. Theologians were to be specialized ethicists to serve a liberal political agenda. Pilate asked, "What is truth?" Well, in a liberal society, truth is what wins in a free and open encounter. The foundational grounds for the Enlightenment project were the natural sciences. Thus, truth was to be found by being logical and objective. This worked in its day. It's just that the project no longer works. The only real change was that people no longer killed each other in the name of God, but now in the name of the nation-states. Since the states were protecting and ensuring our freedoms, we must kill others to preserve this great freedom.

Hauerwas seeks to turn us away from a false universalism and to recover the particular. Thus, the church must address the world by the church being the church and thus make the world the world. Salvation is a political alternative that the world cannot know apart from the existence of a particular people called the church. Hauerwas is so bold to say you cannot even know you need saving without the church being a political alternative.

Prior to Constantine, Christians saw themselves confronted by hostile powers which were personified in those who persecuted the church. Christians knew, as the New Testament proclaims, that these powers were already defeated. This enabled the church to be strong enough to challenge the vast and powerful Roman Empire. The early Christians believed the church has a cosmic mission to proclaim to the world: the rule of the risen Christ. Thus, without the church, the world is doomed and there is no hope of salvation. The church existed over against the world.

Thus, John Howard Yoder says that the church precedes the world epistemologically. We as Christians know more from Jesus than we know from any other source. Nature and science are best looked at not alone, but in the light of the confession and the Lordship of Christ. The church also precedes the world axiologically; the Lordship of Christ drives and plots the critical value choices we must make as we live life.[32] So again, there is no salvation outside the church. This salvation is not meant to confirm what we already know, but to make us a part of a story which could not be known apart from a community formed by that story.

Salvation is the enacted narrative of God's ongoing care of Israel through the calling of Gentiles into the promised people. We need to take this history into account. For Paul, the question was not, as we have been taught since the Reformation, "How can I find a gracious God?" but "How can we trust in this God if he abandons his promise to Israel?"' Paul's proclamation presents the righteousness of God not as some new soteriological novelty but as the manifestation of a truth attested by Scripture from the very beginning.

The early church witnessed powerfully to this truth and many were martyred. The witness of people willing to die for their faith was powerful. It meant that Rome does not get to tell the story of our deaths. The church claims to be the triumphant political power which knows the truth of our existence better than Rome. The church, exactly because it does not seek rule through violence, triumphs by remembering the victory of the Lamb through the witness of the martyrs. Rome could not stand against that. But look at what happened: Rome did win after all when the Christian was 'brought in' to the hegemony of the rule of the state and thus accommodated itself to the rule which entailed the way Rome had always ruled—through violence. Christians are always tempted toward theocracy. When we 'joined' Rome, our witness became weakened. So we came up with an anemic, individual salvation of various beliefs. When we took up Rome's project, the history of the West was set in place.

Now to Augustine—the problem here is that there is Augustine, and then there is the way we have interpreted him who had the vision of the two Cities.

In our day we have the reading of Augustine as justifying a 'realist' account of church and society. All is sin (R. Niebuhr). Augustine's account

---

32 Yoder, J.H. (1985). *The Priestly Kingdom: Social Ethics as Gospel.* University of Notre Dame. 11.

of the worldly city invites a Niebuhr-like interpretation. Yet missing in Niebuhr's account is Augustine's strong insistence that the church is the only true political society, because only in the church are we directed to the worship of the only true God.

Augustine does not think of the two cities as two distinct human associations. The opposition is not between public and private, church and world, but between political virtue and political vice. Augustine says Rome cannot be a commonwealth because a commonwealth is determined by justice—that is, where each gets his or her due—but Rome does not give God his due. Only the Christian community offers sacrifice to the true God, and it is a sacrifice only Christ could make possible. A society which fails to give God his due fails to give its citizens their due. For Augustine, societies devoid of the church cannot have authentic conceptions of virtue. Rome is based on pride—is built on disorder in which passion is restrained by passion, therefore violence.

Augustine says this incredible thing: the City of God can never go to war, even in self-defense! The church cannot use war to preserve itself since she knows the true bonds of human speech are preserved in God's eternal will and the *ordo* (order) of the universe as a whole. The church does not depend on any human system for its survival. This means that sacrifice and martyrdom will occur. Hauerwas says genuine politics is, then, the art of dying. That puts the church at cross purposes to liberalism, for it is built on the denial of death and sacrifice.

As Christians, we will not serve such a world as we have well if we pretend the church is only incidental to the world's salvation. The issue then is how on earth can we witness to God's rule through church without ruling?! The church's main task is then to be who we are—God's salvation. Hauerwas writes that Jesus' salvation does not have social and political implications, but that it *is* a politics that is meant as an alternative to all social life which does not reflect God's glory.

Sehnsucht

Our souls "thirst for God" (Ps. 42). I believe everyone has deep within himself or herself a profound, unquenchable yearning—it is a God-shaped space, as Augustine said—and only God can occupy that space. C.S. Lewis used the German term *Sehnsucht* to name this longing for fulfillment for something which can satisfy in a lasting way. I believe we are created in this way.

Some think if they set a goal and achieve it, then that will satisfy. But that does not last. Some repress this yearning only to find it keeps popping up. C.S. Lewis said that if nothing in the world satisfies it and nothing in the world can push it under, then we must conclude we are made for something else. As long ago as Ecclesiastes, this vanity of trying to deny or repress *Sehnsucht* has been noted. We who have realized what we were made for know we seek for God's presence in God's Kingdom. The trouble is, we live in a Post-Christian society today. Thus, the way of coming to Christian formation is no longer understood or accepted in our culture. As I have noted, in a way, this is a good thing. There is nothing gained by the church returning to the old understanding of being accommodated in the nation-state culture, something which used to be assumed when we were a 'Christian' nation. If Christianity is an alien nation in the current culture, then we may return to primitive Christianity. How did it operate in early times?

We ask folks to come with us to church. What do they find there? Well, they usually don't grasp what is going on. Which church, which 'style' of worship? Rather, it is important that each Christian be concerned for the neighbor in the way Christ taught us to be. We see folks who yearn and are caught up in the culture. What do we then witness to? How do we adequately witness to and exemplify the alternative which is life in the Kingdom? It is clear that a 'seeker' must be trained if they are to gain the language to express and internalize the faith offered by the church. If they only attend a worship service, that is not enough. To their minds this is only another 'experience' (read: entertainment) which may or may not be readily enjoyed. This is something I have realized as I would invite people to St. John church. If I can get them there in the first place, they think that must be the point, to try it and you 'like it'. That is not enough. What I must witness to is the faith Becky and I have come to through years of formation, and how we love the place we call St. John, where we may continue to grow and reach out to others. It's not enough to offer them yet another experience in a culture so saturated with experiences. That is not the point. We can only point to the faith which is everything to us. If 'they' can sense *that*, then they may want what we have. I have learned my evangelism in the program, and the rooms, and in the people of Alcoholics Anonymous. The problem there is that a random person out in the culture may not know that salvation can be found only in the church. They have been seeking, but they are 'getting by' OK. They don't know how deadly toxic life is in the good old US of A. They think they are already 'getting it' if they are generally successful and "happy." In fact, they already have a religion, a kind of nebulous state religion of secular goals and feeling good. Their church is TV. The news there is we are going to hell quickly, though there is hope if you can buy this or that product. The average person out there 'worships' in the general state religion service of TV for most of the week. Then I come along and say, hey, you ought to drive downtown for one hour on a Sunday morning and catch our 'show' at St. John. There they find a deeply traditional worship service. The music and preaching are as good as it gets, *but*, and it's a big but—

Worship is not evangelism. Evangelism is one person (who presumably has some 'experience') telling another where along the trail of life some nourishment may be found. In our day we are all on this trail and the abyss on either side is dark and deep. First, the one who seeks to help stragglers needs to know what she is talking about. That's why I find AA helpful. The one who seeks out AA already knows what it is like to fall off the trail into the bottom. They can hardly believe someone like them has managed to climb back up and actually make progress. We love it when some poor soul comes to be with us. We tell them, well, I fell off also, and what I found out is that I had to change everything about the way I 'did' the trail, and I found that out here in this room, and if you keep coming back and hook up with a sponsor, your sorry ass may make it. The point is, if you want what I have and are willing to go to any lengths to get it, then watch what I do and do it too.

This is not what I have come to understand as warm Christian evangelism. I remember a lifetime as a pastor and the desperate longing to be thought a success. I went to many evangelism conferences and tried to learn how to get a church to grow. Growth was the goal. If one could 'pastor' a church of multiplying bodies and dollars, you would be favored by the bishop and move up the corporate ladder. These convocations on evangelism were really only sales conferences and success and being the top producer in the conference was the thing. They never offered an opportunity on how to become a failure in the eyes of the world, yet how to be faithful in the Kingdom process. Am I being too harsh here? No, not harsh enough. The above is the practice and praxis of the accommodated churches of North America, and the consequent fall of those institutions has been great. What do we do? Well, we can turn to the statement made in the United Methodist hymnal (for those churches which still use the hymnal).

> The church is of God,
> and will be preserved to the end of time,
> for the conduct of worship
>   and the due administration of God's
>   Word and Sacraments,
> the maintenance of Christian fellowship
>   and discipline,
> the edification of believers,
> and the conversion of the world.
> All, of every age and station,
>   stand in need of the means of
>   grace which it alone supplies.[33]

33 *The United Methodist Hymnal*. (1989). Baptismal Covenant III. 45.

We mourn the loss of our former, favored station as churches in America, where it was widely assumed that any reasonable person would come to believe and be a part of the Christian faith. Drive across this great land and observe the landscape and the villages and cities large and small. By far the most distinctive architecture in most towns (like Augusta) is the tall steeples of cathedrals and churches. They poke up above all as symbols of what a city is and should be about. So, go into the town and look close up at the conditions of these edifices and evaluate how esteemed these places are. In any large and 'thriving' city, the church no longer pokes up the most. They have been eclipsed by glass and steel towers of business as usual. One must go to the suburbs to find the churches that offer what people want (market churches).

I thrill to the previously mentioned statement from the hymnal. It expresses exactly what I most want. But as I sit in my study early on a Saturday morning I must ask, what do my neighbors most want? How do they handle their Sehnsucht? Well, I must return to my AA experience. There is nothing I can say or do that will change them into what I think they should be or do. That would be 'shoulding' on them, after all. If they come to me I can try, based on my strength, hope, and experience, to explain what I can about the church, which is more than half of what I am about. But (another huge but) God can be trusted to handle the universe as well as the people I know in the houses I can see out of my study window.

God of my understanding, help me to live in your kingdom in such a way that your purposes get advanced. Above all, help me to be playful and engaging as I limp about the trail that leads to your true church and when I finally get there may it indeed by your true church, and thank you.

What is the Good?

For the Greeks as well as the Christians, virtue was the central concept for moral reflection. Since the word has fallen into dis-repair today, it is important to follow through history how the *good* has been discussed and known. For the Greeks, the word virtue—*arete*—meant "that which causes a thing to perform its function well." *Arete* was an excellence of any kind, denoting the power of anything to fulfill its function. Later, Aquinas defined virtue as simply a "certain perfection of power."

Stan Hauerwas shows us we lack a clear and satisfactory moral definition of the virtues. Plato said "virtue of knowledge," but this knowledge involved is not easy to acquire or identify. Aristotle, by contrast, said virtue "is a characteristic involving choice, and it consists in observing the mean relative to us, a mean which is defined by a rational principle, such as a man of practical wisdom would use to determine it."[34] Aquinas agrees, as he usually does, but addresses also "a mean between the passions." And Kant spoke of "that which brings inner rather than outer freedom under the laws."[35] So, and this is important, the very variety of different notions of virtue indicates that any account of the virtues is context dependent.

There is, perhaps, a stronger emphasis on the significance of decision associated with the language and concept of duty than that of virtue. Duties imply matters which may or may not entail decisions. To be a person of virtue, therefore, involves acquiring the linguistic, emotional, and rational skills which give us the strength to make our decisions and our life our own.

Plato emphasized in the *Republic* the virtues of courage, temperance, wisdom, and justice. These became known as the "cardinal virtues." Plato

---

34 Hauerwas, S. (1981). A Community of Character: Toward a Constructive Christian Social Ethic. University of Notre Dame. 112.

35 Ibid.

considered them central to the functioning of the Republic and also to the soul. Aristotle was no less insistent than Plato that ethics was but a branch of politics; yet, unlike Plato, he made no attempt to establish a list of central virtues. In Christian theology, accounts of the virtues, called 'fruits of the Spirit' by Paul, were even less systematic. Augustine argued that in a real sense virtue cannot be a possession of the soul. The fourfold division of virtue in Augustine's writings must be understood as four forms of love. The object of this love is only God.

Aquinas is, in many ways, the high point for reflection on virtue; his compilation combines Plato, Aristotle, the Stoics, and Augustine in an extraordinarily complex manner. Aquinas maintains, following Augustine, that the theological virtues of faith, hope, and charity must be influenced in us if the "natural virtues" are to be properly formed and directed. Thus, it is through our habits that we acquire a "second nature" if these habits are virtuous. "Virtue as its own reward."

I finished another Murdoch last night. A sexy dark comedy about 'muddles' so common to human nature, but presented in such a way that the reader is not only caught up in it all, but also taught about characters in a definitive way that few modern authors have ever achieved.

Dame Murdoch was not a Christian, yet she realizes Christian language is certainly pervasive; our culture and her characters are responsive to Christ oft-times. She has a quasi-mentor and an "ineffectual" character say to a damaged student about to enter Oxford: "'It doesn't matter what you call it.'" (The boy had been trying to pray.) "'Keep trying. And stop being afraid of Christ. He's just the local name of God. If it's natural to you to cry out "Christ, help me!" cry it and then be quiet. You may be helped.' (Boy:) 'But how do I know what it means, how do I know what's true?' (Man:) 'That sort of truth is local too.'"

As the conversation continues, there is this paragraph:

> 'I mean just that one's ordinary tasks are usually immediate and simple and one's own truth lives in these tasks. Not to deceive oneself, not to protect one's pride with false ideas, never to be pretentious or bogus, always to try to be lucid and quiet. There's a kind of pure speech of the mind which one must try to obtain. To attain it is to be in the truth, one's own truth, which needn't mean any big apparatus of belief. And when one is there one will be truthful and kind and able to see other people and what they need.'[36]

Fairly Christian, that language. I'm so very grateful that Stanley Hauerwas turned me on to Iris Murdoch and Anthony Trollope, both of whom I had completely missed until my seventh decade of life.

I will begin a new Trollope tonight.

Trollope, of course, goes on and on about the church, but it is a church where one would dare not get saved. It is the church of England, behaving badly. The bishops get appointed by the government, of all things. There are some people of faith, but they are not leading characters in the novels.

---

36 Murdoch, I. (1984). *The Sacred and Profane Love Machine.* New York. Penguin. 350-51.

Life and Death

We pause in the midst of life's ever-rolling stream and ask, *is this it?* We cannot hold on to a single moment. Every present passes, and what is past never returns. What are we talking about when we speak of these things?

When we ask about a life after death, I believe we are at the same time asking about a good life before death. If someone cares not about this life, what would there be to take into future existence? What remains of life—what endures? Also: where are the dead?

It seems clear to me the experience of death is not what we know. We know about and experience life. We come to love life, then have pain over those we love and lose. Death is the enemy; we don't accept death. Death is the destruction of a beloved life. It is love which rises up in rebellion against death. The life of love is eternal life.

We turn to the Bible. No help there, *if* you are looking for a definitive, *oh yeah!* doctrine with an abstract concept for life and death. Those people handled things the same way we do. What we find in the Bible are testimonies about life with the living God.

In the theology of the Christian church, however, we do find two views expressed. First, original sin. Second, finite life. Our faith teaches that death came into the world through sin. Original sin was followed by hereditary death. From Paul through Augustine, because of the link between act and destiny, death is not to be escaped and we deserve it because of sin. Before the fall they *could* die; after the fall, it was required. Because of sin, we were cut off from God. All the fathers of the church followed this doctrine of the Fall (Genesis 3). Think of all the fear and guilt we become heir to from this. Fear of death and hell. Eternal death after death of the body, death then judgment. Think of the guilt of the ages that has been suffered through the ages.

Then, apart from the history of doctrine, through the ages, we look at the death of the body as the natural end of earthly life. Do you really want to live here forever? Isn't there a shelf-life of things built into the universe? So, maybe a physical death is not, in itself, an evil. If we had no guilt, could we escape much of the inheritance of the doctrine of the Fall? Thus, Finitude means mortality, and death is the natural end of limited human existence. If faith in God's grace frees us from the fear of sin and death, can we also be freed for "a natural death"?

What if we don't look back, but forward? What if our emphasis is on the future of redemption in the creation of all things? Well, then, out of the remembrance of Christ's resurrection, we see on the horizon of our expectation a new world in which "death will be no more" (Rev. 21:4), since as the "last enemy" of God and of life it will be destroyed (1 Cor. 15:26); through the power of resurrection it will be swallowed up in the victory of life (1 Cor. 15:55).

But what of violent, undeserved death through that which is certainly sin? Murder, starvation, war. What of sin as a violence against life? Tyranny is an organized violence against life based on the fear of death. It is joining death against life. The death of mass victims of violence is not a consequence of their sin, nor is it a natural death. It is a suffered crime. The blood of the victims cries out to heaven. We think of the beasts of Daniel 2 and 7. This great evil is overcome only by the loving kingdom of the Son of Man.

We turn now to old ideas which are 'religious' ideas of the soul flying away on angel's wings and stuff like that. What do we mean when we talk about the soul as a part of our life which is immortal? This is Plato who thought the soul is essentially and in substance immortal. Death does not kill it. Death merely divides the soul from the body. For those of us who loved the body with all its senses and passions, this can be bad news. Why is the soul immortal while all else is mortal? If it only occupied a body until death, it could have never been born in the first place. The soul could have finally nothing in common with the physical, sensory world of this life of birth and dying. If it is cut off from the body, can the soul suffer?

No, well, if it cannot suffer it cannot eat and drink and thrill and be joyful and have sex, well then, what good it is? In the sense of what we call life, the soul is dead. So finally, the doctrine of the immortality of the soul offers no help to the question: what remains of life? I remember those Masonic funerals with their Platonic notions. The trouble there is that so many seem comforted. This doctrine of the Greek Stoics and the Bhagavad Gita do not help me much.

When we speak of an ensouled life today, we speak of a wholly and entirely living life, not life that is unlived. We don't follow Plato here. The real human problem is not the dualism of an immortal soul and a mortal body; it is the conflict between love and death. In both the Old and New Testaments, immortality is always spoken of as the divine Spirit (*ruach*; *pneuma*), which gives life to us and to all the living. In the Bible, this Spirit, who is the giver of life, is a relationship out of which life and the blessings of life proceed. If God is God, his relationship to his human image cannot be destroyed, not by human sin or recalcitrance. Only God can dissolve the covenant God has established with his creatures. So, we have a kind of immortality established by God.

When and where do I experience death?

As Moltmann reminds us, I shall not experience my death on earth, because I will not survive it. But I experience the death of my friends and loved ones, mourn their passing, and go on living in spite of it. Also, as a pastor, I have presided over hundreds of funerals. I have learned from this experience and have seen all kinds of displays of grief and a great variety of ways to grieve. I have seen great faith and strength of character, and certainly I have encountered the opposite demonstrated as well. Life is good, but to be a survivor can be hard. Also, I have been asked as a pastor, "Where are the dead?" We had all witnessed the dead one placed 'there', but the bereaved meant more than a hole in the ground by the question. I said a variety of things over the years, but here is a more comprehensive answer from my perspective and other perspectives as well (bear with me).

First, what is really meant by purgatory? We Protestants muck this one up considerably. The dogmatic starting point can be found in a declaration made by Pope Benedict XII in 1336. He rejected the idea that the dead sleep until the resurrection at the Last Day. The notion was that after death all are judged and confronted with the life they have lived. If someone dies in Christ, his or her sins have certainly been forgiven; yet the consequences of sin remain. Life before death is a continual repentance, and life after death is continued as a similar process of purgation and purification. This is purgatory. It is not hell, and it is not a place. It is a process! The basic idea is from when Christ said, "the pure in heart shall *see* God."[37] Thus, this purification must be ongoing. Now, aren't you sorry about all the disparaging things you have said about your Roman sisters and brothers? In the world of religious ideas, heaven and hell are end of the line places. The idea of purgatory lets God's history with a person continue after death. Read Dante's Comedy to get a sense of this journey. A tenet of faith says that in Christ the living and the dead are a great communion. We believe this is even a penitential community. Of course, this is where the notion of indulgences arose in history. Remember old Tetzel's fundraising campaign? "When the coin in the coffer rings, the soul from purgatory springs."[38] Luther famously condemned this and, of course, old Calvin chimed in calling this a "pernicious invention of Satan."[39] The reformers thought what Christ had done sufficient for our sins. The point which can and should be made is that God's history with human beings continues after death. We all believe this, right?

So, Luther (and modern Catholics) had the idea that the soul sleeps until the resurrection. When the dead are raised by Christ on the 'Last Day,' they will neither know how long they have slept nor where they are. The Bible says we will rise "suddenly;" trumpets will sound.

Luther calls death a sleep. What he means is, first, death has lost its power over human beings and, second, it is not the last thing which awaits us. Death still has its form, but not its power.

---

37 Matt. 5:8

38 Attributed to Johann Tetzel (1465-1519).

39 Moltmann, J. (2000). Is there life after death? In Polkinghorne, J.C (Ed.), *The End of the World and the Ends of God.* Trinity Press International. 248.

Juan Ramón Jiménez said, "the worst thing about death must be the first night." Well...

Moltmann tells us "the Last Day is 'the Day of the Lord,' so it is not just the last day; it is 'the day of days,' the time of the eternal present."[40] Just think about that.

So we answer, where are the dead? They exist already in the world of the resurrection. The resurrection is "today," not "on the Last Day;" "*today* you will be with me in Paradise." That's what Jesus said (Luke 23:43).

Now if we want to visit a range of options, we can turn to my personal least favorite, the thought of Reincarnation. Plato and Goethe and new age people choose to go there. All the reincarnation theory has the individual life placed in the wider community of the generations. Everything is related, connected. "The Abrahamic religions, in contrast, have linked their conviction about the counterpart of a personal God with a belief in the uniqueness of the human person, and the individual life that can never be brought back. People are not just 'part of nature'... They are also the image of the invisible God. Before God, every human person is an original, not a replica, and God never clones."[41]

We also must factor the understandings of *person* and *nature* in Western and Eastern understanding respectively.

What the Bible brings to us is the principle of *grace*. Instead of destiny, we get: his mercies *"are new every morning"* (Lament 3:23); and *"He who forgives all your iniquity, who heals all your diseases"* (Ps 103:3). He is himself "the power of life that breaks through the laws of karma and destiny, and replaces retribution by a new beginning."[42] There is no other way to address the suffering of our present times. Karma has no place in the framework of grace. Moltmann frames it this way: "The dead of Auschwitz: what karmic guilt are they supposed to have expiated? The dead of Hiroshima: what karmic retribution are they supposed to have suffered?"[43]

---

40 Ibid. 249.
41 Ibid. 249-50.
42 Ibid. 251.
43 Ibid.

We return to our belief that God has an ongoing history and relationship with us after death. The dead are not at rest! Again, as a pastor, I have been there to baptize a baby that was stillborn, never had life after the womb. Where is the child now? I have been there as a young person died rather than having fulfilled their great potential. We think of persons raped and murdered. How can their lives be complete? Where and how will they find "rest?" (Don't even dare say 'closure' around me.) Certainly, if those lives have no meaning, then the whole world is absurd. Most deaths I have experienced have been a 'natural death'. By that, the departed had died 'full of years'. They lived lives of ease. They did not starve or suffer a premature death like most people on this planet today. How do we then affirm an ongoing history with God in the light of these harsh realities?

I believe God will complete the work he has begun with a human life, with you and with me. If God is God, even violent death cannot stop God from being God. I believe God's history with us will go on after our deaths, until that completion has been reached in which our souls find rest. Now, this is *not yet* the life of the world to come. It is a place of grace between the life which has died here and eternal life there. I don't want to think of this as sleep. I would rather think of Quistorp's "great 'waking and watching of the soul' after death, with which it 'perceives' its healing and its completion, and 'experiences' its rebirth for the life of the future world."[44] The dead are not lost. But they are not finished either. They exist in a community of hope we call church. Each All Saints Day we come to a celebration of this, and we experience what it means to be a community of hope shared by the dead with the living, and by the living with the dead. If in worship Christians celebrate the presence of Christ who "is the Lord of both the dead and of the living" (Rom. 14:9), then they are worshiping in communion with the dead also.

44 Ibid. 252-53.

Eschatology

Eschatology as a technical term was not coined until probably around 1550, but apocalyptic thinking is often filled with talk of end times and is ancient.

Why look at the end in the beginning? Where is Christ? (He is, after all, the reason for the season.) He is coming. When? First advent, second advent. The end is our beginning. The one who was, who is, and who is to come. When? Where? What? Who? Why? We begin at the end, which precedes the beginning. We begin at the end in expectation of the Second Advent. He came to them; he will come again to us.

Mary stares at the manger. She, still pregnant, speaks of her child's mission as already accomplished, and it is! How then indeed shall we cast the characters at the annual Nativity Scene? Mary was poor; we don't have any idea what she looked like. Let's see. We must have "Mary blue," that particular blue associated with the virgin. That's not in the Bible. We get it from paintings. How old is she? She has to have a great voice to sing the Magnificat. Which setting shall we use this year? We always insist on having the scene to take place outside. The weather is nearly always bad. Can we hire the donkeys and sheep and goats from the guy we used last year? Don't forget to borrow a doll baby from some kid. We always have one, but don't really want anyone to see that it's just a doll. We don't really have to have Wise Men, and camels cost too much to rent, and they don't arrive until January 6th anyway, historically speaking. Shepherds are easy. Getting them to behave is the key. And Joseph, anybody can do that part.

The hardest thing is to have Mary representing her people, those who don't belong to the church anyway. They are in the poor neighborhoods. We want to be true to the Bible. Hannah (1 Sam. 2:1-10) is one of the four poems sung before Mary's. We also have Miriam (Exod. 15), Deborah (Judg. 5), and now Mary. All of these songs are revolutionary. They are *Israeli songs of protest* and deliverance of God's people from oppression. Today, how can we stage the scene so Mary can show a true solidarity with her people? Could we just bring busloads of poor people to come and have this all be for them? I see great difficulties there. The song clearly says God has already accomplished much through Mary's lowliness and her willingness to say "yes." God has shown strength, he has scattered the proud and brought down the powerful. God has lifted the lowly. God filled the hungry with good food. The rich had to leave the premises. They left hungry. God has helped those who fear him. This has been agreed upon from Abraham on. How on earth can we depict all this on the parking lot of the church?

Well, I'm glad to be retired and would never have agreed to be on the Nativity committee anyway.

It's a better image simply to proceed down I20 to just this side of Atlanta. There in Conyers, GA is the Monastery of the Holy Spirit. In the church is a majestic *Theotokos* (the God bearer), depicted in a magnificent rose window above the altar. The first time I saw it, I was even put off a bit by the proportionality of Mary's womb! It is huge! Mary sits in this glorious stained-glass circle with outstretched arms and a womb so large it contains Jesus standing as a grown man, his arms also open wide with enough room left over for God to rebirth all who seek him. I have been there many times, and it is always a powerful experience. As a Protestant, I have even come to realize how the Mariology of the Roman Church developed. If the Magnificat is being chanted by the monks, one realizes, here is your manger scene; here is the part Mary plays. Her role and her song are certainly not minor. All the Advents come into focus as one knows Christ will come to restore all the broken places in the world where healing is needed. The vast circle reminds me we are all pregnant with the possibility of new life, for God is with us and God is in us. That's a manger scene! Mary sings because she has new life in here. *Theotokos*, important role!

There is a poem by Philip Appleman which expresses so much of what I am thinking and feeling in this great season of all the stuff in the yard wilting from the cold, and people entrenching their shabby and ill-considered beliefs, and just being an American in Advent. Part of it goes like this:

> ...grant me wisdom, will, & wit,
> purity, probity, pluck, & grit.
> And forgive, Ye Gods, some humble advice—
> these little blessings would suffice
> to beget an earthly paradise:
> make the bad people good
> and the good people nice,
> and before our world goes over the brink,
> teach the believers how to think.[45]

This poem would be a great invocation for the annual gathering known as the Southern Baptist Convention.

45 Appleman, P. (2009). From "Five Easy Prayers for Pagans" in *Karma, Dharma, Pudding, & Pie.* Quantuck Lane Press.

Bible "Prophecy"

Through time, two tendencies emerged—first the pre-millennialists thought the kingdom would come through tribulation. Postmillennialists thought end times would emerge through evangelism and social reform.

Jonathan Edwards, the premier American theologian, taught the kingdom would come when Christ's kingdom would be established by the power of the Spirit and would become universal. He expected the end to be around the year 2000—in some ways, he was clearly right.

Many were to interpret Revelation literally and project elaborate codes to promote their notions. There were Seventh Day Adventists and Jehovah's Witnesses and Branch Davidians, etc. These folks finally came up with the notions of the Rapture, Tribulation, and Armageddon.

John Nelson Darby (1800-1882) thought up a system which became hugely popular because Cyrus Scofield included it in the Scofield Reference Bible (1909). Hal Lindsey was to follow.

These folks were dispensationalists, because they divided history into periods which would bring the Thousand-Year Reign of Christ. They were also pre-millennialists because conditions would be worse until better. These folks like big words and puzzles. They also exclude most everyone except themselves, because only a relatively small group of them would be whisked up to heaven. This seems to many an attractive escape from the real task of Christians to walk with the Lord in the real world. The main problems with their various schemes is that they aren't biblical. Darby imposed material on Daniel that isn't there, and one finds in Revelation that, although Revelation is full of Old Testament references, it *never* quotes it verbatim. The book says God *will* do certain things, but never *how* these things get done. Neither Daniel nor Revelation refer to the Rapture. And the sharp distinction between Israel and the church certainly is not to be found. All New Testament writers see Christian history to be a continuation of God's history with Israel. The Darby group confuse the literal and the symbolic. Tim LaHaye and Jerry Jenkins have gotten rich from a false reading of the scripture.

If one looks at the Bible accurately, one senses Revelation to be an *apokalypsis* (revelation) written to an intended audience. It is like Daniel in its visions. Other apocalypses include 4 Ezra, 1 and 2 Enoch, 2 and 3 Baruch, the Apocalypse of Abraham, and other extra-canonical writings. These forms of literature are similar in form. They speak of supernatural worlds and salvation at the end of time.

People think of Revelation as a mysterious book. John's readers would have recognized the form of the book and could interpret the code. Our lectionary includes only six short passages. These are not the controversial parts. Of interest are the many sections which have been set to music. It is important to read the book in whole rather than jumping from it to other passages like Dan. 9, 1 Thess. 4, etc.

The book is itself not linear. It presents threatening visions overcome by the Lamb while playing the music of the heavens. The progression is that through their faithfulness, God's people are brought to God's victory in the Lamb. It is written to seven actual churches "that are in Asia". Its message is to actual Christians living in actual history. It moves from Asia to the heights of heaven.

I once heard Tom Key 'read' (he had it from memory) the book in a single evening. That's the way to 'do' this book. The presentation produced visions, all right! The mind made a movie of the thing which moved to the triumph of God letting down the true Jerusalem. The book is a revelation in the form of a letter to seven congregations. The understanding is that Christians would 'get' the message which could slip past Roman censors. The author knows that the prophecy is more than predicting the future. Every prediction of the end has been wrong for all this time. One must take the book and good commentaries and go through line after line until victory is achieved.

Barth

Paul, in Romans 12:1-2, says "present your bodies [*somata*, plural) as a *living sacrifice* (*thysian*, singular), holy and acceptable to God. *And* do not be conformed to this world, but be transformed by the renewal of your mind..."

The community, in its corporate life, is called to embody an alternative order which stands as a sign of God's redemptive purposes in the world.

It is important to realize how the church has faced its relation to the world throughout its history. In modern times there was a development in which the notion of Christian ethics arose. At one time Christian ethics did not exist. The early church simply did not distinguish between theology and pastoral direction. Aquinas exemplified the inseparable unity between the ethical and theological dimensions of Christian living in *Summa Theologiae*. Neither Luther nor Calvin distinguished between theology and ethics. The birth of modernity is coincident with the beginnings of 'ethics' understood as a separate sphere of human life. Immanuel Kant wanted to separate the two and to ground ethics in reason. Thus, he wanted to turn ethics into universal law. Barth believed there could be no ethics that are not theological. Again, I did not get Barth in seminary but studied ethics as a separate function from the rest of theology. For Barth, notions such as 'the good' or the 'Categorical Imperative' (Kant) are far too abstract to give the guidance which can come only from the concreteness of God's command as found in Jesus Christ.

Barth has not won the day. Today most theology is *prolegomena*, sort of essays on the theological method, showing how theology should be done in case anyone ever got around to doing any. First, they want to create a respectable 'system' and how Christians should act is not something they ever get to. What we must witness to is the Trinity. We are to live the Christian life in such a way that it would be unintelligible if the God of Jesus Christ did not exist. Existence is not a given into which God must then be situated or otherwise accommodated. Rather, existence itself is an analogical term which can be properly displayed only as God's free gift.

Language and Doctrine

Now I turn to language, word, text, witness. Wittgenstein claimed there is no more basic foundation for language than the conventions of the community which uses it. Thus, we do not really know what language (doctrines) means unless we can see how it is enfleshed in human life. Furthermore, doctrinal claims fail the test if they cannot be lived out. Both meaning and justification require exemplification in life.

The Church's one foundation is Jesus Christ her Lord. If this is true—and it's always been true—then the church at worship is the place to begin. If we live in a world without foundations, all we have is the church. That such is the case is no deficiency since it is all we have ever had or could ever want.

Hauerwas has written:

> The proper way to construe human knowledge of God is neither from "the bottom up" nor from "the top down" (insofar as this strategy merely reproduces the epistemological dualisms upon which modernity founders) but is according to the mutual interpenetration of grace and nature as exhibited in the inescapably analogical and historically ordered uses of language by which God's relation to God's creation is articulated.[46]

46 Hauerwas, S. (2016). *Sanctify them in the Truth: Holiness Exemplified*. New York. Bloomsbury. 48.

We recognize our 'nature' as creatures only when "we discover we are constituted by a *telos* not of our own making."[47] Thus, we come to the church. The church proclaims the Creator who presides over a graceful dominion of creation (nature/human nature) is the same God who has revealed himself in Jesus Christ. This self-disclosure entails the eschatological necessity (though perhaps not the temporal permanence) of the church. The 'natural' cannot be separated from the political any more than the theological can be separated from the ethical/ecclesial.

In presenting ourselves as a living sacrifice (Rom. 12) we come to church and celebrate the *virtue* of worship. Worship keeps nothing. Worship gives everything back to God, hangs on to nothing. Worship forbids any finite accumulation which will always engender conflict. Confident worship also knows that in offering we receive back all that we need. The temporal world is not denied, but its temporality is restored as a gift and thereby rendered eternal. Only the vision of hope of heaven and citizenship in the Kingdom makes us socially and politically just on earth. How could we ever think otherwise?

For both Karl Barth and Thomas Aquinas, the important thing is to show that what God primarily reveals is God's own self in Jesus Christ. For Barth, Jesus Christ is the primary form of the threefold Word of God, incarnate, written, and preached. For Thomas, Jesus Christ must also be the real, life-giving aspect of the Revelation in order to ground the new *scientia* of sacred doctrine, as other revelations grant to other Aristotelian disciplines, the first principles which give them rise. According to Thomas, proceeding from the first principle is not a deficient science for proceeding from Revelation; it is for that reason a proper science! For both Barth and Thomas, scripture is the place from which one mounts arguments.

Both Barth and Thomas would also follow *Augustine*. In his tenth book of the Confessions, the saint interrogates nature, all the beauty and splendor of finite creation, in search of God. The "sea and its deeps, and the living, creeping things... the moving air... the heavens, the sun, the

---

47 Ibid. 49.

moon, stars" join in unison and deny their divinity: "we are not the God whom you seek."[48] Thus, God, the highest good of one's life, cannot be discovered in anything merely finite, anything which can be found "in the world." If we follow Aquinas here, the soul is urged to look for God not within, nor *in* the world, but rather only in that power which is fundamentally transcendent—only in the "unmoved mover." If it moves at all, it is moved by God.

---

48 St. Augustine. (2014). The Confessions X: The examined life. In *Three Ways of Loving God*. Brewster, Mass. Paraclete Press. 8.

Sin

Dante and Milton found it so: for anyone who has written about the extremes of heaven and hell, good and evil, God and the devil, and so on, the problem persists. How to write about sin without making it more interesting than God? This is certainly true in our time. First, we are quite fond of our various sins; second, we use the word 'God' as some generalized concept to refer to anything which remains inexplicable. Do not most folks step up to admit they are sinners, but seem less enthusiastic to believe they are in the hands of a gracious God who is the beginning and the end of all, but who also refuses to abandon us to our sins? Lately I think again and again about all this and in particular my own copious sinning.

"*Christ Jesus came into the world to save sinners*" (1 Tim. 1:15). Where I grew up, there was a "tent culture," revivalistic kind of religion. I don't know why this had to be done in a tent when there was a perfectly good church just down the road. Perhaps it was because this troupe would feel the need to hit the road pretty quick. The point is/was (talking about making sin interesting!), it was simply more entertaining than church in a substantial building. Yet even in the south, one cannot always dwell in a tent. When we came inside, we were re-schooled to believe the problem was not our 'sins' (an entertaining list), but *sin*! So better theology allows us to believe that since *sin* is the problem (not just our favorite list of them), what does getting saved mean? How the hell are we made holy? When we left the tent, we did not know how to take inventory of our lives; we could not tell the truth about ourselves.

Now, I would rather be in a neo-Gothic building to talk of them than in any tent ever made, but the point is... wherever we wound up, we still remained basically individualistic. Thus, we still had our own entertaining list of individual *mea culpas* with no clear idea of *sin*, nor of how to be honest about all of this. Why not turn to scripture? St. Paul's account of sin calls upon the actual naming of sins in the concrete practices of the community of the baptized. This way we learn to speak truthfully with one another. Left alone, we just continue to fiddle with ourselves.

OK, I went to seminary; there are views of sin which still smack of Augustine's battles with the Manichees and the Pelagians. They are still with us, and they are still incompatible with our Christian faith. After Augustine, anyone who delved into all this could no longer doubt the concepts of sin and salvation are systematically related. One cannot be formulated without the other.

The modern dilemma is that most believe in the essential goodness of the human and in the presumption of human freedom and autonomy. On the one hand, sin is not regarded as belonging to essential human nature and therefore not something for which we can be responsible. On the other hand, sin is inherited corruption and, thus, inevitable. We can trace some of this back to Kant, and have looked to this earlier in these journals. The whole modern, liberal stance remains. Again, what of sin really? It's like the theories of atonement which don't quite 'get it.' Satisfaction theories of the atonement have been used to underwrite pretentious, universalistic accounts of salvation that make unnecessary the actual existence of a reconciled people. This cheapens crucifixion, making it seem to be simply an overdraft in God's Cosmic Bank and now, after crucifixion, humanity is solvent again. If we go back to the tents, this is just a more sophisticated version of what was taught there.

If we look at scripture, we gain what we have lost to modernity. Read all of Eph. 4:25-5:2 several times. (We need to use words carefully!) Obviously, in the Ephesus church, some have been stealing. What then is the context of people speaking truthfully with one another? (Think of the wonderful image in Eph. 2:14-22.) Jesus is the cornerstone, and in him we dwell in a temple not made with hands. We cannot see clearly if we do not look from this temple 'holy to God'. Not even the knowledge of sin is our contribution to salvific understanding. Sin is not a negative human achievement to be pointed to in some Faustian pride. We only know our sin when we are saved from it! God's light must shine if we are to see the long shadow cast by our sin. So, we are now not surprised to find Ephesians speak of stealing in a passage about telling the truth. Right now, sitting here pre-dawn, I feel the need to roll my wheelchair down the altar next Sunday morning. It's not that the church needs to know what a sinning scumbag I am; it's that I need practice in telling the truth. If there is Salvation even in Sin, there is need for us to be Sanctified in the Truth.

Look to Ephesians again. There is not a list of requirements addressed to individuals; rather, these are reminders of the practices necessary for the common life of the church. Lying (v. 25), allowing anger to lead into temptation (v. 26-27), stealing (v. 28), destructive speech (v. 29), grieving the Spirit (v. 30), along with bitterness, rage, wrath, quarreling, blasphemy, and the like (v. 31), *and* the inability to forgive one another (v. 32) are all potentially mortal wounds to the common life of the church. All of this stands in opposition to the life of agape commended in Ephesians and exemplified by Christ (5: 1-2).

For Christians, the ability to name, recognize, and remember the connections between our sins is a theological achievement. And it is not easy, nor is it obviously even achievable apart from the church. We have to be taught these things. That which the world thinks wrong, immoral, or in some cases even commendable, the church calls sin. It is thus a 'privilege' for us to confess our sins to one another. This is "out loud", before God. Where else is this done? We are not just 'saved even in sin', but because of our sin.

This is not some fideistic thing the church does in private. When Christians learn to speak truth to one another, they are now able to speak truthfully to those who are not Christian. This is a new job, not a result of 'going to church'. We can never claim to be superior to others. We simply can confess that by learning the skill to confess our sins, we at least have been given the means to discover our lives. We then can see more clearly this sin in which we are immersed. Again, the scriptures... The law is the way to righteousness, but through the law we are able to discover our sins. Then Paul would say, "*Is the law sin? Certainly not*" (Romans 7:7-12), but in the problem of trying to sort out the 'Pauline conception of grace,' we always fall short. Could it be that Paul simply means what he says? Could it be that, short of a practice of a people formed by living faithful to the law named by the Decalogue, we are not able to make the law serve the purpose of the worship of God? And it is once again lifted up that, therefore, the confession of our sins, which the law makes possible, is thus intrinsic to the sacrifice constitutive of worship. We still are not to impute mortal sin to those who have not received Jesus' graceful invitation. They cannot reject what has not been offered any more than they can come back from where they have not been. God has not abandoned us, nor is God not present to those who have not heard the Gospel.

Rather than being a condemnation, 'original sin' is the hopeful affirmation that when Christians faithfully witness to the Gospel through word and sacrament, those who are given that witness have the means to locate their lives within that witness. This is as good as it gets. This is the great joy that there is 'salvation even in sin.'

This is, after all, not theoretical. This is meant to be lived.

December 16. I remember on this, Kandinsky's birthday, the wonder I felt with art early on in my life with the wonderful, colorful, geometrical shapes which went so well with a white modern house and a black concert grand. Well, I've never lived in such a place, and haven't thought much about all of this for fifty years or so. Thus, on Kandinsky's 148th birthday, I goggle up these amazing colors and enjoy. Music was important to the birth of abstract art, since music is, itself, an abstract art.

It's the Bauhaus stuff I like most (1922-33). He taught there the course on basic design as well as the course on advanced theory. The paintings from this period most intrigue me, but what do I know? (See "On White" - 1923.)

The fucking Nazis ran all the stuff off of the continent. Living in an apartment in Paris, 1934-44 brought a great synthesis in his work at the end (Composition X, 1939). Anyway, along with Klee, his stuff thrilled me as a young man. I had to call Dr. Bob, and he assured me just now he had the same fascination early on, early Schoenberg, et al.

There is this wonderful story about Kandinsky, who while working on Composition IV, left his studio absolutely exhausted and went for a walk. While he was out, Gabriele Münter tidied his studio and inadvertently turned the painting on its side. Upon returning from his walk and seeing the canvas (while not yet recognizing it), he fell to his knees and wept, saying it was the most beautiful painting he had ever seen. You gotta love that!

This stuff brings in around $20 million today, but what does a 148-year-old man need with all that?

Our old friend Stanley Hauerwas is long on record as thinking the loss of Christendom to be a good thing. By that, we think of the Constantinian hegemony the church has suffered and what Christians have thought we gained thereby. If social stability and the encouragement of the Dow Jones numbers have been that which is most important in American Society (and who could doubt it), then the church's accommodation in the culture has led to the loss of much that the church *must* be about. Also, the presumption *is* that war is a necessary evil to be endured if democracies are to survive. Thus, we rush to destroy those we think not in favor of our type of democracy.

Church must always be a work of the Holy Spirit if church really means church. The world is to be made world, as well (Hauerwas). Church and World are all tangled up in our day. Dualities such as faith and reason, grace and nature, creation and redemption, are to be framed in the light of the church/world alternative. In this manner, the world might recognize itself as world. This is good news all the way around.

Time

Yoder says that, from a New Testament perspective, we live in two times (aeons) simultaneously. The difference in the ages is not temporal; they represent two different directions. Sin characterizes the old age; the new age, made possible by Christ, is redemptive. For Yoder, it is simultaneously true that Christ triumphant reigns and is to be anticipated by the world, and also that other powers are still rampant. Yoder states that this rendering of time is the point of eschatology. *"The preaching of the gospel is why time does not stop."*[49] This then is the meaning of the kingdom. Jesus is ruling over creation in all the movements of time. If the church *is* a politic, then every area of the Christian faith has an eschatological dimension. This means Christian Theology always is unfinished as well. So much for systematic theology, right?

In one of the last interviews he gave before his death, Karl Barth had this to say:

> I am not ultimately at home in theology, in the political world, or even in the church. These are all preparatory matters. They are serious but preparatory. We have to learn to stand in them, to do so fully, and I want to do this quite cheerfully, but we have also to learn to look beyond them.[50]

He then said, in answer to a question about grace:

> Grace itself is only a provisional word. The last word that I have to say as a theologian or politician is not a concept like grace but a name: Jesus Christ. He is the grace and he is the ultimate one beyond world and church and even theology... In him is grace. In him is the spur to work, warfare, and fellowship. In him is all that I have attempted in my life in weakness and folly.[51]

---

49 Hauerwas, S. (2013). *Approaching the End: Eschatological Reflection on Church, Politics, and Life.* Eerdmans. xi.

50 Ibid. xv.

51 Ibid.

One must have one's notions of creation sorted out. This might be best done as we approach the end, and we do find all bound up in the Trinity. Creation is not a timeless truth; it's just that, as noted before in these volumes, we know there was a beginning because we have been shown the end. Real time, eschatological time, is the lifetime of Jesus Christ. Barth said, "His life is the turning point, the transition, the decision which was accomplished in His death and resurrection; together with the time preceding and following this event in the history of Israel and the existence of the Christian Church."[52]

The post-Nicene doctrine of the Trinity stated it was 'heresy' to claim that different revelations could come from the Father, Son, and Holy Spirit. Yoder made that in the Incarnation and in Pentecost and in the continuing life of the church, there is *one* God. One need not be concerned to 'balance' the doctrines of creation and redemption; one needs to find the interconnectedness of all we get to believe. This means, again, that we start at the end. God seems to create through the Son in the power of the Holy Spirit. It's all the same, and it's all God.

For me, the *time* categories we encounter must also take into account the 'science' we have learned from science. By that, I mean it is completely true that Jesus rules the cosmos from the Cross. That is an extraordinary claim we make only because it has been revealed to us, as we then view history eschatologically. Along comes science, who says "oh yeah! The sun is going to flame out in five billion years or so." To that, I reply: "Well, God has overcome greater problems than that!"

Then along comes Yoder, who says we can see history doxologically because we are given the gift of participating in God's rule of the cosmos. Talk about extravagance! We don't have to usurp the Emperor's throne, nor do we have to be in the halls of Congress constantly 'pastoring' the speaker of the house. We instead sing the songs of Zion and celebrate the Lord's lambship, or the lamb's Lordship (Rev. 5:7-10). Yoder's stress on the lordship of Jesus Christ means the politics of Jesus is from the beginning and shall continue beyond the end. If Jesus is at the right hand of God, he has already won the cosmic victory, but also, he is in charge of

52 Ibid. 12.

current events. Yoder would say for Jesus, "I am King but the servant kind of King."[53] This way, he says the hopes of the Jews are fulfilled. In Jesus Christ, the politics of the church can refuse to accept the claims of earthly kings. *Also*, if we ask, 'what kind of politics?' we can point to the nonviolent kind. Nonviolence shows history is determined not by kings and empires, but by the church (another incredible claim). This enables Yoder to claim any attempt, for example, "to justify war for the individual Christian citizen, after it has been judged incompatible with the ministry of the church, is a refusal to be honest with the absolute priority of church over state in the plan of God." Wow! As Stan puts it, "the church knows better than the state what the state is to be and do." It's not that the church should enable the work of the wider society though; rather, "it is for the sake of the church's own work that society continues to function."[54] Glorious words. One finds the whole meaning of history in the church. But do we actually believe God can use the power structures of this world for his purposes, even when they stand opposed? Well, do we believe the Trinity and the Bible? Where then is this church? I have little trouble believing Yoder, since his interpretation is revealing truth which we accept by faith through the power of the Holy Spirit.

---

53 Ibid. 26.
54 Ibid. 27.

Peace and War

Hauerwas has said *Sanctify Them in the Truth* was a book which fell stillborn from the press. It is to me one of his most helpful books. It has a bunch of Methodist material in it.

We are to keep trying. To stop with some satisfaction at any place along the trail is not what we can do. It is a journey, and our destination does not loop back. We keep on keeping on. We, "forgetting what lies behind and straining forward to what lies ahead, press on toward the goal for the prize of the upward call of God in Christ Jesus."[55] Paul is explaining to his favorite church this process of perfection. He claims not achievement but progress. At the end of chapter three, he tells the Philippians we should live our lives in a way that is *"consistent with whatever level we have achieved"* (v. 16). Paul is still growing in his faith. Christ has grabbed him (v.12) for the purpose of 'growing up', of moving into a mature relationship with Christ. That is what it is about.

The problems with perfection are well known. Mostly, perfection conveys too much of a sense of accomplishment, as if a goal has already been achieved. There is no goal; we are talking about a qualification of our Christian character. In Wesley's time, a world was just beginning to be born in which one need not be Christian to live in a decent manner. Our world is truly different from Wesley's. We are better at seeing ourselves as troubled sinners than righteous saints. We are also embarrassed at some of Wesley's thoughts about how we are to live, which are so thoroughly unmodern. We today would rather not be seen as too moralistic or pious. That is perhaps part and parcel of my fascination with the novelists of Wesley's era. These writers were acutely concerned with the virtues of constancy and integrity as the hallmarks of the moral person.

55 Phil 3:14

For both William Law and John Wesley, this constancy of character and singleness of intention are the things which make our behavior consistent with a life devoted to God. Perfection requires the wholeness of a human life.

If we are serious about all this in our personal lives, we are compelled to consider these things in our corporate lives as well. We are to be in but not of the world.

But here is the test: are we consistent and constant in our citizenship in the great statehood we call the US of A? We look at our presidents to tell us some things about what it means to be a good American. If the nation is in crisis, then we turn on the TV to see how the terms are to be defined. For example, *terrorist*. In the Middle East, we find it simple to tell the difference between a freedom fighter and a terrorist. In our own country, a terrorist is certainly clearly discernible. If you threaten our 'way of life' you are thus branded. We don't stop to say, 'Well, you may have a point; our way of life is not always as righteous and just as we suppose it to be. Let's sit down and reason these things out.' And, of course, there is little time to do that after the fuse has been lit.

If war and violence can be seen as compatible with living as a Christian in a society, then that is the place to begin. If you provoke me sufficiently, you can expect a reaction. If you really come up against me, you can look for a certain violence from me. I have been thus enculturated. Even though I have gone to church each Sunday and regard Jesus and what he said in red to be the whole point, if you do unto me, I'm gonna do back. Thus, it is absurd for me to declare myself a pacifist. It's just that I think I *should* be one. If war and terrorism are incompatible with Christian discipleship, then one must live non-violently. Most folk I know would say under certain circumstances, war is not only necessary but a duty, even a 'sacred' duty, for God and country, our way of life, conserving our sense of place into the future, protecting our women and children, all that sort of thing. Logically I follow Hauerwas and Yoder in that if terrorism is prohibited then so is war. If the normality of war and violence are challenged, then our Christian beliefs (if they are directed against such use of force) must seem quite as fanatical as the violent side!

It is even true that we have a hard time defining peace and violence, war and terrorism. Often, peace is just another name for the absence of overt hostilities. Then we are led to have a huge, international conference to sort these things out—to define our terms, if you will. It is true, however, that if Christians are to really help the world live more peacefully, it will be by being who we are as those who worship Jesus Christ.

The thing is, we cannot even know what violence (and war) is apart from the practice of non-violence. By extension, we know little of this, because where may peace be found and where is the church which practices peace?

Is it true that one community's terrorist is another community's martyr? If one seeks to define acts of terrorism, one can only do so from a set of moral practices and presumptions. It is to me false to define terrorism as an act or actions so discontinuous with traditional warfare that the 'ethics' of war as we have had it in our experience do not even apply. Actually terrorism, like the many enlargements of violence before it, is a direct lineal descendant of 'traditional warfare'. This is an important thing to consider. When we drop a bomb on brown people somewhere and "collateral damage" occurs—that is, we inadvertently kill women and children—who can say this is not an act of terrorism? If the PLO blows up a busload of school children, is it a 'terrorism thing' as opposed to the Israeli's response to bombing a refugee camp where women and children are killed? The US Department of Defense defines terrorist activities as that committed by those other than duly constituted governments. Our nation has overthrown duly constituted governments; is that not terrorism? And so, we are in the position of inheriting terrorism. Perhaps it goes back to the 'honorable' tradition of the British Army orderly marching around in bright red coats and we colonists hiding behind trees with squirrel rifles. Think of our own civil war. Warfare changed. Our technology should have outlawed war long ago. Again, it's like one of the Popes said upon hearing about the invention of the crossbow: "Ah, here is a blessing in disguise, a weapon so terrible it can never be used in war." And so on, up 'til nowadays. The 20th century certainly has proved that everything can, will, and has been used in warfare. The bombs we dropped on Japan. We were tired of fighting. The Manhattan Project program was a matter of success and pride. Will not history regard it as the greatest act of terror in modern times? War is hell and more and more will terrorism be seen not as aberration, but as the degenerate progeny of conventional war. Conventional warfare is conventionally inhumane. We have come too far and we have gone too far, and as I look at it, there is no cure. From where can help come? Can this new Pope address St. Peter's Square in such a way people everywhere will say, "oh yeah, it's time to quit killing each other?" Can our President say something among the nations? No, he is Commander-in-Chief. He's got Navy Seals doing stuff we peaceful Christians applaud, and therein lies the difficulty. No, I must not get a gun, for I would use it, for I am deep down a terrorist if you mess with me a certain way. The question is, would I rather be a victim? Well, it brings the whole deal down to, how do I 'feel' about my own front yard? For example, what if there were a bunch of black guys with their hoods up coming at me; what would I do? Well, shit my pants, I guess. Could I find the means or authority to establish warm Christian dialogue? Would I not say, 'damn if I only had an Uzi?' or whatever. Am I not a racist terrorist myself?

To me, if I am honest, there is no way war and terrorism can be shown to be separate things; no clump of theologians or departments of government can be found to sort out these things. If you look at it, words like torture, murder, war, terrorism, abortion, do not these words all work the same way? Does not all of this have the same inevitable conclusion? Our prized attitudes about the benefits of a hegemony of our cherished Western cultural beliefs being accepted as universal is wrong and will lead to inevitable difficulties. Only more war and terror will come of it. There is no basis in our world to come up with a clear, rational stance from which to distinguish war and terrorism or any other forms of violence. Is the answer then some form of universal civilization? Well, everyone I have ever met would not only vote against such a thing but would rush to their gun cabinets ready to defend to the death our cherished notions of western democracy which would then compel our commander-in-chief to scramble the jets; 'we need to kill some brown people somewhere, right?'

No, there are deep problems with what I am writing, and we are led to epistemological quandaries. Why is it not possible to find a Christian position which can powerfully proclaim the proposition of peace on earth, good will to all men, women, and children? Certainly such a thing is not only possible, but the only possible chance we have. Right? How will the whole wide world respond to such a proclamation?

It was the central responsibility, to present the rational basis for judgment, that was the whole project of the Enlightenment. No one should appeal to any authority anymore. Each person can now be counted on to appeal to principles of Western rationality and thus to sort out any difficulty which may emerge. Well, that whole project has failed us. The problem is that the way we can judge the failure of the project is only through the rational processes the Enlightenment provided. Thus, we have a historical situation. Anything we can look at is itself a concept which comes with a history. We are caught up in a web which clearly shows the immense diversity of any tradition of inquiry. So, if we cannot avoid relativism, are we not condemned to continue to live in a world of war? There will continue to be disputes and the only way to resolve a dispute is to fight, right? I raised my kid to stand his ground. Fortunately, when he was asked if he was the biggest kid in the first-grade class, he was able to say, 'no, the teacher is bigger.' He muddled through and in college learned eastern martial arts to a deep degree. Thus, I like being in his company should we find ourselves in a 'dark' neighborhood.

As an example of how his (Brian's) peacefulness is more profound than mine, I turn to that which happened about a decade ago. Brian and I went to a movie together and behind us a few rows this dude was seeking to impress his date by making comments and being disruptive in general. I got up, went to him, and implored him to shut the fuck up. When I got back to my seat, Brian said, "Dad, I will not protect you if you do something like that again." Well, did I learn from that valuable lesson? Probably not.

I am not only violent, but my emotions are falling apart. Could not get through my two sermons last Sunday without having tears in front of all those dear people. I nearly choke up all the time. Also, as I read back through a few of these pages, it sounds racist both in being directed against people of color and in the implication that 'they' are the ones we would bomb if the opportunity would present itself. Why not bomb some white folk now and then? Well, I think I know why.

We, me and people like me, own about 3/4 of the world's goods and services and yet 'we' only constitute about 1/4 of the world's population. The vast majority of the world's people subsist on just a small portion of the world's goods. So, at times, 'they' get pissed about all this, right? Well, 'they' must not complain too loudly, nor must they hide behind a tree and shoot at us as we drive by in our big vehicles. If they do, we will destroy them, lock, stock, and barrel. If this is not true, prove me wrong, both in statistical reality and in clear moral principle. You say, well, the US of A gives more to *others* than anyone; I reply, true: what we give for others exceeds what other nations like us give. But what we give is such a small part of our national GNP that we lag way behind almost every other nation-state 'like' us. President Carter says it's a very small amount of 1%. Thus, we lag behind many others *and* what we give is always politically motivated (we make sure the cameras are rolling in Darfur) or in service of our defense department (we give more for the defense of Israel than nearly all the rest of our giving). If this is not true, then prove me wrong. Becky and I give more than most anyone I know, if you are talking about a percentage of what we 'own'. But the camera crews don't come to watch us write a check to charity. The Augusta National makes big news when the press conference is held to show how much they give to help those in need. I have some idea of the percentage of their wealth that is thus represented (and I think you do too), but we shall never be able to find out because 'they' would kill us rather than tell us and 'they' are the few who really own most of everything and they gain year by year as the poor lose the small portion they have.

If you take offense at any of this, dear reader, then pick up one of those Bibles which have what Jesus said in red. You will really get pissed at that old radical rabbi, and if his reality becomes manifest in our society, we are ready to kill him again. This, then, is the state of affairs I thus proclaim before dawn on this last day of the year. New Year's Eve, only a coincidence of numbers. You say, what event could mean less than that? Well, you have then never heard of TV and football, parades and parties. Actually, I plan to celebrate, not tonight but certainly all day tomorrow as I sit in my big chair and watch it all. I may bitch and moan about many things, but the reality is, I am a big, fat American and as violent as the next guy, but I will enjoy the day. God help us all.

Resolutions to be made, hell no; I'll wait for Easter for that.

Damn, it's now 3:30am on the first day of 2015, yes, a coincidence of numbers. I missed the party last night, and if they set off fireworks at midnight, I didn't hear it. As I read back over the last few pages, I should be ashamed of myself (I guess). The last news item I can remember for 2014 last night was a horrible accident. Lady in Hailey, Idaho in a Wally World where I have stopped and shopped myself on the way to the ranch. Shot and killed by her two-and-a-half year-old. She had one of those purses designed for those wise Americans who have a concealed permit. That is the last Walmart before one enters the vast southern Idaho area wherein no Wally World can be found. One needs a lot of protection there, doesn't one? Kid fished the gun out of her purse and blew her away. Terrible, you say. I wonder how we can prevent such an awful accident from happening. Well, I think I know one way...

We have, again, an epistemological crisis. Nicholas Lash puts it well: epistemology is what we do when things go wrong. To share a culture means we share schemata, which are at once constitutive of and normative for intelligible actions—i.e. it means we can get a joke, or we can 'get it' when such a thing as the one described above occurs. There exists the possibility of different interpretations of what is going on around us. So, how is it possible that such a *horrible* and/or *preventable* accident could happen in a Walmart? Some may say 'damn, I gotta teach my kid to shoot like that' or one may say 'we must melt down all the guns' (turn them into plowshares) so the culture has then the opportunity to establish dialogue. Here then we have the problem of having too many schemata for interpretation. I believe if we even try to discuss what went wrong in Idaho, we have a situation wherein it is impossible to really understand what is going on around us. It's actually a demand for us to stop and start over again. Such a lack of understanding makes it impossible for us to know what is going on around us. Such a lack of understanding makes it impossible for us to make our own lives intelligible. Such a lack of understanding makes it impossible to even distinguish normality from madness. We had best discover a new narrative to deliver ourselves from such a true tragedy as what happened in Idaho. New concepts are required to enlighten our schemes, to furnish solutions to things and problems which seem intractable.

Relativism is the doctrine we have been using. It is not working. We need a whole new thing. What about Christianity as a whole new thing? Has that been applied to the continuing crises of epistemology?

Our problem as Christians is not that we come into conflict with the world, but that we do not. Is it true Christians have been sent out into a world to challenge such notions of violence and warfare and concealed carry? In the state of Georgia, our wise politicians have recently agreed you can carry a gun anywhere you want. Yes, you heard that right. Or, if you are a black guy, you may wave one around in front of a convenience store. This helps the police become as effective as the two-and-a-half year-old in Idaho (target practice). This must be our goal, after all. Is this even seen as a crisis by our Christian brothers and sisters? Not in my experience. It seems to bother no one I know.

We Christians are sent out into this world of violence. Jesus would have us armed only with the weapons of love. The problem is, we don't believe this. We may pretend to do this and, every once in a while, to provide 'peace', but we don't even recognize such a concept as the peace of Christ. Oh, we may have a seventh inning stretch in church occasionally to stand and 'pass the peace with one another,' but that is not really what is meant by the peace of Christ. If we were to really represent the peace of Christ in our world, we would be regarded as radical as any radical Islamic fundamentalist would be. This is why I do not want to be associated with traditional 'liberal' Christianity. I want to be thought radical. I'm just too much a coward.

If this is to be the year about a book, then I'll need to spend time within that book *each* day. The Bible is not designed to answer our questions. If anything, the book helps us ask better ones. In fact, the Scriptures sit in judgment upon our questions. One may certainly bring incorrectly asked questions to the Bible. This happens chiefly as we try to get it to see things our way. Why can we not get support for our argument therein? One can wrench a thing from its context, but it falls flat if we try. It amazes me how it remains the sovereign word over and against any words of my devising. In short, the Word remains directed to me.

didascō – I instruct you

parabalō – I urge you

agapaō – I love you

So, my interpretation rule for 2015: the concrete before the theoretical, the communal before the private, and be open to constant rearticulation.

Epiphanies

Epiphany – from Greek *epiphaneia,* lit. "the shining forth"

If a people in any age have light, it is a reflected light.

God's people themselves do not generate light; they must instead gather it up. They can only disperse the light that shines upon them.

The Old Testament passage tomorrow has then *"lift up your eyes and look around"* (Isa. 60:4). The gifts have already been given, but we refuse to see. The light of the glory of God is a gift of the kingdom; it is already breaking into reality around us, but we often fail to see it.

The day of the sun, first one of the new year; the Sunday of the manifestation of the light of the star which came over the place where the poor baby lay. On this day, early in the year, we want to build upon a firm foundation. Well, Jesus Christ *is* the foundation; others are shifting sands and the baby was poor only to those who were/are in control. That baby was the son of God.

Here is the deal: we came into a crisis when the modern world view floundered upon its alleged foundations. René Descartes (1596-1650) had sought to build up a new structure of knowledge. If human reason was everywhere the same, certainly a new structure could bear the weight. Why not a solid one based upon pure reason? If science and religion are two different things (as far as knowledge was concerned), we can surely reason things out. In Descartes' lifetime, the Thirty Year's War had not garnered much support for religious traditions (why not come up with a new firm foundation?). Well, why not? We know now that mistakes were made. The modern experiment has failed us. Here was the modern deal—the ideal of human reason: let's build upon the general, the universal, the timeless, the theoretical. In pursuit of those admirable concepts we bypassed the local, the particular, the timely, the practical.

The truth is, the foundations have not held. In science, the more we learn the more elusive become the basic elements. The basic atomic theories have given way to particle physics in which things refuse to behave 'scientifically' and the foundational elements are weirder than we can even conceive. Thus, the very large and the very small will not obey our modern foundational philosophies. In religion and theology, we have the same challenges. God seems to remain resistant to our eager efforts to tame and understand 'Him'. We have been unable to do 'systematic' theology. Theology, if it is based on God, is not a finished product. It is, like the language upon which it is based, an ever changing way of looking at what the Creator has revealed in the past and what the Trinity leads us to in the present, based upon what Jesus Christ will give when the time is right, all informed by the Spirit. Wherein lies the foundation of all that?

So, the metaphor of foundation (like a building) will not do, even though much of our speaking assumes it.

Wazoodial Reflections

As I look back in these volumes, I see a tendency to nitpick metaphorically. So I want to shift gears and dwell on some basic, honest stuff. I googled 'wazoo' yesterday, and so I choose to term these musings *Wazoodial Reflections*.

Wazoo is a Frank Zappa album. It was a live album published after his death. This could happen after my death, you know. I imagine a whole generation of scholars poring over these works, trying to separate the original from the stolen, the insightful from the literal product of the wazoo. If they made a movie of all this, it could be called 'Wazoo Gone Wild,' but who would play me? It would have to be someone who could fake deep inner peace. I'll think on it.

The thing I have discovered about writing in the last three or so years of retirement is that writers write. You say, 'Oh?' I reply, 'you bet your sweet wazoo.' Write is what I do. I am prolific, even. First one must sit still. You must wait. 'It' is in there straining to emerge. You don't know where you are going. You are being led. You must often get out of the way. What's up with all that? Well, as a Trinitarian I would say, 'it's the Spirit.' That Spirit which teaches me to pray with 'sighs too deep for words.' You are limited in the process with words, after all. Words, mere words, are not enough; yet words are what we have.

I return constantly to T.S. Eliot: "Where will the word be found, where will the word resound." He then answers, "not here, there is not enough silence."[56]

One starts with silence. That is why I rise up early in the morning. It tends to cause me to nod off during the day, but I find the Benedictines have been right for centuries. One wakes to pee and then one remains up.

---

56 Eliot, T.S. (1930). Ash Wednesday. Faber & Faber.

Something is going on at 3:00AM. It's when the drunk finally staggers off. It's when the monks can perceive the cusp of the day. It's still the day before and not yet the new day, in terms of circadian rhythms and such. The body and the mind must adjust. Again, the point is that this is the time of silence. How to discern the 'sounds of silence'? Well, again, we are led. One does not google it. It is mysteriously given. One sits still, staring at the page. Eventually symbols appear. You don't know where you are going. You are not given directions. You wait. You stare at the page. The page is not empty. It has the power, the page. You'll see.

One sits still and waits until the gift gets given. It should *always* happen, after all. It's what we call regularity. If one has writer's block, what can one do? Well, sit and wait. If one is 'spiritual', one is waiting on the Lord. She will always show up. That is the promise. I believe it simply because I have experienced it.

Here we turn to François Rabelais (look him up). From *Gargantua* we get wazoodial reflections. Here he wipes his ass with the neck of a goose. He recommends it as the ultimate experience of that sort. Why they call it 'taking a shit', I don't know—I have persistently preferred to leave one there. But Rabelais helps us with the various attempts to ascertain the abstersion of the fecal matter. This may be thought of as gross and adolescent. But I think it deeply related to the muse and the spirit.

Someone once said: "He writes so well it makes me want to put my quill back in the goose." Again, it's all related. I remember my old border collie. Her name was Lucille. No fit name for a dog, so I called her "goose." She was such a wonderful animal, although she got me drunk. In my first year 'in the program' a quarter century ago, I had violated all the rules (I mean suggestions). Instead of a nine-month chip (the green, least given out chip in AA), I asked Goose did she want to go get some Tennessee sipping whiskey. She did what she always did when she realized she was getting to go: she jumped up and ran around in circles as border collies do. Damn dog got me drunk. Relapse, it's what we do after all. Drunks drink: the wonder is when we don't. I don't. Thank you, Jesus.

Bach, Beethoven, Mozart, but the greatest of these is... Barth played Mozart each day and declared him super-human. All I can say is in my unlimited opinion, these three are in a category all by themselves as the greatest.

What are the three words, nine letters, each which begin and end the same way, whereby such matters as those above can be wazoo-lized? Well, how about:

resonance

re— relevance —ance

resiliance

(that's resilience, for those of you who know how to spell and count)

A Mozart piano concerto is playing as we speak.

The Complete Wazoodable Analizations. By way of anal-yzing, a whole anal-gram thereunto. What the wazoo!

I seek to write with *a scathing wit and scapular wisdom.* It can happen, has happened, but will it continue to happen? *Afflatus* is a Latin term for poetic inspiration, derived from a Latin word meaning ‘to blow upon’.

Cicero (106-43 BC) thus wrote, “no man was ever great without a touch of divine afflatus.” A creative power—a divine *ruach*—must enter the writer from outside herself. This mysterious force then inspires. Of course, afflatus need not be confused with the old Playboy cartoon wherein the man advised the maiden, “blow is just an expression,” nor do we have here any wazoodial ramifications; we are blown away from the outside in, not the inside out. Thus, we dispense with blow jobs and flatulence. (Flatulence: flatus expelled wazoodially.)

You produce 500-1500 milliliters of gas per day and deal with it through 10-20 farts. Can you imagine the grant proposal for the controlled study which produced this vital statistic?

After Christendom, Again

Hauerwas argues that what we thought we had was not working. It was broken and we could not and should not try to fix it. It was a time we called modern and the church fit in nicely with that culture. But now, the times have changed. The shaking of the very foundations has occurred and wherever it is that we are, it is clear we must not try to go back to where we were. We used to have Christendom; we were a 'Christian nation' and thus were taught the principles of an abiding, civil religion. That day is done, and good riddance!

Christian adherence to foundationalist epistemologies—that is, the kind of position we find exemplified in thinkers such as Kant—was what suited the old world we were taught to call the modern world. It has failed us, and the church must step up and grow a pair. Only the church as revealed in scripture can train us up into the way we must go.

Where there is freedom of religion, we have a hard time separating our responsibilities as citizens. Our jobs as those who live in this country are to be thought of as being good citizens. We would hate to be thought of otherwise. We are Americans, and we are supposed to be a certain way. Our citizenship is in the US of A. But we are Christians. That is clearly another citizenship. We go to church and there are the damn flags. I never had the courage to throw the things out. It was supposed to show that in the US of A, we had a separation of church and state, and we were free to wave the flag of our faith and all. But there were rules about the flag—the flag Old Glory, I mean. It must be on one side if on one level, etc. We could do what we wanted with the Christian flag. Hell, no one had died for that flag, but we all knew folk who had died for the stars and stripes. It was to be treated a certain way. Which flag do we really wave in the churches of my experience? Well, it was not the Christian flag. Our cherished way of life had been fought for under the banner of the American flag and long let it wave. Who would lead a parade under the waving of the flag of Christ? Who would be the grand marshal of that procession? Do you see where I am going here?

Well, I never had the courage to say to my people what we were really called to. I am a big pussy. We are not an 'established church' in America. You don't need an established church if everyone believes more or less the same. I live now in an area where you "cannot sling a dead cat without hitting a retired Colonel." I thank someone for their service whenever I meet a person who has served in our armed forces. I actually mean it. I am pro-soldier and anti-war, but it doesn't seem to make a big difference.

The church should have the strength of Christ. If we would wave the Christian flag, it should have the power to trump all other flags. We stand for that which moves the sun and the stars. What we are after as Christians is to find a way of life which would not only enable us to act effectively, but also move us to act in a manner that who we are and what we do are of a piece. Most of us now live lives we do not understand. We must rediscover the politics of salvation. It was once revealed; we lost the reality of it in the modern world. Now we must recover and discover the fact that our citizenship is in the Kingdom of God. That can *only* be our primary and real citizenship, and any flag waving not under that banner is of the world and not of Christ. If we are Christians, our politics *must* change. We must undergo a conversion to a new way. It is the way of Christ, after all, so it is really an old, new, yet to come way. It is the way that saves. We are delivered into a salvation which changes everything about the way we live. If we are not changed, we are not saved. If we are not saved, we continue to flounder and be lost and be caught up in that which we do not even understand! If we are to live lives which demonstrate truth, we have then a politics which has as its *telos* the one who alone is worthy of worship. This whole process of salvation takes place in church. The church is necessary for this salvation. There is no salvation apart from the church.

Baptismatus Sum

In the beginning, when God began to create...

creatio ex nihilo—creation out of nothing

imago dei—humans in the divine image

We can find in Hebrew texts this creation out of nothing idea. In second century, BCE—2 Maccabees urges the faithful to *"look at the heaven and earth and see everything that is in them and recognize that God did not make them out of things that existed"* (2 Macc. 7:28). This is a new thing, a forever new thing; it is *all* from God and the Genesis account reminds us that 'in the beginning, God.' That's the whole thing. The waters were it seems always there. When we remember our baptism, we remember our sins washed away. When Jesus was baptized, he reopens the world.

Luther said, 'Baptismatus sum.' That means 'the whole thing.' In baptism, I am given my DNA. If all came from the stars, all the elements of creation, then I am intended from the beginning. What a concept. I am christened to creation.

To express all this, we are only left with figures of speech. God spoke the world into existence. He spoke and creation was commanded into being. God speaks and God acts. God is best revealed not as a noun but as a verb. God certainly did not *have* to create.

> The poetry that started it all said:
>
> When God began to create the heavens and the earth—the earth was without shape or form, it was dark over the deep sea, and God's wind swept over the waters—God said, "Let there be light." And so, light appeared. God saw how good the light was. God separated the light from the darkness. God named the light Day and the darkness Night. (Gen. 1:1-5a, CEB)

This started time. The first words ever spoken, then, were "Let there be light." God was pleased with God's self.

By the time John told his story of how God spoke the world into existence, he wanted to include the very best thing that had ever happened in the created world. He (John) wanted to speak of how the true light came into the world. He gave us his version of the Christmas story this way:

> In the beginning was the Word
>   and the Word was with God
>   and the Word was God.
> The Word was with God in the beginning.
> Everything came into being through the Word,
>   and without the Word
>   nothing came into being.
> What came into being
>   through the Word was life,
>   and the life was the light for all people.
> The light shines in the darkness,
>   and the darkness doesn't extinguish the light.
> (John 1:1-5, CEB)

There is still darkness. Here at my study desk at 5:08 on a Friday morning, it is still dark outside. Soon, a blue cold light will be seen through the window before me; it will slowly reveal itself and grow and shine into a new day.

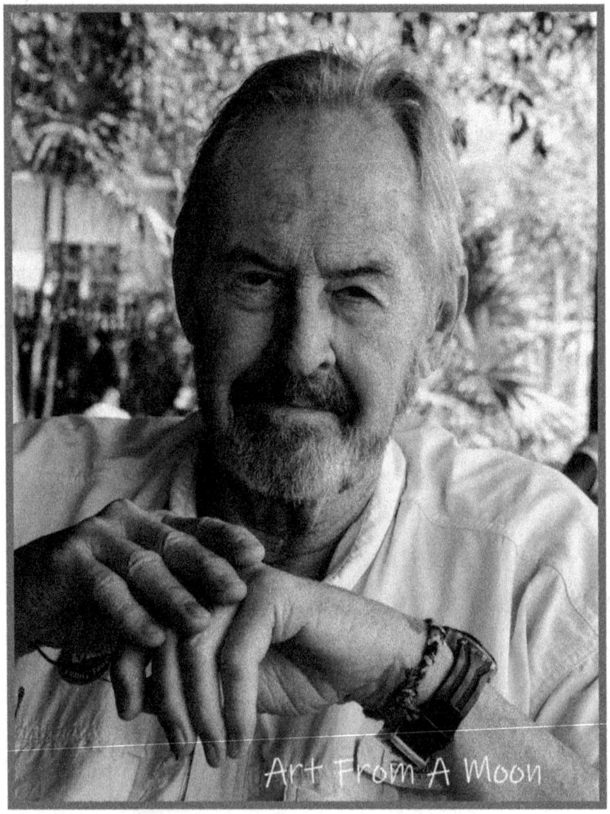

Rev. Charles F Moon III

Conclusion

I was 16 years old when I met Chuck and Becky. Chuck was our new pastor and, like any good Methodist, the first thing my father did was invite them out to dinner at a local buffet. A few weeks later, at another restaurant, Chuck was already shamelessly picking french fries off of my plate. I'm sure this says more about Chuck's personality than about how quickly we bonded, but I think even then, in all the terribly finite wisdom of a teenager, I knew there was something incredibly special about this quirky, six-and-a-half foot tall, Jeep-driving old man who was, in that moment, pouring black pepper onto his coleslaw with reckless abandon, the shaker cap forgotten on the table beside him.

When Chuck gave me his first journal to type up, he asked me to flip through it and make sure I could read his handwriting. Skimming those first few pages, I stumbled upon a line spaced slightly apart from the surrounding paragraphs: Chuck's sobriety date. I had known him for over a decade, but I had a sense when I read that line that I was diving into something special. At the time, he was actively working on his tenth volume of journals, and in my hands I held a tiny piece of a huge and daunting project. I can honestly say I don't regret a minute spent with his work.

If you've made it to the end of this book, you have had the privilege of experiencing a bit of Chuck's soul in the words he wrote morning by morning. You've seen his wisdom and wit, his successes and shortcomings; he was, after all, shamelessly and unerringly human. I suspect you've learned a thing or two about theology, or physics, or any number of subjects. You might feel you have a bone or two (or three) to pick with him. (If he were alive, he would engage you with relish; he isn't, but I know that he would be delighted to see you furiously scribbling arguments in the margins of these pages.) But I hope, above all, you have shared in his wonder at the magnitude of the God who loves us beyond all reason.

I had the privilege of knowing Chuck for fifteen years, and I can think of no greater honor than uncovering the truth of this absurd, irreverent, wonderful human being in the (only occasionally illegible) ink of a black fountain pen.

~ Alex Eash

Powerful Potential and Purpose
PUBLISHING
www.PPP-Publishing.com

CPSIA information can be obtained
at www.ICGtesting.com
Printed in the USA
LVHW020207100221
678887LV00008B/163